THE GENTLE PATH
OF SPIRITUAL PROGRESS

THE GENTLE PATH
OF SPIRITUAL PROGRESS

by
Master Ni, Hua-Ching

The Shrine of the Eternal Breath of Tao
College of Tao and Traditional Chinese Healing
LOS ANGELES

Thanks and acknowledgement to:
Abe Sprinsock and Janet DeCourtney for the charts
and tables in the appendix.

George Robinson, Liza Hughes, Judy Waxman and
Cathy McNease for help in editing.

Shrine of the Eternal Breath of Tao, Malibu, California
College of Tao and Traditional Chinese Healing
117 Stonehaven Way
Los Angeles, CA 90049

First Edition - Copyright 1987 by Ni, Hua-Ching.

This book is dedicated to those who are experiencing the roughness of internal and external elements in their lives and who have the positive intention of taming the wild buffalo of their own unrefined nature, as well as that of the world in which they live.

To female readers,

According to Taoist teaching, male and female are equally important in the natural sphere. This is seen in the diagram of Tai Chi. Thus, discrimination is not practiced in our tradition. All my work is dedicated to both genders of human people.

Wherever possible, situations of using masculine pronouns to present both sexes are avoided. Where they exist, we ask your tolerance and spiritual understanding. We hope that you will take the essence of my teaching and overlook the triviality of language. Gender discrimination is inherent in English; ancient Chinese pronouns do not have the difference of gender. I wish all of you might achieve yourselves above the level of language or gender.

Thank you, H.C. Ni

CONTENTS

PREFACE

THIS BOOK is part of the collection of my talks from the world trip I made in 1986, the Year of the Flying Tiger. All of the talks were originally published in one volume. When we were ready to reprint the book, suggestions came to divide the talks into two volumes for the convenience of readers with modern busy schedules. I have taken their advice and distributed the material that was originally under the title, *The Gentle Path of Spiritual Progress*, and published it in two separate volumes. One book retains the same name; the other book is called *Spiritual Messages from a Buffalo Rider, A Man of Tao*. Now, I would like to quote what I have said in the preface of the first edition.

"Now that this book is finally accomplished, I would like to survey the work that I have done. This survey should be called the afterward or the conclusion, but it is a funny human custom to arrange things so that the tail turns out to be the head.

In these lectures, I have expressed the motivation and intention of my global trip and my work as a spiritual teacher. I think this is a great time for human beings to be alive. One can witness the creation and trouble-making of heroes who are much greater than those of earlier days, but who nevertheless rise and fall just as their predecessors did. We can also observe the political ambition of strong leaders who subject entire countries to their individual control, just as religious authorities previously enforced their ambitions on society. Some religions today have taken on the disguise of worldly ways, but whatever their form, all ambitions must fail. Why? Because there is a subtle law in the universe which aggressive people do not see. No one person or group of people can bring the world under their control. Time after time, egotistically based power has collapsed and will continue to do so, because the subtle law of the universe does not support anything that is unnatural. Although you might think of this as the cycle of history, it is actually something much deeper and more subtle.

Some people may take the subtle law to mean that a person of strong intelligence should never interfere with worldly troubles or disorder, but this would be a misunderstanding of the subtle law. It is true that virtuous leaders are not self-assertive. It is true that they do not do anything to establish a policy or doctrine that might obstruct the natural development of all people. This is not to say that they sit still and do nothing. Their wisdom comes from attunement with the subtle law.

Unfortunately, it is not easy for a hasty, dogmatic mind to see or understand the subtle law. Nor is there a book that average people can read to learn about it. Widely-read individuals might think that the works of Lao Tzu contain the subtle law, but they are only the finger pointing to the bright moon. The pointing finger is not the moon itself. People can and must look for and discover the subtle law for themselves. To do this, you need to be open-minded: not to the aggravating troubles of the world and the stubbornness of undeveloped individuals in high positions, but to the underlying subtle truth pervading everything and everyone.

It does not take a high level of spiritual development to recognize the source of trouble in society. It is people themselves. Nature's threats diminish as human intelligence grows, but unfortunately human troubles increase proportionally. The problem is narrow, shallow visions that are fed by the fuel of self-assertiveness. When people apply their personal or collective ambitions to humanity or to anything else, they violate the subtle law, and evil is the result.

Although the subtle law is not a written document, its existence is as prevalent as the air we breathe, and its effectiveness is far-reaching. The more highly visible religious and political laws made by man, like colored smoke, are much easier to recognize and follow.

My purpose in this book is not to tell you more about exciting, but confusing, colored smoke. You have experienced enough of that in your everyday life. Through reading, through contact with others, through education and work, your mind has been exposed to it since childhood. What I wish to present to you here is simply the plain truth.

Some people make trouble for themselves, and some develop their problems to a scale that includes the whole world. As students of Tao, we take care of the mess that we have made for ourselves because of our own childishness in an earlier stage of our lives, and we also take care of the problems that were created by others who were or are in power, no matter how vast or deep the scope. This is the number one responsibility of a student of Tao.

I do my work for you and your friends with the wish that everyone will someday attain self-awareness and be responsible for living in harmony with the subtle universal law. In this way, people can counteract the vicious trend the world is following by working on their own spiritual growth and helping those around them without going to an extreme, such as waging war.

I promise that you will find the traceless footsteps of the buffalo along the path that leads to your personal subtle light. The sole concern and contribution of the buffalo rider is to help guide those who study and closely follow the subtle footsteps of the ageless and universal subtle truth.

Ni, Hua-Ching
March 21, 1990

LOOKING FOR TRUTH IN FOUR SEASONS

(A song written by Master Ni to his young students)

In beautiful Spring,
The colors of red peach blossoms deepen.
The truth-seeker walks on his long journey,
Walking, walking,
More than ten thousand miles.
He continues on his way.
He continues on his way.
Walking, walking,
Moving on the path with no end.

In the sweet Summer,
The fragrance of lotus blossoms softly deepens.
The truth-seeker walks along his path,
Patiently, steadily.
No light comes to him.
Heavy-hearted, sorrow comes.
Heavy-hearted, sorrow comes.
Sadness, sadness, darkness is all around him.

In the soft Autumn,
Pretty mums bloom all around him.
The truth seeker walks.
Time goes by, passing, passing.
Helpless, he sees it going by.
Tears begin to fall like rain.
Tears begin to fall like rain.
Searching, searching,
How can he find his way?

In the gentle Winter,
Snow begins to fall upon the meadow.
The truth-seeker walks broken hearted.
Snowing, snowing,
His path is covered by white.
Home seems just too far away.
Home seems just too far away.
Homeless, homeless,
Where is the road to follow?

In the beautiful Spring,
The colors of red peach blossoms deepen.
The truth-seeker walks.
No more seeking.
Calmness, calmness.
He has found his way home.
He has everywhere to go.
He has everywhere to go.
Flowers, fragrance, seasons, snow.
All the truth is around him now.

INTRODUCTION

For the past ten years my direct service has been limited to healing, teaching and writing books in the United States. 1986 was the Year of the Tiger, according to the ancient twelve-year cycle, and the special tiger of that year was a tiger of fiery energy: a tiger with wings. So by riding the energy of the flying tiger in 1986, I traveled to different places and made personal contact with many people who are looking for the truth of life and the universe. It was very encouraging to hold these great meetings, so I am putting these lectures and dialogues of timeless value into book form to share with all my friends in other places.

This work has come about through personal contact with people in the world. As I answer different questions, you can see that it is my personal spiritual response to the sincere search of people of the world, all of you. As a person of Tao, I am interested in examining the differences among all religious doctrines, disciplines and commandments. In the tradition of Tao, we always discuss what Tao is instead of imposing external discipline on people. It takes a long, long time just to discuss Tao, and I need to use simple words to point out the right direction, taking a sweeping route, wider and wider, that eventually leads to the vast sky. People still may not know what Tao is, but they will have been lifted out of the original pitfall they were in. In this way, they come to their own true spiritual nature.

If the great tradition of Tao does not offer a rigid discipline, but only guides people in a broad direction, then what is the way? I think it is better not to apply the intellectual mind to it. If we try to explain it, we only move further away from it. If we set Tao up as an established doctrine among many others, we only add more conflict to the existing spiritual confusion in the world. Tao, therefore, is a "strange philosophy" with an empty or neutral content. No one can establish anything with it or for it. If anyone says, "This explains the truth of Tao," it would only be one more way established by different people at different times and places, not the wholeness of Tao. Tao is not an "establishment."

What, then, can I tell an individual seeking Tao? In a practical sense, I myself consider Tao worth looking for. Tao is the absolute power that expresses itself in an effective way of life. It does not deny happiness, power, material wealth or intellectual achievement. Tao is the pointing finger and, at the same time, the direction. It is both living and realizing an effective way of life.

What is an effective way of life? There are two important things to understand. First, no waste; live your life without wasting your time or energy or anything else. This is the first part of living effectively.

The second important principle is balance. We sacrifice too much for the sake of emotion and for unhealthy cultural or religious concepts that create all kinds of prejudice. Our lives end up being sacrificed for something totally unrelated to our beingness. You do not live for life itself. This is what is called "sickness," because it deviates from the truth of life.

The well-being of any individual is Tao, and the well-being of an individual is always connected with the well-being of the whole society. If there is no well-being in society, then the individual is not safe from negative influences or interference. Tao, therefore, is the total well-being of both the individual and society.

There is no defined way to reach Tao because each of us is a different age and gender, with different customs and beliefs and tendencies. Revolution may seem like the most effective way to bring about total well-being, since advanced civilization itself is the result of such revolution, but in order to bring about true well-being, there must be no negative waste or sacrifice involved. A useful revolution would produce only an effective life for individuals and society.

Negative sacrifice can also be caused by looking, searching, reaching for and creating conceptual spiritual fantasies. This deviates from Tao just as much as everyday waste and sacrifice in life at a more material level. Spiritual fantasies waste the time and energy that could be directed toward real self-development and spiritual achievement. People need, first of all, to learn the way to live effective lives and realize Tao in their everyday lives. Effectiveness is supported by no waste and no negative sacrifice. But on the other hand, if you do not make a sacrifice of any kind, you might become selfish or self centered, and a self-centered life is itself a waste most of the time. You must understand that no negative sacrifice must be realized at the same time as no waste is realized.

Tao actually turns out to be a direction, a goal which can only be realized in the process. You cannot separate the goal and the process, otherwise you deviate from it. This is a new direction for intellectual people, because learning Tao involves the true reality of life. It demands total devotion. In general, people misapply their devotion to artificial religions. That is a waste and negative sacrifice of their own healthy emotional energy. Artificial religious and political doctrines do not encourage people to live effectively, thus they deviate from the truth of life. Devotion, correctly applied, should be to life itself, not anything else. When you apply your devotion to Tao, you apply it to an effective way of life by pouring your energy into effective living, being and doing. This is the new but ageless religion called Tao. It means correctly applying your devotion to life itself and realizing your goal in the process of each moment of living. This sounds strange to modern people, because we are used to deceiving ourselves with the dualism of cultural confusion. Life is not naturally confusing. On the contrary, it expresses its own nature quite clearly and purely. What I am saying only seems new, because we have deviated so far from the truth of life. We need to regather all of our energy to bring our focus back to the essential direction of life itself.

If you wish to use the word "religion" to describe Tao, then what are the traits and attributes of this very old, and at the same time very new, religion? For one thing, it is a religion that advocated becoming rich. Everybody would like to become rich, but do people need a religion to tell them to become rich? That is not the point. The point is, if you can be rich, be rich. If you cannot, then what do you do? The ordinary way tempts you to sacrifice your life just to become rich without ever looking into whether that is a worthy exchange or not. Tao, the "new" religion of the long stream of life, teaches people to become self-rich. By learning to effectively use the richness of what you already have, you can enjoy something far greater than money. You can enjoy the richness of your own self-nature. The interesting thing is that the richness of self-nature also brings with it a materially rich life. People think that it is just the opposite - that material wealth will give birth to a self-nature - but it is not so, and much waste and negative sacrifice are spent on trying to create something real out of untruth.

Lao Tzu teaches that feeding the hen, not looking in her nest, will give you eggs. In other words, people look for the fruit instead of tending to the tree. Paying no attention to the root of their spiritual nature, they are blocked from the richness of their own being. The material richness they seek is something totally external. By making something external more important than life itself, they make an unworthy exchange and thereby lose their vital balance.

This "new" religion of eight thousand years' development also advocated becoming noble. If you become very important and respected by all people in society, you enjoy being a noble among people. It is your achievement. Simply, if you can be noble, be noble. It is alright, unless the nobility is gained through cunning tricks or other practices that cause the waste and sacrifice of your own life's true essence. How, then, do you become noble when everyone else competes for nobility? The integral truth of life teaches self-nobility. External nobility is not what one should value; rather, value the nobility of self-nature.

This "new" religion of a million light years advocates longevity. If you can live, live as long as possible. Discover longevity and immortality within your self-nature. An external number of years is not the essence of living. True life is not measured in numbers of years, but by the enduring essence you gather through an effective way of life.

This "new" religion that respects all moments advocates being holy. Who should be holy? Each person should be holy. If your holiness is not recognized by others, you can still enjoy the holiness of your self-nature, because self-nature is holy with or without other people's recognition. Colorful religious uniforms and practices are false; public recognition is secondary. More important, do you nurture and develop your own self-nature? It is important for yourself and the well-being of the entire world. Personal sickness or lack of achievement weakens the world's well-being.

This religion of ageless origin also advocates being beautifully paired. People should enjoy sexual fulfillment. How do you achieve that goal? Not everybody has the good fortune of finding a good husband or wife. Is that so important? It is not. True marriage, true harmony, starts from inside the individual. If you discover the harmony within your own nature, but do not have the chance to be happily married or paired, you can still be a harmonious being, happily married to your own self-nature.

So, in the pursuit of all human desires, special achievement is supported and approved by the new religion of penniless rich origin. But, be careful. If anything causes waste or damages the completeness and fullness of your self-nature, then it is not an achievement and not worth attaining. Anything that does not embrace the completeness of each individual's own self-nature only pulls a person down.

It is not easy for me to organize the important guidance necessary to teach Tao. The messages I have put together in the above lines are important and are meant to express the simple essence of life. If any sentences, paragraphs or suggestions I make do not appear to guide you toward the simple essence of the integral truth, examine your intellectual patterns of thought and dualistic preconceptions that may be blocking your connection to the great truth.

These simplified remarks are the introduction to this book. Other holy books offer promises of heavenly kingdoms, last judgments and great revenge on your enemies, but the integral truth of Tao remains indescribable and indefinable: the harmonious reality of one great universal life. The suchness of an effective life can only be expressed as the suchness of truth in each individual's life.

The new dawn of ageless truth expressed in this book puts the horse in front of the cart. Instead of trying to use a conceptual God to drag living people down an imaginary road to nowhere, this new tradition teaches you to develop yourself to reach God and be God. This new religion may make you feel strange at first, especially if you are used to the other way. Nevertheless, I present these talks for the honest inspection of your universal conscience. Thank you."

CHAPTER ONE

Munich, West Germany: April 12, 1986

It is a great honor to meet all of you. I did not expect to enjoy such popularity in a new place, but I feel like a great star with all of you good people crowded inside here and the heavy snow outside. I have not come for any reason other than to assist your spiritual life, and serve your mind and spirit.

By misinterpreting and over-emphasizing collective worship rather than individual spiritual achievement, conventional religions have been a hindrance to most people. As a result, people have some awareness of their natural spiritual energy, but they do not work on developing and refining it. God is not something apart from you. Each of you has your own spiritual energy; in reality, this is God. I hope that, through developing your awareness, you will come to respect this personal, spiritual energy as well as the collective spiritual energy of universal life as a whole.

Most of the world's problems can be traced to two causes. The first is intellectual denial of the existence of the spiritual sphere. The second is the mentality which, though cognizant of spiritual energy and reality, insists upon conceptualizing them. When people try to conceptualize spiritual energy, many different interpretations arise. Then people hold onto their personal interpretations and get caught up in the differences, which results in strife. This is the pattern that has been established by religious division and antagonism throughout history.

There are different stages of spiritual development. Long ago, people were both mentally and spiritually backward. They conceived of God as a monster, somewhere out there, who punished their transgressions. At this stage of development, such a view was effective in maintaining order and harmony among primitive, undeveloped people during the stage of humanity's childhood.

As humanity evolved, there were those who developed a different type of culture. As a result of examining life with an objective outlook, they realized that a person is a combination of three spheres of energy (body, mind and spirit). They also discovered that when these three work together in unity, a person's life goes beautifully. Conversely, when one's being is out of alignment, then internal and external disharmony ensue, and the result is what is called "punishment." Suffering is not something imposed from outside; it arises out of disharmony between the body, mind and spirit of a person or group of people.

What causes conflict and disharmony? One thing is insatiable physical desire, the kind of desire that can never be satisfied. Once an individual gives in to it, it creates conflict within one's spirit and causes one's life energy to be squandered. This is like letting the air out of a tire.

When the mind oversteps its bounds, it becomes like a spoiled child or a tyrant who wishes to have its own way and control everything, yet is unable to control itself. The struggle for superficial academic achievement is one example of mental desire. When you finish high school, you go on to get a bachelor's degree, and then you want a Master's and a Ph.D. Your body may say, "I don't like all this studying." Your spirit may say, "What is this for?" But the mind says, "Do it for me; I want to prove that I am tops. I want to be the best!"

A small businessperson usually begins with one shop and maybe one helper. As the business grows, he or she might open two shops and hire more employees, then three shops and many employees. Even though there is enough money to provide a good living from the income of the first shop, he or she still wants more. An ambitious mind and swollen emotions can drive a person beyond any physical or spiritual need. As you well know, the world of business always puts people under pressure for the sake of achieving the empty goals of the mind. People achieve what does not benefit them and miss what really counts. When the mind's authority is over-extended, the body and spirit suffer. This is clearly illustrated by nations that allow the unlimited expansion of their military forces. Under the selfish domination of undeveloped minds, more and more weapons are designed and produced by those who are eager to do battle with other swollen egos. This is not just an empty metaphor.

In your society, men and women who do not know each other have a way of meeting called a "blind date." You need to meet people, but how do you feel if your blind date turns out to be a disappointment? You want it to be a good date, so your mind begins to imagine all the details in advance so that it can plan what, how, when and where, etc. Then you become anxious and frustrated if things do not go the way your mind has planned. But do you know something? Many people probably do not even know the person they have been married to for twenty or thirty years. That is certainly an expensive blind date!

It is not much different with the rest of life. A man or woman puts all one's time and energy into developing a business, continually directing each aspect so that everything is carefully worked out. But one day, many years later, he or she may wonder: "Do I really like this? Is this what I truly want?"

A student may go back to school and work hard for self support while earning a degree, only to realize when it is all over, that it was not of much benefit at all. Such a person followed his or her mind, and where did it lead? Well then, if the mind is so knowing, then how is it that so many people end up missing the mark of a correct and balanced life, even after recognizing mistakes they made in the past?

Since most people overvalue and trust the mind, their lives turn out like blind dates, even when all the details are worked out perfectly. The real problem is one of spiritual undevelopment.

The most that the mind can achieve by itself is half the truth. However, when you are guided by your own refined spiritual energy, life is not a blind date. Good, healthy, normal energy attracts good energy in turn, and things done with the guidance of one's clear, strong, subtle light naturally turn out well. If a person's own developed spiritual energy takes the lead and acts as the guide, the person will be in the right place at the right time. He or she will prosper and find happiness and success. You should, therefore, cultivate and refine your spiritual energy, and let the mind fill in the details rather than try to set the stage.

The reverse of this process is disorder. Why? Because the mind can never attend to every facet and detail of life; it inevitably leaves out something vital and the spirit is then left with the task of patching things up. This is how negative religions of the mind operate.

While the intellectual mind provides some service, it is partial. It cannot be relied on for everything. For instance, when someone invites you out to eat, you do not know whether the restaurant will be good or bad. There are two ways of looking at this. You could say that such a thing is not important, because it is just a social occasion and you should not be too picky. Or you could just enjoy whatever restaurant you go to by eating a moderate amount of the food it serves.

Then again, if you decide to go to a movie that has not been recommended by anyone, you may like it and you may not. Such things are not what I call blind dates, though. My general concept of a blind date is when you have a big goal in mind. In such a case, you should not worry about all the details; they will fall into place of their own accord. Some may be unexpected, but you can always manage them. What is important, and what I wish to emphasize, is that while surely in the beginning you can exercise your intellectual mind and decide what you are going to do, you cannot plan every little detail. The fulfillment of a goal does not happen exactly the way your mind imagines or expects it to. In most things, it is the subtle response that makes things go well.

You and I have never met before now, so this meeting is a kind of blind date, yet it is harmonious and fruitful. Why did it turn out so well? Because we met as a result of the light of our spiritual energy.

I am sure that all of you know that the mind is programmable, but it is even more important to remember that once it is programmed, it is not as open or receptive to other things. There is some language barrier here between me, a Chinese-born Universal citizen speaking unrefined English, and a large group of Germans. Yet it is not a barrier at all to your unblocked spiritual energy. What is it that supports us in this way? It is our harmonious spirit in action.

When we first met, perhaps your mind was suspicious and skeptical of me, but I think you felt easier as your spiritual energy began to know me. Language and concepts are products of the mind and thus are limited, but there are no width or depth too great for your spiritual energy, which is unlimited. Whatever one's age, race or culture, the long-closed window of one's being can always be open to let spiritual light reach deeply into the heart. I would like you to remember two points. First, always respect the harmony between your individual energy and the universal, communal, spiritual energy. Second, always let the spiritual light lead you and set your direction. The mind should serve life at the level of details. Do not lose yourself in someone else's tailor-made program. It is unnatural. It is like predetermining a child's life all the way through kindergarten, grammar school, high school, college, graduate school, marriage and a career. Is the child's real happiness considered in such a plan? A person's parents and society may spend a lot of time and energy forming an idea of what a person should be like, but life is individual. It is natural and cannot be designed. Things do not happen by design; they happen naturally. If happiness could be attained by design, then you should be happy all the time, because you could design everything. If everything is planned from the time you are little, then you grow up to fit the world just as feet grow to fit shoes.

Q: Master Ni, suppose someone asked you why you came here to Europe? Did you come to look for a woman or a female spirit? How would you answer?

Master Ni: I am interested in this part of the world because it has suffered more tension than any other place in the world. I come here hoping to find men and women who will work together toward improving their own spiritual condition and that of all people. I love you as human beings. We have all suffered greatly from world tension. I have faith that people will develop themselves individually and jointly, growing toward spiritual goals. As that happens, the world's troubles will dissolve.

The nature of worldly problems in the past is quite similar to those of the present. Today, people with strong intellectual minds rule over others, whereas in the past the rulers were those with the greatest physical strength. But any conqueror is inevitably challenged and overthrown by

someone stronger than himself. People with strong intellectual minds try to dominate others, but how can a person
be happy when another mind tries to suppress him or her?
The world is like a family whose brothers and sisters are
trying to impose their intellectual minds upon each other.
What happens to such a family? We should change this
direction and not worship the contentious nature of the mind.
If people surrender to the spiritual energy of unity and give up
their mental differences, they will create a more supportive
environment for everyone.

A family is society on a small scale; it is also a unit of the
society of which it is a part. Society is made up of its units,
and anyone can always tell what the problems of a society are
by the problems of its individual units. In primitive times,
when physical strength was uppermost, battles were settled
by physical superiority. Now that the ground of competition
has shifted to the field of the mind, families have become
among the worst battlefields. Because of the competitive,
intellectual mind's drive to be victorious, fathers and sons
compete; brothers and sisters compete; husbands and wives
compete. When everyone tries to win, our environment
becomes inharmonious and discordant. Such an atmosphere
makes people insecure, and one who feels defeated upon the
battlefield of mentality becomes vulnerable to nervous
disorders, cancer and many other problems.

Please respect your own spiritual energy as well as that
of others. Spiritual energy is communal. This is the true
meaning of God. God means harmony and peace. Each
family has its own family God. Each company has its own
company God. This meeting has its own meeting God; not
because I talk well, but simply because of the Godness of our
meeting. If we discuss some petty matter with our intellectual
minds, disagreement and friction would soon arise. You
would go home with an upset stomach or an intellectual
ulcer. But when you can recognize and respect your own
spiritual energy, you also recognize the spiritual energy of a
family or group. To the extent that you identify with that
communal spiritual energy, competition and strife will
diminish. This approach does not try to suppress anyone. A
spiritually achieved one embraces many people. The mind's

nature is just the opposite; it always differentiates between what is mine and what is yours.

The world's problem is that people have become disconnected from their own spiritual energy. When people see others excelling materially or intellectually, they feel threatened and react. If you are wise enough to live a healthy, simple life, there is no reason to revolt or try to acquire what someone else has. There is no reason to compare yourself to someone else if you already have what you basically need.

If your mind is always going, it will become weakened. When you expect everything to be under your control, you get all frazzled and shaken when it is not. Thus you are easily disturbed by traffic or by your relationship with others. When you lose your good foundation, your reactions are no longer normal.

So stop worrying. Once you let go of your mind's expectations, everything will go much more smoothly. Things will evolve naturally on their own without worry. People often have broken hearts because they are so nervous with each other. They could make friends easily, and things would go well, but the tension created by expectations prevents the very things they expect. An excellent mind is associated with high spiritual energy, but you cannot trust the mind with everything one hundred percent. Thus, our goal is to nourish personal spiritual energy.

In ordinary life, people are ignorant of the fact that there are some things that the body must handle and some things that belong to the management of the mind. But the overall responsibility of one's entire life belongs to one's developed spiritual energy, because the mind is unable to perceive the reality of the spiritual dimension.

My friends, I respect my own spiritual energy and I also respect your spiritual energy. I adore the spiritual energy of naturally developed beings who were here on earth before me.

People everywhere can be inspired by learning the truth. I wish I spoke all languages so that I could offer to everyone what I offer here to you. I have written many books in English and I hope that they can serve you throughout your life. First one attains understanding; then comes practice and after that comes real personal growth. This is different from conventional religions that just tell you to have faith in someone else who is almighty and who will do things for you. In the great tradition of Tao, you need to work on and develop yourself so that you can ultimately achieve true knowledge first hand.

Every individual is a miniature kingdom; thus it is important for you to know how to govern yourself. Once you know what your goal is, you will find the practices that will enable you to achieve it.

Q: How do we achieve this understanding?

Master Ni: Spiritual knowledge differs from intellectual knowledge. If I could give you a formula such as one plus one equals two, I would do it at once. Regretfully, I cannot, because spiritual knowledge is something that comes with personal unfoldment and development.

Q: How do we develop?

Master Ni: I offer you the ancient teachings contained in my books. Although my service in the world is not yet complete, my spiritual contribution through my books is complete now. Use them for your spiritual development and you can eventually become a divine being with a full heart.

I wish to recommend in all earnestness and sincerity that you read my books. Since I will be traveling frequently now, I will send helpers to assist you in your efforts to understand and grow. You have everything you need to achieve yourself spiritually.

I love you all with my full heart. Even though I leave your presence physically, I am still with you. You can always have a spiritual connection with me as you look for support to develop. I hope that all my young friends who have spiritual aspirations will become teachers and help the world. Do not be disappointed, do not despair or be discouraged with yourself. In your own time, you will become a person of spiritual responsibility and attain achievement. With your good understanding and sound mind, you will be able to promote harmony among all people and initiate a harmonious and beautiful, spiritually advanced epoch.

I did not mean to evade the question of whether I came here looking for a woman or a female spirit. I would like to sincerely answer this question. I have come to the world to look for a woman. She is a country with awakening people who can be responsible for themselves and for the long-term future of all people. I come to search for the female spirit that gives up fighting and embraces the entire world to her bosom. This is the purpose of these untiring trips.

This has been a great opportunity for me to meet and get to know you. As you understand the content of my books better, and as you begin to develop, you will discover that Master Ni is not a remote individual. Master Ni could be your important inner friend. Master Ni is also your external friend. You are also my internal and external friends.

So, to my truly good friends I say farewell, but I never really say goodbye. So long for now.

An individual can be either the slave of the material sphere and spiritual underdevelopment, or a master of spiritual freedom. The pursuit of enlightenment is what enables one to attain spiritual freedom.

To end our meeting, I offer this poem from an ancient achieved one in the great tradition of Tao, the path of wholeness and naturalness.

> **It is suggested that you**
> **who are looking for enlightenment**
> **do not be greedy to learn**
> **so-called esoteric teachings.**
> **Once you dissolve your impulsive mind,**
> **you will naturally embrace the Tao.**
> **Once your mind is with Tao,**
> **there is no need**
> **to single anything out as "Tao."**

CHAPTER TWO

Munich, West Germany: April 13, 1986

(This talk took place in a private house in Munich after showing the videotape of "A Broken Heart.")

Master Ni: Did you enjoy this story about broken hearts? People who love each other can bring good, positive things into each others' lives, but a person who loves all people will never have a broken heart. I would like to respond to your questions now, since they will allow me to see how I can best help you.

Q: I was raised and educated to hide my true feelings. Now that I've finally begun to accept them, I wonder if a spiritual discipline will just repress them again.

Master Ni: The word discipline has many implications. Most often it creates the impression of restriction and a denial of personal freedom, as in cases where a patient is forbidden to drink alcohol by a doctor or when a soldier on duty is not free to come and go as he pleases. But there are two kinds of discipline: one is healthy, while the other is unhealthy and unnatural. By developing your own spiritual discernment, you will be able to distinguish clearly between them.

Healthy self-discipline is a matter of personal responsibility. You cannot blame your father, mother, teacher or anyone else for using the wrong kind of discipline in the past. The level of your own spiritual development is what determines your judgement and choices now. As an independent individual, it is up to you to recognize which disciplines are healthy and appropriate for your life. If you are more spiritually aware than your parents, you may see their mistakes, limitations, and conventional shortcomings. Forgive and help them, if you can; they are your mother and father. They need you to understand their unhappiness.

People often feel conflict within themselves when their desire for unrestrained freedom exists equally alongside their understanding that they cannot do everything they please. The true purpose of healthy self-discipline is to enable you to safeguard and develop what is essential in your life.

Now what if discipline is imposed on you from the outside? For example, the government may require your support to increase its military power and raise your country to the top of the political heap. It would be up to you to decide whether or not such disciplinary measures were wholesome and constructive. If a discipline is healthy and its purpose worthy, you should accept it; if not, then you should reject it. Such understanding is usually within you on a subtle level.

There really is no need to feel conflict around the issue of discipline. Healthy discipline can be enjoyable and can yield tremendous happiness by allowing you to reach new dimensions of freedom and choice. For example, a person who is sick, debilitated and suffering might be forbidden to touch any form of sugar, alcohol or favorite foods. There is an element of selection and choice in these activities. A person could let oneself feel badly about having to practice self-discipline, but with some spiritual insight, a person will see that disciplining oneself is simply a necessary means of achieving a good life and good health.

It is a question of developing clarity to set priorities and make right choices. Good discipline actually strengthens the power of a person's will to execute wise choices. If a person is spiritually ignorant, he will resent such disciplines and fail to see the repercussions of too much personal freedom. Many people sacrifice their own physical and spiritual health for the sake of better financial circumstances, without realizing that the things they do and the choices they make are undermining their lives day by day.

All of you, at least, are interested in developing harmonious spiritual energy within you. Harmonious spiritual energy is much higher than physical and mental energies. Spiritual energy is unfettered by the apparent conflict between discipline and free will that exists at the lower levels of awareness.

Q: Why is there no conflict on the spiritual level?

Master Ni: Knowledge that is intellectually acquired through learning, hearing or reading is fragmentary and partial. It may help one thing, but harm something else. On the other hand, spiritual awareness and understanding is whole. Thus it is beyond the mechanism of conflict. It can be cultivated and developed through a combination of learning, practice and discipline. To achieve the capability of whole-knowingness, we must work on ourselves with healthy forms of discipline. Our life-energy is like electricity which is easily scattered unless it is harnessed and channelled through the appropriate circuits.

Q: I have heard you say that emotions cost energy and that we should keep away from them. Can you say more about that?

Master Ni: Emotions do disturb a person's energy. In general circumstances, a person is peaceful and his or her energy grows stronger as it remains in the normal flow. There are various causes for emotional disturbance, such as inharmonious living situations or hormonal imbalances. If there is a hormonal imbalance, the problem can be remedied by practicing specific cultivations from the great teaching of Tao. It is normal for a man to long for female companionship and sexual partnership, just as a woman longs to be sexually satisfied. But when this does not work out as well as you would like, or you cannot find the right partner, then you feel unfulfilled and unhappy. In the great tradition of Tao, we have special techniques for resolving hormonal imbalances of this nature on an internal level and refining them into spiritual energy.

Attitudes are also important in a person's emotional life. In general, it is important to maintain a calm and peaceful internal life. It is not possible to dissolve one emotion with another emotion. If you have a problem with another person, you should keep utilizing reasonable measures to tackle the difficulty rather than allowing the mind and emotions to be continuously troubled.

When you are emotionally troubled, there is a strong tendency to wallow in the mud of the emotion rather than strive for a cool, objective overview that could reveal a positive solution. When a woman is stuck in emotional trouble, she may develop a cyst in the breast or uterus. All kinds of cancer and serious illness are caused, in part, by the toxic by-products of extreme emotions. We need to take responsibility for our own emotional lives, because emotions can profoundly influence the physical body and other aspects of our being.

If you do not manage your emotions well, you invite crises and pressures, internally as well as externally. For instance, if you remain angry with your spouse or a friend, you might have an accident while driving. Even if no one is harmed, the emotional shock to your entire nervous system can affect your waking and sleeping patterns. You punish yourself this way, because you never learned how to respect a peaceful way of life.

Generally, society, parents, friends and schools all teach one thing: to push yourself and your life relentlessly and endlessly. This is not the way to live, but a good number of us live the better part of our lives this way. When you were small you were pushed into pre-school; then you were pushed to elementary school. When you finished that, you were pushed to high school and then college. Now you push yourself to marry someone. It may be someone you hardly know. It may not be a happy union, but you have to get married because you have that desire. Now you must push for some job, which you might even dislike, but you have to take it. Why? Why do you push yourselves in this sad way? It is because you lack the spiritual guidance that could direct you toward what is beneficial and away from what is not.

People have suffered from mental confusion for a long time. They have also suffered from broken hearts for a long time; not over losing loved ones, but because they have lost the connection with their own souls.

Q: What about intuition? Is that part of our spiritual energy?

Master Ni: The intuitive mind functions differently from the intellectual mind. The left side of the brain is the seat of intellectual functioning, while the right side controls the intuitive functioning. Intuitive processes are largely non-verbal, metaphorical and pictorial, as in dreams. The intellectual mind is needed to interpret the images of the intuitive mind. This is where much confusion and misinterpretation can arise; there is a literal and a symbolic interpretation. If you take it literally, you may worry that your house may actually catch fire. But interpreted from a metaphorical or symbolic perspective, fire could have any number of different interpretations, depending on the individual situation. It could be a metaphor for unharmonized sexual energy, or it could express your sublimated anger. You need the intellectual mind to help decipher the meaning. There is never a set formula for interpretation. Each case is new and unique. A rigidly intellectual or materialistic person might say, "I can't know this for sure," but a more developed person would integrate intellectual and intuitive functioning to find the appropriate meaning.

As I said before, your intellectual mind depends on the natural intuitive side for balance.   You understand the language I speak, but what I say does not depend one hundred percent on language. The subtle meaning of what I express becomes more vivid and vitally relevant to you through the understanding of the intuitive mind.

The intuitive mind can read the heart. You may deny it, but that is just the intellectual mind trying to be the boss. Generally speaking, we are always reading the heart and mind.   When someone is angry or sad, we often recognize these emotional conditions without any verbal exchange. When a man and a woman meet, they will intuitively or psychically know if they want to allow a friendship of whatever depth to develop. If the mind works well, these impressions are usually correct, but overly strong desires and demands can confuse one's intuitive sensibilities.

The intuitive mind is important and is closer to spiritual energy, but it is still not spiritual energy. It is only the function of one side of the brain. It depends on its partner, the other side of the brain, to give explanations.   Accurate interpretation depends entirely on your development, and partial development is the single greatest cause of most difficulties. In the great natural tradition of Tao, we value total and complete development.

If you go to a psychic, she might "see" you at a gambling table winning a lot of money.   There may have been more images and pictures that she did not see yet. If you go ahead and do it, you could lose all your money if she only saw you winning and did not perceive the entire situation. Sometimes an image means something else altogether, and the psychic completely misinterprets it. There are very few people in whom both sides of the brain are equally developed. Throughout history, religious prophecies have been mostly matters of misinterpretation; intellectual minds that cannot interpret things correctly render intuitive visions useless or even wasteful. It is good to move in the direction of the developed intuitive mind, but how?

I mentioned electricity earlier. Water, if its flow is unchecked, can cause damage; dammed, it can produce electricity and be useful. All natural energy needs to be channeled in order to become useful. It is the same with the mind. In order to maintain the natural, healthy balance of your mind, you need not apply unnatural discipline. Neither your emotions and desires nor your scattered, overactive intellectual mind should be allowed to flow unchecked. You need to control your energies in the right way in order to achieve more on a spiritual level. If you think you are intellectually accomplished and therefore do not need to practice meditation, you will remain incomplete. You need to follow the important practices which were developed by the ancients who achieved themselves naturally. Otherwise, your intellectual and intuitive mind will always cause confusion.

Q: Is it true that I should not listen to the voice within because I may delude or misguide myself? If this is so, then it would become absolutely necessary to have a Master.

Master Ni: Master or no master, you need someone of a similar or higher level of achievement than yourself. Such a person is free of the confusing elements that obstruct your objective view and can thus be of greater service to you than you are to yourself. As the saying goes: "The fortune teller can read everyone's fortune but his own."

It is also beneficial to study and practice the I Ching. It educates the intuitive faculties of the mind and can help you with your personal development. You may at times get a particular line and jump for joy in the belief that it is a wonderful portent, or you may respond in the opposite manner and get depressed. At this level, an unclear mind can affect the practice and you can be self-deceived. In order to have accuracy, you must have a pure, clear attitude without any expectations, demands or preconceptions. Therefore you need cultivation. This is why you need spiritual practice.

Q: So, I cannot rely on my own practice if I am not clear enough?

Master Ni: If you do not know the right direction and you have an intuitive sense of it being to the left, it is still better to inquire from one who is sure. The other day, as a friend was driving me someplace, he came to a part of the road where he was no longer certain of the direction. My friend had an intuitive picture in his mind and insisted that all was well, but we did not really know how to proceed correctly and had to ask a passerby for directions. It is the same when people confuse recognizing a "picture" with knowing how to proceed rightly in this "picture."

Q: Can you describe a wholly integrated and spiritually developed person? What would he or she be like?

Master Ni: Like you. They would have two eyes and eyebrows, in the same place as everyone else; two nostrils, not three, pointing downwards, not up.

The recognition of another person's spiritual level depends entirely on your own spiritual development. If you take a child to see a great art collection, give him a dollar and tell him that he could have any one of the great paintings he wished for that dollar, the child would more than likely prefer to spend the money on sweets, because his artistic or aesthetic sense is not yet developed. If you had no familiarity with Chinese calligraphy or Tai Chi Ch'uan, you could not tell the difference between a student of three months and someone who had been practicing for thirty or forty years. When you are developed in an art, you can recognize ability and mastery in that form. When you are spiritually developed, you can recognize another spiritually developed person.

Q: At another time you spoke of an organization of spirits within us. What is our relationship to them as individuals? Are they independent of us?

Master Ni: To illustrate the spiritual reality of a human individual, we can use the metaphor of a photograph. A picture is composed of dots: some darker, some lighter, in different gradations. Our being is composed of component particles like that. These component particles can be spiritualized through a natural process of cultivation over a person's lifetime. As you can see, the truth of life is not as limited as it appears to be in general physics. Each small, individual life forms a totality in the larger life of a human being. That is to say, an individual human life is composed of numerous individual spiritual lives. The matter of life and death to an individual is the reality of integration or disintegration among these infinitely smaller spiritual components. Modern medicine has never developed this sort of knowledge, but ancient developers of natural medicine understood it deeply.

Spiritual life thrives on the natural condition of one's life being. In this culture, one's intellectual capabilities are overly taxed and stretched, which causes a splitting of one's spiritual unity. Material and intellectual knowledge serves an important function in our lives. The mind develops in both an intellectual and spiritual dimension. It is the balance between the two aspects of the mind that will lead human culture in the right direction.

The natural world is filled with spirits and gods. Just like human beings, they need to be further educated and developed, especially those that have formed within a person's being. The spiritual elements within an individual can best be illustrated by a picture I saw in the museum of one of your great cities. It was a figure that was half-human and half-goat. Because a human being is a combination of energies, one particular nature or another can be fostered. You can be a cat, a fox, a goat, a goddess or a god. Which would you choose? Foxiness? Goatishness? Demonic energy? Which will you allow to drive you? We can choose to follow a direction in life that emphasizes and develops our goat half or one that leads to spiritualized purity and sublimation. If you indulge yourself without restraint, your high spiritual energies will depart and low spirits will come to live in your body in increasing numbers.

The spiritual energy with which your body is originally endowed can be increased by your positive attitude toward life and by real practices, but, it can also be darkened or lost by engaging in spiritually depleting behavior such as lying, cheating, murder, etc.

Q: Can one's spiritual energies leave completely? I mean can a person lose his own soul?

Master Ni: You can lose it if you do wrong things.

Q: Who is it that loses the soul? Is it the body that loses it or the spiritual self?

Master Ni: Yesterday I talked about the makeup of the self. Spiritually and scientifically speaking, there are three aspects of energy. You can do something to increase your level of energy in one aspect, but the resulting imbalance would make you lose energy from another. Once you lose a part of your soul, your body becomes weak, you lose your memory, and your life begins to wither.

Everyone is half-human, half-animal. Only you can empower your animal part to be the dominant force in your life. Once you increase your low animal spirits, your lower appetites become insatiable. You always want more: more food, more sex, more things. Subtly, without your awareness, your internal partnership shifts its emphasis and balance through the guidance of your mind. You might open yourself up to influences from a lower sphere or from a higher sphere. If, on the other hand, you increase your spiritual energy, your craving for sexual contact decreases and material possessions do not hold the same attraction.

I suggest that you open yourself to universal spiritual integration. Close the basement door of your body and do not let any cats or dogs come in to make a mess everywhere.

My dear friends, after you have attained intellectual maturity, you can employ your mind to make better judgments and decisions. You can make more mature evaluations that differentiate between the logical and illogical, the emotional and unemotional. You cannot apply your intellectual mind to investigate the relevance of universal reality because you have not yet put your energy into developing yourself spiritually and so have not attained the pure, natural capacity for spiritual discernment. I do not approve of training young people by forcing them to swallow bulky encyclopedias of intellectual information. First I help to strengthen their spiritual unity. Will you always need an encyclopedia or someone else to answer your questions? You will always find someone who will answer your questions; perhaps you will get the right answers, perhaps not. You may be misguided.

A person may say: "I will not have the opportunity to find a teacher who can reveal to me the secrets of the ancient developed ones." Another may say: "I do not have the time or the finances to develop myself." These are common problems, common impediments.

In ancient times, real spiritual discoveries were not given in public talks. Before receiving spiritual instruction, a student had to develop himself through special cultivation. The spiritual sensitivity that enables direct knowingness was required of a student in ancient times in order to receive instruction concerning spiritual truths.

I recommend the study of Tao to everyone. Tao is not God, Tao is not un-God. Tao is whole. Different places, different times and different generations have invented different names and ways of expressing and explaining it, but none of them contain the entire truth of the universe. Do not follow partial truths. Your father tells you one thing; your school tells you another; your friends tell you something else. Then you go to many different spiritual teachers and they present other perspectives and you get even more confused. You may stay with some viewpoints, but you still are far from the truth, because truth is not held in viewpoints. If you have learned partial truths, you will always carry conflict within your mind.

In truth, academic achievement is secondary. What matters is your beingness, what you are. How do you live your life? This is the foundation. Refining this can bring you to a brighter sphere of life and higher spiritual stages. This true knowledge is not decided by what your mother and father say, or by the dictates of religion or culture. Insisting on one partial religion or another means that you will attain nothing in truth. It is like looking at your feet but forgetting your step; it is misguiding.

Because of the importance of complete spiritual knowledge, I have written my books for those who have become aware of how costly it can be to follow something or someone they do not truly know. Even so, they can only be comprehended by you through your own judgement.

Q: Would you elaborate on what divine energy is?

Master Ni: Divine energy is never an isolated phenomenon. It is universal. It is not the property or possession of Hinduism or Judaism or any "ism" at all. No one can lay exclusive claim to it, because it is natural and universal. It belongs to no one, yet it belongs to all in every age and in any place through enlightenment.

Universal divine energy is natural inspiration. It cannot be imagined or described in a limited way. It is not created by man. What can be described and put into images is what man has created. These images then become the false lure of religions. The universal divine energy is the root of all life. It is the root of my life and the root of your life. With this root people never die, but if you have been severed from this root, you are dead already.

My dear friends, the restoration of your unity through your own spiritual energy is so important, because your spiritual energy is closely associated with universal divine energy. I tell you, not one of all your worries, pains and troubles is worth remembering or repeating. In your mind, you feel you have been mistreated by the world. All your troubles are insignificant once you reconnect with the universal divine energy. If you meditate daily, you will have no use for psychoanalysis, even though there are small vexations to be dissolved. If you channel your spiritual energy toward the universal divine energy, large and small vexations disappear, and more important things emerge in the right order. No one can attain unlimited enjoyment or exercise unlimited freedom, yet one who achieves himself spiritually has unlimited joy, profound freedom and boundless life.

Look where you invest your energy. Is it in transient worries, bothers and small vexations? You will find you have more to give people when you connect your personal energy with the universal divine energy. Then you will have attained spiritual richness and you will have your own root. No winter cold or storms can break your branches or wither your leaves; your life will remain unharmed and sustained by your deep root. There is no need to wait for Spring to come; you are ever-Spring. You can blossom and bear your fruit in Winter as well as in Summer.

The helpers I shall send will be able to assist you with your particular problems. From this day on, do your best to study Tao so that you can restore total union to your being. Where will you find a friend who can tell you the nature of spiritual truth? Or where can you find such a book? In ancient times, no spiritual master would give away the secrets of spiritual truth. Knowledge brings responsibility. I would like to share the spiritual truth with you. I would like to help you. Have you read the *Tao Teh Ching*? Have you read the books I have written for you? Reading is like eating. A single meal will not sustain you forever. As you keep growing, new doors keep opening; you need new nourishment, new teachers. I work hard to assist you as your spiritual friend. At my stage of life, I do not have to work for material needs any more, because I have achieved success in that area. But I cannot forget those of you who wish to attain spiritual truth so that you may become sages during your life in the world. Therefore, I offer myself.

Q: Which book do you recommend reading?

Master Ni: It all depends on your own subtle response. Read two or three pages from each book and you will know which one is for you. Not only do you change constantly, but new books can open new doors.

Q: Why do you say that Taoism is not partial when it is only one of many ways?

Master Ni: When food gets stuck in your throat, do you blame the food and say that you will never eat again? Most religions do just that sort of thing. Normal life is rejected because of a few problems. Sex or marriage becomes condemned and one is told to avoid them.

Most religions prepare you to die, not to live. The teaching of Tao is concerned with the wholeness of your living body, mind and soul. Sex, if properly fulfilled, is not considered bad, and married life can be spiritual too. The tradition of Tao only shows you the right way of doing and living. If you make a mistake, you need not be burdened by the feeling of worry or guilt; simply correct yourself. If you get sick, look for a cure from natural medicine. If bad food causes a problem, eat good food.

The tradition of Tao does not use negative scare tactics to restrain you. It encourages you to live your life fully. The word "Taoism" was actually brought into use by English-speaking people with little true knowledge. In and of itself, "Tao" means the path of enduring life or the path to a healthy, enjoyable life. Nothing is beyond it and no one can avoid it. It does not remove you from life; it guides you to live well at all times in all circumstances.

In conclusion, Taoism is not an established, conceptual "ism." If I were to call it something, I would call it the Path of Universal Natural Spiritual Truth or the Path of Universal Subtle Integration. But for simplicity, let's just call it Tao.

Q: What about Zen and Yoga?

Master Ni: Zen is a form of Buddhism. It focuses on the mind and on breaking away from religious shells. But what about your spiritual development? What about the physical body? If yoga is defined as putting your head this way and your legs that way, do you think that is spiritual development? There is something missing if you cannot be married, cannot hold a job, cannot have money or a social position. In Zen and yoga, you need to renounce aspects of the world in order to become spiritual, but this has nothing to do with the total truth of life, Tao.

Ordinary religions can turn you into a pole: the naked electric pole on the side of a busy street, stark and barren. On the other hand, Tao makes you sprout, blossom, and yield fruit as you sway and dance in the breeze of life.

I do not agree with the commercial approach of different religions. I will not push you to buy my medicine. If you say you would like to live spiritually, I will tell you, as I tell most of my young friends, not to neglect the development of the four major supports in your life. These supports are your rational ability, intuitive ability, emotional harmony and physical being. These four fundamental elements branch out like limbs on your trunk. How would you feel if you had only the trunk of your body without any arms or legs?

Trust me! When I was young, I was just like you. I was always eager to learn one thing or another, but I neglected the whole. I served my emotional needs as if they were the king of my being. This caused a conflict between the upper spiritual mind and the lower intellectual mind that did not serve me well. The intellectual mind is not bad. You need it for survival and creativity. These "four horses" would be no good without the mind. It's just a matter of using it properly. Neither can you say that material things are evil. How can you decide such a thing? There is nothing wrong with anything material. Again, it is just a matter of right usage. You need your physical strength or else you will die. You may react to things emotionally sometimes, but that is because you are alive and not dead. Just do not get bent out of shape about anything.

You have everything when you have the living strength of Tao within you. You are an organization of the following five aspects of being; the wellness of physical being, the harmony of emotion, intuitive ability, rational strength and intellectual mind. You need a leader, and that leader is your developed soul. Do not worship only one aspect of your being. Become the whole of yourself. When you are your own person with a strong organization or integration of these five aspects of being, you can do anything. If standing on your head today makes you spiritually developed, then stand on your head. If your understanding of life takes you in a different direction, then do what is in tune with your understanding. A person who follows the path of living a whole life is free to utilize and enjoy all available concepts and methods at his or her own discretion. When you asked me to participate in your Christmas party here, I said, "Yes, why not?" This is April. There is snow outdoors. The weather is right for your mood. If you have a flexible mind, high spiritual truth can be meaningful on earth. The whole universe is our destiny, and right understanding can enable us to truly enjoy it.

I was born and raised in China, but I never say that I only like traditional Chinese art. When I come here, I want to enjoy the European museums. You do not insist on eating only potatoes; you enjoy Chinese food too. Everything serves a normal life. Read my books. The *Tao Teh Ching* is important. So is the *I Ching* or *Book of Changes and the Unchanging Truth*. Everything in the great tradition of Tao is important, because you are the one who is being served by all its teachings. The elements of your life are peripheral to its root, your indiscriminate spiritual essence. This essence never dies, but continues to evolve.

It has been very nice to be here with all of you. I love you and hope to see you again in the future. Our friendship has just begun.

An individual can be either the slave of the material sphere and spiritual underdevelopment, or a master of spiritual freedom. The pursuit of enlightenment is what enables one to attain spiritual freedom.

To end this meeting, I offer this poem from an ancient achieved one in the great tradition of Tao, the path of wholeness and naturalness.

> **We all have something within us**
> **that is no different**
> **from each other.**
> **Although it is small and gentle,**
> **it produces, permeates and**
> **transpierces the entire universe.**
> **I point it out to you as the true source**
> **of universal spiritual nature.**
> **Your experience of emptiness,**
> **loneliness, brightness and**
> **far-reaching is one of**
> **closeness to the subtle origin.**

CHAPTER THREE

Innsbruck: April 19, 1986

It is great that all of you are so interested in your spiritual development that you have come to see whether this person from a very different culture can contribute something to your life.

Most people have been trained by their churches to handle spiritual questions according to a system of religious belief. Unfortunately, conventional religion does not address itself to the issue of individual spiritual achievement, but emphasizes obedience to the church which handles spiritual matters in an assembly line fashion. This method is advantageous to the ruling classes of a society, because it can control people through fear. This is not the way that spiritually developed people approach the problem. Religions can hold people's minds at a collective, social level, but they do not affect individual spiritual development. In reality, "God" is the name for a spiritually completed person, and "man" is the name for a God before he has accomplished himself spiritually. Ideological concepts are something altogether different from the reality of God.

In the tradition of Tao, a person's individual spiritual achievement is respected, rather than social trickery or manipulation. In the natural society of ancient China, there were great temples where regular celebrations and festivities were held. While these celebrations satisfied the need for an emotional expression of harmony between people and their spirits, each person's awareness came from his or her own spiritual cultivation. No separation was made between God and man. When there is a separation, God is God and you are you; God is all-powerful and supernatural, while you are sinful and can share no part of his Godliness. This is a great ideological mistake.

My spiritual lineage dates back to Fu Shi and the Yellow Emperor, long before written history began. The Yellow Emperor established the first College of Tao to train his descendants to be Gods and Goddesses. In the rest of the world, only one person in two thousand years ever declared, "I am God," and he was crucified for talking that way.

Spiritual self-development and religious mass control are very different matters. In a natural society, everyone is encouraged to develop themselves to the level of a God or Goddess, since the source of suffering is a person's incomplete development. No matter how materially successful you are, your spiritual light will not be strong and bright without good spiritual development.

If you fail to meet external religious requirements, there is no real problem in life. It is a problem if you fail spiritually. People should worship and respect the universal, natural spiritual truth rather than religious cosmetics on the face of truth.

Do not let anyone tell you that you cannot know the truth for yourself or that you cannot achieve yourself spiritually without being tied to a temple or church. You were not born a spiritual slave; you were made into spiritual weaklings by temples and churches. You are the authority who distinguishes what is true and untrue, spiritual and unspiritual. The problem today is that not enough people are spiritually achieved. If they were, they could never be misguided.

You are the very treasure of the world, yet the refined expression of one person's spiritual view is not enough to shift the consciousness of the world. There must be more spiritually achieved people in order to change the world for the better.

My advice to you is to strengthen yourself spiritually. Break through your obstacles and clear away the clouds. As you develop, you will naturally become better able to help yourself and the world. You should meditate for some time each morning and each night, gradually increasing the time you spend concentrating on your life being. As you do, your spiritual vision will improve. If your mind is disturbed, you may silently recite either the first chapter of the *Tao Teh Ching* or the words, "The Great Path of One Undiscriminative Truth." In this way you can tame the snake of your mind. Do not be too ambitious and meditate too long in the beginning. If you feel drowsy, it means that your energy is sinking. If, during meditation, you enter a state of quiet, calm purity, know that you are close to the natural, universal spiritual unity. When your mouth fills with liquid, swallow it. If your mouth is dry or bitter to the taste, it means that you are sick. Do not meditate when you are sick. You might consider helping yourself with other natural ways. Once you begin meditating regularly, you will find that you get sick less often, that you are better able to control situations that caused you to seek outside advice or counsel in the past, and that you are on the path of attaining high spiritual awareness.

I travel a lot and am welcomed everywhere I go, because spiritually developed people recognize each other and extend respectful friendship among themselves. They also help others who are less achieved than themselves but who also aspire to spiritual development. About forty years ago I went to Taiwan where I worked for twenty-seven years planting and nurturing good spiritual trees instead of painting them different colors and hanging plastic fruit on them. Ten years ago, I was invited to the United States. I have served people there through traditional Chinese medicine as the means of self-support which has enabled me to do my worldwide work as a spiritual teacher.

As a result of my travels these past few weeks, I feel I understand the particular suffering of people in this part of the world much better that I have before. Since we may not have time to go into all of your problems in depth, I would like to share with you some methods from the great tradition of Tao that you might find helpful.

First of all, *The Book of Changes and the Unchanging Truth* or *I Ching* is very valuable for resolving emotional and psychological difficulties. There are many different spiritual and psychological workshops which help people with their problems, but I believe you would find that the *I Ching* also has many advantages.

Q: Do you differentiate between the use of the I Ching for emotional and psychological problems and its use for spiritual development?

Master Ni: It can help people at all levels. It guides people who are having a difficult time and helps them learn how to handle themselves emotionally, psychologically and spiritually as well. Initially, one can use the *I Ching* to settle the mental or emotional level of a problem. Once this level is clear, one is then able to enter a deeper level and use the *I Ching* as a spiritual mirror.

Many of you have problems on your mind, but you are shy and reserved among strangers, so I think it is best if I just keep talking. Please do not hesitate to interrupt me, though, even if your questions are unrelated to my topic.

Q: I know that the mind is the basis of many troubles in life, but what can I do about it?

Master Ni: Through the use of the *I Ching*, you can learn to be reasonable and balanced. Through training in defensive martial arts in the tradition of Tao, you can learn to be calm and confident. Through practicing the spiritual discipline of Tao, you can learn to be virtuous.

You should notice whether you follow the guidance of some rigid, external system of thought or whether you trust yourself to be the judge of what is right for you. The capability of independent judgment comes from nourishing an independent mind. If you refer to the *I Ching* in specific situations, it may respond by showing you the obstacle, either in yourself or in the situation. Learning to observe problems more objectively trains your mind to penetrate deeply into circumstances and respond appropriately.

Some negative religious practices have you sit in one place like a stone and focus on the cessation of thought and action. You turn into a fossil this way. In the great tradition of Tao, the mind is valued as an important tool and a good servant that enables us to live in the world and use material support to further our spiritual development. The mind is really a great asset. It all depends on what thoughts and guidance you feed it. It could be a source of negative as well as creative influence. You need to guard the mind well in order to foster its positive achievement. A healthy mind can support you in rising above any difficulty to gain success and fullness in life.

The physical practices of Tai Chi Ch'uan, Chi Gong and other martial arts are actually applications of the *I Ching*. Winning is a matter of maintaining good balance. One loses when failing to keep balance in any sphere of life whether it be emotional, political, economic or military.

Balance and calmness lead one to the path of natural truth in which spiritual well-being and harmony with the entire universe are experienced. One of the elementary practices of this path is the avoidance of an acidifying way of life. Acidic conditions created by food and emotions cause rapid aging, devitalization, illness and disease. The first acidifying influence comes from improper eating: the over-consumption of meat, dairy products, pickles etc. The second acidifying influence comes from emotions like jealousy, resentment, hostility and hatred. I know that people feel jealous, but once a person is spiritually achieved, he or she can love another without being fettered by the mind or emotions. Even if you had a preference for someone special, you would not try to bind them to you alone or label them as yours. The problem is not love, but trying to bind one another. You have a subtle choice when you love someone. You can either let go of your emotional grip on the person or you can hold on and acidify the sweet relationship. If you hold on to jealousy, resentment and so forth, your eyes will get wrinkled, then your face will get long and the muscles at the corners of the mouth will become loose; then your internal organs will begin to suffer and become twisted.

Often, when you feel that you have no control over the love of a friend, you attack him or her. When you are developed and you care for someone, then you love the essence of that person and would prefer not to hold onto them as a possession. You need, first of all, to keep yourself balanced and know what kind of love is nourishing.

Emotional indulgence can ruin your life and cause you to develop cysts and tumors. You have a choice whether to be wise and refined or narrow and dominating: whether to enjoy love by giving up control or to love with fiery, destructive excitement. Letting go of the controls and choosing to be natural is important in any human relationship, whether it is family members, friends or lovers. The closer you are, the more friction there may be; but no matter how much you want to get back at the other, the only one you will harm is yourself. We must learn to smile and take everything more lightly. There is no need for fighting.

Often in relationships, at the peak of beauty and sweetness everything turns sour or acidic. We need to understand to what extent we may let our emotions go without overstepping the boundaries of health. In other words, it is alright to be jealous, alright to be angry, alright to feel what you feel, but do not let it go to extremes. In order to maintain healthy emotions, one must allow and accept them, but one should also know when to put one's foot down so that the emotions do not get the best of you. You must be in control of yourself and not let your emotions control you. When you are a slave to your emotions, you actually bring harm to yourself, because any extreme emotion can cause you to acidify and affect your nervous system and internal organs in a bad way that invites danger into your life.

It has been said that man's greatest enemy is himself. People punish themselves constantly. I hope that you will reflect on your past emotional experiences. Has acting from strong emotion brought you victory and success or fear and desolation? You must have noticed that when you are upset with someone you do not sleep or eat well. When your entire system is upset, what further spiritual development can you achieve? We should maintain peace and harmony internally as well as externally.

Q: Does this mean that it would really be better not to have emotions?

Master Ni: By no means. I am simply saying that you should cultivate   emotional harmony. You are the driver of your vehicle; do not drive it recklessly. Know your machinery and manage it wisely so that it will not crash or burn out. Do you know why you do not manage your emotions? Because you accelerate all the time. You have never learned to slow down and shift gears. You are too tense and push yourself forward because you are afraid of being hurt by someone. This is due to spiritual weakness. If you were spiritually strong, you would have no reason to be afraid. You would know that all things follow their natural course and turn out for the best if they are not forced or manipulated. You have all seen American westerns at the cinema. Someone comes along and says, "You have an ugly face!" This is clearly a challenge to a shoot-out. If you have a balanced disposition and someone tells you that you have an ugly face, you say, "So what! I like it!"

A tense mind creates tense situations, like the relationships between most countries in the world today (at least among the political leaders of those countries). You would recognize that to do your part to harmonize with the natural flow of life, you need to let go and give up your spiritually blind nervousness and tension. I recommend daily meditation to accomplish this end. Training yourself to be calm and composed will help you achieve balance. A good life requires the steady condition of a peaceful mind.

Life is precious. Do not spend it as a slave to emotions or to spiritual undevelopment. The next time you begin to get upset, stop; take a deep breath; exhale. Then take a walk and remember that once a strange friend of yours told you something interesting about this matter.

Q: If we should follow the natural flow of things, then what is the purpose of karate and other martial arts?

Master Ni: Karate, Kung Fu and martial arts in general are taught as a means of self-defense and discipline. They were not developed for violent purposes, but to give people a sense of security and confidence. People acquire weapons and learn how to use them out of fear. The benefit of martial arts is that they give you enough confidence to overcome your fear and seek harmony and peace within yourself and with everyone else. My understanding of martial arts always brings me opportunities to make more friends.

Q: What can you do about the humiliation that results when you can't defend yourself and later must live with it?

Master Ni: I believe you are speaking about things like rape. The cause of such violent action is a person of no spiritual development. The answer to eliminating this sort of thing is to first focus on your own spiritual awareness and development and then extend your understanding to help others in developing their spiritual energy. This is especially true of one who has had the experience of being the "victim." You need to realize that your pain has been experienced by others and it will be experienced by more people in the future. If you want to heal this wound in human society, you must resolve to devote the rest of your life to spiritual development and to inspiring others to reach for the same. This is the only useful answer to your question.

Q: What can you do about an earthquake? Is it just fate?

Master Ni: Because of intellectual over-development, we have lost our natural intuition. Animals know instinctively to evacuate a danger zone in time. Only humans will remain in a dangerous situation.

What is fate? How does fate come about? Even if it is your fate to be a man or a woman, it is still up to you what kind of man or woman you will become and whether or not you attain happiness. If your fate is filled with hardship, it is up to you to find the key to the door of happiness. The door to true happiness lies in your own spiritual cultivation. As a human being you always exercise your free will in the midst of your present fate. You can set yourself on a course of betterment or one of tragic self-destruction, either of which will manifest in the future as your fate.

I would like to discuss one more point. It is what I have observed about sex. You must all realize that sex is not a sin. It is a natural right that cannot be taken away from you. You have to be responsible. You need to ask yourself if you can be responsible to the man or woman you are attracted to. This does not necessarily mean marriage, but the role you take on in an emotional relationship or partnership is significant. You must be responsible with the other person's emotions. Man needs woman and woman needs man, but a woman can get pregnant. Too often the man disappears from her life at that point; this is irresponsible. One must assume more maturity as an adult and consider the consequences of one's actions.

Irresponsible sex is a great hindrance to spiritual development. If you have many sexual partners, your heart cannot stay whole. If you can manage more than one partner, you must be sure to be responsible at an emotional level in each relationship. Can you cause no one to fall and remain clean in the matter yourself? Of course, in the event of a child being born, you must take responsibility. You cannot let a child grow up fatherless or motherless. Unless we take care of the next generation, what will the future of humanity be? So long, and I hope to see you again.

An individual can be either the slave of the material sphere and spiritual underdevelopment, or a master of spiritual freedom. The pursuit of enlightenment is what enables one to attain spiritual freedom.

To end this meeting, I offer this poem from an ancient achieved one in the great tradition of Tao, the path of wholeness and naturalness.

> **Maintain your mind as a spotless mirror**
> > **hanging in a cloudless sky.**
> **It takes in images of everything clearly.**
> **Keep your spiritual energy**
> > **like water in a cold, deep lake.**
> **In all twelve hours of each day's cycle,**
> > **always keep yourself awake.**
> **Do not let your clarity**
> > **fall into darkness.**

CHAPTER FOUR

Vienna: April 20, 1986

Worldly life, without fail, will come to an end. However, self-cultivation, self-refinement and self-integration can bring about a life which will not be extinguished. By maintaining and refining one's spiritual energy rather than scattering it through meaningless or temporary interests, one's being can be transformed at death in a whole state.

Long ago, people of self-cultivation kept to themselves in the high mountains, letting the world run its course while they tended to their own spiritual work and development. We cannot afford to do that today. The world needs us to remain in its midst and offer whatever help and understanding we can. Nevertheless, like the sages of old, we can still tend to our own spiritual work and development as we realize the ephemeral nature of changing events around us. I realize this is easier said than done; we are all still bothered by small things and people. We need to take time out each day to cultivate ourselves, reflect on our virtuous fulfillment and become ready to receive the spiritual truth of immortality.

Q: Can you tell us your view of physical immortality and whether it is a serious consideration for this civilization?

Master Ni: People ask me questions like this one often. The answer is always, nothing physical can endure without change. All physical life has a beginning, a process of growth and an end. The achievement of immortality depends, however, on physical energy. It is a process by which the visible is transferred to the invisible. The task you have before you now is to prepare for that great undertaking. When you are ready for it, the spiritual truth will open itself to you. There is no one and nothing in the universe that can grant you spiritual development or immortality; it must be gained by your own efforts.

In order to help your understanding, I have made the accumulated experience of the ageless tradition of Tao available in my books. My helpers are also available to assist at the emotional and psychological level as well as with their own level of spiritual experience. All in all, as you satisfy your intellectual needs and gain understanding, you begin to work on your spiritual self in order to actualize your life being. However, without engaging in the process of cultivation, you are left to face your unachieved mind and the various troubles it creates.

Exercising virtue toward others and yourself is the foundation of proper growth. Take care not to let your energy scatter. One should fulfill the necessary obligations to one's family and friends without going overboard or meddling in the affairs of others. A person's energy can be scattered in many ways. I hope that each of you will work at furthering your own understanding.

Q: How necessary is seclusion for spiritual development?

Master Ni: I would say that it is best to remain where you are, although you do need to create an environment for yourself that is supportive of self-cultivation and subtle transformation. In the beginning, it is helpful to have a teacher who can guide you in overcoming the difficulties you will encounter. That way you can check with the teacher from time to time to ensure that your practice and progress are correct. Eventually, though, a student must find his or her own way and become self reliant for everything. Like a child who is learning to walk, at first the student's hands are held; then he or she takes his first steps without help and eventually, he or walks on alone.

At this point I would like to say something about spiritual purity. Many people develop certain prejudices from beliefs they learn from churches or spiritual teachers. This is not constructive. Natural development does not lead to prejudice because it contains no bias of any kind. It is fully saturated with the reality of universal truth which is natural and unstained by any conceptions of the human mind.

I encourage you to embark on a path that allows unlimited development.   It will be a path of natural, universal, spiritual truth that is free of competition; a path in which each person helps the other.   In order to better serve those of you who come from different cultures and different religious backgrounds, the name "Fellowship of Integral Truth" or "The Natural Spiritual Path of Life" can be used instead of the term Tao.

If you wish me to help you, I will give you a meditation technique that you can use to begin your cultivation.   You can do this in the morning and at night.   First you need to set aside your emotional troubles.   Then go into a room by yourself and eliminate any possible sources of disturbance. You may wish to disconnect the telephone or tell other people in the house to leave you alone while you are meditating. Then, clear your mind of any mental disturbance and simply sit in stillness.

Do not meditate if you are experiencing emotional turmoil that you are unable to dissipate.   (A person with serious emotional problems should work on eliminating these before embarking on a spiritual path.)   Do not meditate if there is a bitter taste in your mouth, because that indicates some problem connected with your liver which will promote anger. Do not meditate if your mouth is filled with too much saliva, because it indicates that your energy is running low.   A dry mouth, on the other hand, means that your internal secretions are not functioning properly.   Rather than meditate under these conditions, you should consider some other natural means of self-adjustment.

There are three main practices in meditation:

1) Establish and maintain communication between the two sides of the brain and body.   Position the fingers of the hands so that they touch the fingers of the opposite hand and allow the energy to flow between the two sides of the body.

2) Keep spiritually centered and do not allow the mind to wander.

3) Keep the mind directed by repeating the subtle phrase, "The Path of One Truth."

I would like to explain the Path of One Truth. Truth cannot be found in any particular thing or idea unless one discovers its connection with the wholeness of life. This is especially important to remember as one sets out to embrace the whole truth. With the use of these three principles, one can attain natural spiritual integration.

In the initial stages of meditation, one's pure spiritual energy will not be sufficiently nourished if one's mind is scattered or lacks clarity. This pure spiritual energy is without color, size, shape, gender or weight. By nurturing it, one creates a "whole presence" which leads the achieved one toward spiritual freedom.

Q: Would you please tell us more about how to conduct our lives in order to grow spiritually?

Master Ni: There are five main observances of the natural spiritual path of life:

1) Limit or avoid acidifying foods such as red meat and dairy products.

2) Avoid unnatural or violent sex, such as rape, abusiveness, homosexual activity or masturbation. (The companionship of friends of the same sex is respected as much as the companionship of friends of the opposite sex. Marriage is considered a serious commitment of at least twenty years between a couple who decide to raise children. People who remain single for spiritually healthy reasons need to be respected, as well as those who choose celibacy for spiritual purposes.)

3) Find an honest and honorable livelihood. This discourages evil schemes, theft and making excuses for one's weaknesses or failures.

4) Avoid artificial stimulants such as alcohol, drugs, caffeine, sugar, honey (sweet fruit is alright) and salt.

5) Do not be a false witness for anything that you are going to promote or sell; do not defend yourself or treat anyone else with strong preference. (In other words, do not lie, especially with the intention of using spiritual conventions to create competition rather than cooperation.)

All the personal disciplines suggested above can be adjusted according to one's life situation. Since some of them are more important than others, you need to develop your own capacity to discern and adjust to them through your life experience.

Now we come to the Three Fundamentals of the natural spiritual path of life:

1) Avoid excessive physical contact or touching, especially one hour before and after meditation or any other kind of spiritual cultivation. It is better to express one's friendliness, love or respect by holding one's palms together, bowing, nodding the head, or some other simple gesture.

2) Remain silent just after rising and just before going to bed.

3) Remain still and quiet, or move slowly, at high noon.

The total realization of the natural spiritual path of life can be achieved through the balance of studying and practicing natural truth, and by simply being natural. It can be studied in the work of the ancient developed ones that I have gathered and presented in my books. It can be practiced according to one's purpose and level of achievement, through the Eight Treasures, Tai Chi Ch'uan, Chi Gong, Wu Tao and other practices. By observing the five elements, the Three Fundamentals, and the three practices in meditation, one can become a being of natural spiritual truth.

Other skills and techniques that can assist one's spiritual integration and help with specific problems can be found in *The Workbook of Spiritual Development For All People*.

Q: How are these practices related to our responsibility to society?

Master Ni: Some people like to be associated with group practices and others prefer to remain alone. The one who joins the Universal Fellowship of the Natural Spiritual Truth can give direction to and help renew a healthier human society. If the majority of people in the world made an effort to develop spiritually, the harmonious, orderly world that we all wish for could be achieved. Internal and external spiritual cultivation could then be complete and integrated, and all people would be made happy by bringing forth the fruit of conjoint spiritual achievement through their own efforts.

An individual can be either the slave of the material sphere and spiritual underdevelopment, or a master of spiritual freedom. The pursuit of enlightenment is what enables one to attain spiritual freedom.
To end this meeting, I offer this poem from an ancient achieved one in the great tradition of Tao, the path of wholeness and naturalness.

> **The master keeps awakening.**
> **Who stands in the middle of the room?**
> **There is always something that comes**
> **   to challenge his mastership.**
> **This is how one becomes fortified**
> **   and constantly unites with**
> **   the universal spiritual**
> **   source of great oneness.**

CHAPTER FIVE

Sydney, Australia: May 18, 1986

I am happy to see all of you. People here seem more relaxed and less tense compared to those in other cities I have visited. You also seem more interested in spiritual development. You probably represent the greater number of people in this beautiful city as its spiritual crown. If you were in China now, or even a few hundred years ago, you might have found yourself looking for an environment as conducive to spiritual cultivation as this one is. Here on this special continent, far away from the center of worldly political arenas, it is easier to find natural support for spiritual development. When you are not locked into any fixed view, you have a better chance of achieving the completeness of your spiritual development. Like your ancestors who were free-spirited, you are not confined by spiritual misconceptions or religious enslavement. All of these things have laid a good foundation that will support your quest for further spiritual achievement and truth.

I have been working in the Western world for ten years now, but this is the first time I have made a trip around the world to meet people of high spiritual awareness. I come from the great tradition of Tao as a small person of Tao. Tao is a word that cannot be defined, even though everyone who learns Tao makes some attempt to define it. I must admit that I make my own attempts at it. For the sake of convenience in communicating, I define Tao as "the way of universal, natural, spiritual truth."

Religious beliefs often develop in relation to a specific group, tribe or nation according to particular needs at certain points in time. They are not universally applicable or self-evident. The truth has to be fundamental, vital and true for everyone, everywhere at all times.

The first aspect of truth is universality, and the second is naturalness. If something is conceived, it is artificial. Although conceptions may help a person temporarily, the enduring truth is forever natural and dependable. It is independent of any culture. The third condition of truth is that it is spiritual rather than religious. Religions tend to be socially oriented. I hope you understand that Tao is not a limited expression of the temporal conditions of a specific group of people. It is the common fact of life within our entire universe. It is, in fact, the way of universal, natural, spiritual truth.

Munich, Germany, was my first stop on this trip, which began in early April when there was still a lot of snow in northern Europe. The people there suffer from much more tension than you do here, so my service there was directed more toward assisting them with that.

In a few cities, I did nothing other than sightsee, because people there were only interested in fashionable activities. There was no room in their hearts for anything lasting or beneficial. In this city, it seems that many of you have been reading books and searching for opportunities for spiritual learning for some time. What is beneficial in this search is that you can actually achieve yourselves spiritually. It is to this end that I offer my services. If you have any questions, you may ask them now.

Q: Why do you think so many people are turning away from the Judeo-Christian belief system?

Master Ni: I recognize that most of you were probably taught this religion at a young and tender age, probably by your parents, and you may have a certain degree of attachment to these doctrines. I hope that you will forgive me, therefore, if I offend you in any way. Sometimes people can be troubled by hearing statements of the truth that are different than what they are accustomed to.

When the people of Israel lived under the rule of Egypt, they needed someone to free them from the humiliation of slavery. Moses, a student of the Egyptian mysteries, was brought up in the Pharaoh's family, and his own level of spiritual development was much higher than that of the people of Israel. His first task was to raise the dignity of the Israelites, which he did by claiming that they were the "chosen people" of God. Although this was an uplifting thought at the beginning, it turned out to be a poison to future generations. It has caused a lot of suffering to those who have taken it too seriously. The original story may have had symbolic meaning, because religion often expresses things metaphorically, but considering the facts of the matter, did Moses actually accomplish his goal?

You know, most people are slaves. There are all kinds of slavery, and one of the worst is slavery to unreasonable customs and narrow, restrictive ideas. It is the universal truth that all people are children of God. Judaism, as a spiritual and sociological phenomenon, expressed the struggle between slavery and freedom. The Jewish people have continued to live in constant expectation of a savior, generation after generation. Jesus responded to this expectation in a time of adversity, but he was a free spirit and he straightforwardly said, "I am God. I am the light and the way." You could truthfully say the same, once you knew the secret of life.

If we speak of saviors, it should be understood that each person must be his or her own savior. You cannot expect someone else to save you. Two thousand years ago, one man recognized this and was crucified for daring to say it. Conventional society does not allow anyone to become higher than the collective level of development. This is a simple matter of historical fact.

Q: Is a person more free after death?

Master Ni: It takes a long time for energy to configure and manifest as a particular life. Once you embark on the voyage of life, you find that the waves get rough sometimes, so you think it would be easier to get back out of life. Take the example of a person who enters a monastery in order to get away from life's problems. Do you think you can escape life by going to a monastery? The source of one's problems is always within, and the only solution is to achieve spiritual freedom by living life correctly.

Q: I have frequently seen mention of immortality in Taoist literature. Would you say something about this subject?

Master Ni: Within the realm of ordinary thought, it seems like there is an end to physical life, and so there is. To a spiritually developed person, the deep reality is a transformation in which the essence of physical life comes to a stage of independence. It is very much like when I write. I produce drafts and revise them again and again, until only the final, perfect copy remains. A person's life, from childhood on, has many drafts. As the person constantly cultivates and refines his or her being in order to achieve the highest essence, what endures is the final, perfect version of spiritual life.

The purpose of my world trip is to recommend balance in all three aspects of life as a means of assisting the normalcy and well-being of one's life. It is necessary for everyone to learn and practice the basic truths before even considering the pursuit of divine immortality. I generally avoid the subject of immortality, because it is a spiritual achievement that must not be confused with make-believe stories. Immortality is a step-by-step achievement based on special practices that enable you to realize your destination with confidence.

There are two levels to the achievement of immortality. On the physical level, one achieves longevity and many enjoy life for a comparatively longer period of time due to the supportive state of one's spiritual unity. The second level is a higher level of spiritual unification that continues after one gives up the physical body.

In the cultivation of Tao, one who wishes to achieve immortality needs two things: natural philosophical attainment (the integration of intellect and intuition) and supernatural virtuous fulfillment (living like a heavenly being). In this way, one can attain spiritual immortality and the truthful guidance of all immortals.

Q: Can a person with a family achieve immortality?

Master Ni: The initial requirement of life is physical fulfillment, and so most people marry and have a family. If you have a good marriage, your emotional life is supported. If it is a bad one, you can benefit from working on your emotional independence. Many people get trapped by family life or business and find no time for cultivation. It is important to handle family responsibilities conscientiously and still maintain spiritual goals as the center of your life. Some traditions shun worldly life, but the great tradition of Tao recognizes that many people grow through the difficulties of daily life. There is no escape anywhere; it all depends on which lifestyle you choose and whether it is a wise way of managing your life. Once this stage of life is fulfilled, it is spiritual development that matters.

Q: What if your family life is enjoyable?

Master Ni: Then enjoy it, but do not forget about spiritual development. Things that bring enjoyment can also bring pain. I do not want to emphasize pain, because people should enjoy life. This meeting is a pure, enjoyable event, because our purpose is of a spiritual nature. You are not obliged in any way at all. In most human relationships, it is different. You need to be aware of your position and influence in relation to others. If they are younger, help them. If they are children, guide them to grow correctly. If they are your elders, try to make the rest of their life comfortable and enjoyable. With your spouse, keep your mouth quiet most of the time; likewise, with your brothers and sisters.

Q: What do Taoists mean by chi?

Master Ni: In my book, *Tao, the Subtle Universal Law*, you will find an in-depth explanation of chi. Science views life from a materialistic perspective. Recently, it has advanced to the point of exploring ever smaller particles of matter. Chi is not matter, but without it, the physical body is a dead body. If the world were simply a material world, it too would be dead like a stone. People grow old because their chi diminishes, but chi can be developed and transformed into a higher, more subtle kind of energy called Shen which is immortal. Shen is the spiritual level of energy.

You can notice within yourself how the chi changes. Sometimes, when you are mentally or emotionally upset, the normal functioning of the body is disturbed. Then, because of the disharmony of chi, illness and even death can arise. It is important to keep your chi harmonious if you wish to maintain your health. For example, a pain in your stomach or throat is merely a symptom of disharmonious chi. To know your life is to know your chi. Once you know it, you will be able to nurture and protect it.

As I have mentioned on other occasions, divine immortal beings can be summoned by means of their inner chi which is responsive to similar energies. We are gathered here today because of the attraction of chi of a similar, high vibration. If your chi were different, you would not have come here.

Q: What is the best way to control chi?

Master Ni: If you do not want to age rapidly and become unable to enjoy the activities of youth, then you must treat your life energy as you would treat money. Would you spend a week's allowance in one day? Take time out daily to gather your spiritual energy. Once your spiritual energy is gathered. all of your bodily systems work well, your health is secured, and you can prolong the enjoyment of good activities. The subtle growth of spiritual energy supports health and longevity. The opposite way of life only hastens one's physical death.

Q: Is your tradition still active in Mainland China?

Master Ni: Since the Communist takeover, the tradition of Tao is technically forbidden in China, yet it is still practiced widely in the name of health and fitness. Through the popular practice of Chi Gong, people are actually cultivating their chi every day.

Temples and ancient places of spiritual practice in China have become tourist attractions now, but even so, it is still beneficial to visit places where people have developed themselves. Such places have good, strong energy that has supported people in achieving themselves for centuries and is very special.

You can benefit from making your own surroundings serene. You can also support your own and others' spiritual practices by protecting the environment from jarring, inharmonious influences.

Q: How do you keep from drowning in the world's spiritual darkness?

Master Ni: I have given some answers to this great problem in my book, *The Uncharted Voyage Toward the Subtle Light.* Basically, you drown when you accept someone else's spiritual weakness as your own rather than working toward spiritual awakening for yourself and your fellow man.

Q: Is Lao Tzu the originator of Taoism?

Master Ni: No, he is the elucidator of Tao. The tradition of Tao was an essential part of Chinese culture long, long before Lao Tzu. During Lao Tzu's lifetime, clarity had been lost and there was much confusion. Someone was needed to reinterpret and clarify the meaning of the ancient sages' attainment, just as I have done and as someone will do after me. Lao Tzu's work is invaluable. There is no other book so objective and undemanding in its expression of the natural truth.

The essence of Lao Tzu's guidance is very simple, but it is the most profound truth of life. He teaches egoless life. He teaches people to maintain flexibility of mind and attain flexibility of spirit. Surely they are one and the same, but they are experienced at different levels. Any conceptual insistence reflects an immature mind and spirit striking against obstacles caused by one's own undevelopment. Fighting and arguing over conceptual differences will never lead people to the final, indescribable, simple essence which is the root of everything in the multi-universe. It is formless. It is most flexible. It pervades everywhere and is in every one of us. In later times, people have called it chi. Different levels of it have been recognized, but its highest most subtle and most powerful form is what should be most valued and trusted by all living beings. No one could or should conceptualize it, because in doing so a person may damage one's harmonious connection with it.   The teachers of narrow, competitive paths separate people from the essence of life. They are great impostors and frauds. Lao Tzu calls them thieves who make their victims regard them as their guardians.

Lao Tzu teaches us to be unopinionated. He teaches all people to learn to be containable; not narrow, but broad. Containable means to be tolerant or forgiving; perhaps a more precise definition is to have an accepting nature, be allowing or be accommodating. Lao Tzu teaches us to be kind, because kindness is virtuous love. People are seldom kind, even to those they love.

Lao Tzu teaches people to strengthen their bodies, not for the sake of muscular strength, but to increase health and the strength of natural life. He teaches people to respond to the common need of any generation at any time, but not to take credit for it. Once any job, big or small, is done correctly, one should evade the sweetness of its fruits which are produced for people one may not even know.

Lao Tzu's teaching is an inexhaustible treasure in which all the achievements of the ancient developed ones can be seen. I have deep reverence for him. The truth he presents is your truth, just as it is mine and everyone else's. Within it we rest and revitalize. It is plain, not glaring; useful, not dominating.

Q: There is a saying in the Tao Teh Ching: "Beware of the mountain, and keep to the valley." How do you interpret what Lao Tzu said?

Master Ni: A person should not be as arrogant and stiff as a mountain. Be approachable and containable. Be as productive as the valley. Then your life will be enriched by the universe and your life will be filled with beauty, goodness and truth.

Q: What is the proper role of ego in our lives?

Master Ni: In general, do not worry about your ego. You need to do things well. Let that be your concern. If anyone tells you anything about your ego, just ignore it. Mind your tasks so that they are done peacefully and thoroughly. An ego problem is one of exaggeration, as in the case of a politician who glorifies himself and feels justified in subjugating everyone else. My advice to you is to do your best, be responsible and do not concern yourself with egotism. Do whatever must be done daily. Develop self responsibility. Whenever you do anything in life, do it egolessly. There is no such thing, in reality, as a separate self. Everyone is actually connected with everyone else. Even when you achieve spiritual immortality, you are still concerned with the development of others, because you are not separate from anyone. A person who is proud and arrogant obstructs himself. He cannot be open to the truth.

Q: Would you comment on the illusion of separation? I seem to feel separate from other people most of the time, yet at other times I feel a deep unity with them.

Master Ni: For the sake of spiritual cultivation, it is better to maintain a little distance from others. You need some space. If you get close to others, they may find it strange if you do not participate in parties, etc. Since you need your spiritual privacy, it is alright to separate yourself momentarily. Spiritually, the whole universe is one. We are all a part of Nature.

Q: It seems like the more I find out about life, the less I know.

Master Ni: The solution to that is not to look for knowledge. Life is not just an intellectual matter; it covers two aspects - darkness and brightness, that which can be known and that which cannot be known. Once you associate with the aspect of life that cannot be known intellectually, it is not that you know less, it's that you are getting closer to true beingness.

Q: You mentioned the two sides of life. I have heard that Taoism also has two sides, one being black magic.

Master Ni: Black magic? I never learned any black magic. If I had, I would not be here with you like this. I would be trying to change the world to fit my narrow magic. In another sense, though, my life is one big piece of magic, and so is yours. Everything in life has two sides, yin and yang. What I am concerned with is the higher union of pure spiritual development. Please do not think this is not magic.

In China, ordinary magic is practiced under the name of Taoism, but it has nothing to do with the tradition of Tao that I teach. A spiritually achieved person is morally much more powerful than an ordinary person, just as a beam of light that is concentrated through a magnifying glass is more powerful than ordinary light. Any kind of magic is a by-product of the goal. Just as a Kung Fu master has the power to kill his or her opponent, but refrains from either fighting or injuring others, a spiritually achieved person avoids imposing or even displaying power publicly or privately. Do not get involved with black magic in any way. It can be harmful to a spiritually unachieved person who makes it as a goal.

Q: Would you tell us about Fu Shi?

Master Ni: In general, Fu Shi carried on the achievements of the ancient developed ones. In very ancient times, the major problems of people stemmed from incest. People's lives were short, their intelligence was weak, and blindness and disease were common. Fu Shi promoted the system of appropriate pairing (the principle of yin and yang), which is applicable in almost every domain of life. He discovered the system of the I Ching and also developed the domestication of wild animals and birds as a food supply, thereby uplifting people from the primitive practice of hibernation and the threat of starvation in winter.

People who have good genes must be careful in their selection of partners. If you choose poorly, you will be troubled with the wrong mate, and your children will be a constant source of trouble to you. If you choose a partner who is virtuous and wise, you will be emotionally and perhaps spiritually supported. You are all still young, with a long spiritual future ahead of you. If you have made a mistake in the past, I hope you will correct it now.

Q: Would you say something about death?

Master Ni: Death for the average person is suffering. To someone who is spiritually evolved, it is like a snake shedding its skin. Generally when people approach death, they begin to exhibit some clarity, because their spiritual energy is finally preparing to leave the body. Unfortunately, when the physical body is too powerful, the spiritual energy remains trapped there and cannot withdraw easily or completely. When this happens, we call the trapped spirit a ghost. Despite popular beliefs, spirits are actually very tiny and far from frightening. Only when there is some emotional involvement with a ghost is there an amplification or solidification of emotional energy to the degree that the spirit is visible in some kind of form, but this condition is only temporary and illusive.

You spiritual energy is not lost only at death; it is being spent all the time. Death only comes when the body and spirit are no longer compatible; when the body gets too weak or broken down to support the spirit any longer. Death is unpleasant to an undeveloped person. It is a process that involves a very tiny part of you that leaves and changes form. This tiny being is partly your desires, partly your memory, and is partly associated with blood relatives. When it leaves the body at the time of death, its departure is not enjoyable.

Achieve yourself so that someday you can say, "I am ready to go." After having lived a long and productive life, you will be able to say, "My spiritual energy is now complete. My body is no longer compatible with my spirit." At that time you will exuviate, like a cicada breaking out of its shell into a new life.

Q: The word "natural" is used a lot these days. Will you tell us what is really natural?

Master Ni: Too frequently, unnatural products are labeled "natural." Sometimes reading the label does not really tell you anything. You need to develop your spiritual discernment in order to really know what is what. Spiritual discernment means the discerning capability of one's spiritual development. You would like to choose something that not only does not harm the body, but is supportive and beneficial.

Q: What is the relationship between the spiritual and the physical?

Master Ni: Every individual is made up of two spirit groups: one physical, the other spiritual. When one's higher spiritual energies are undeveloped, these two groups lack co-operation and harmony. When disharmony and emotional problems persist, a woman may develop a cyst or tumor. A man may drink alcohol when he's under emotional stress, get angry and then cause his spleen or liver to shrink. Spiritual achievement is the only remedy for all the different problems of life, large or small. Once you are spiritually achieved, you can penetrate to the heart of your troubles, dissolve them, and then go on to higher spiritual growth.

Well, we have discussed many things today in making each other's acquaintance. Details are important guidelines that cannot be neglected, so read my books. They contain the complete picture of total spiritual achievement and the answers for many different questions. I could not possibly be physically at your service all the time. However, if your open heart accepts me as your spiritual friend, this will establish a universal, natural spiritual channel that can assist your growth at all times.

An individual can be either the slave of the material sphere and spiritual underdevelopment, or a master of spiritual freedom. The pursuit of enlightenment is what enables one to attain spiritual freedom.

To end this meeting, I offer this poem from an ancient achieved one in the great tradition of Tao, the path of wholeness and naturalness.

> **When your mind is wildly active,**
> **your spiritual mastery moves away.**
> **When your mind allows entry**
> **to the robbers and thieves**
> **of your true essence,**
> **You are sent back to lower reincarnations**
> **without having to wait for**
> **the next lifetime.**
> **Be firm and courageous**
> **and accept the support of the power**
> **of the universal moral nature.**

CHAPTER SIX

Taos, New Mexico: July 12, 1986

Living here in Taos, close to nature, is not easy for modern people unless they are somewhat independent spiritually and emotionally. It is very important to be independent, because close contact with society through newspapers, television and society at large can be damaging and unwholesome. If you use it well, this place can actually help you cultivate further emotional and spiritual independence. This natural environment can offer emotional support and nourishment. I do not recommend that you cut off all contact with society, but just enough to keep your clarity, balance and objectivity. We all live in modern times, yet we must still safeguard the spiritual benefits of living simply and naturally.

A person's only true privilege and dependable pleasure is his or her own spiritual attainment. Anything else can be taken away from you. You have a very supportive environment here, and you have developed the intuition to recognize true spiritual opportunity. Your concerns are not limited exclusively to material survival; they include an understanding of spiritual survival as well. Generally speaking, there is great hope if you are willing to work and achieve yourselves above the average.

One person will open up and develop so that the entire truth lights up within, while another will cut himself off from the light by creating numerous obstacles. Each individual has different needs, but everyone can benefit greatly from a harmonious approach to life and the practice of Tai Chi. My books can also give you personal contact with the many achieved masters I was able to meet and absorb in my youth.

I would like this meeting to be constructive for you, so please feel free to ask me whatever questions you have so that we can start to unfold your spiritual energy as well as mine.

Q: Would you talk about desire and its negative as well as positive attributes?

Master Ni: Everyone has desires. Some desires are healthy, and some are not. In certain spiritual traditions and religions, desire is considered to be evil and one is required to deny all desire. This view is as unhealthy as advocating the unreasonable and unrestrained fulfillment of desire. What matters is how you handle yourself. You should not use the force of your emotions to support your desires or manipulate situations so that you get what you want immediately. Take time to consider the nature of your specific desire and decide reasonably whether to act upon it or not. If you decide to pursue the desire, then you should consider the right means of doing so.

You are no longer children who can cry and pout to bend your parents to your wishes. As adults, however, many of you still retain some of those childish habits when pursuing what you want. Unfortunately, we have all been victims of our parents' mistakes, but we cannot blame them any more, and we cannot complain. They did not know about spiritual reality. As adults now, we can and must correct our emotional patterns and problems and forgive our parents' errors.

It is not difficult to discern whether a desire is right or not. The difficulty comes in our approach of how to fulfill it. I once saw a comedy in which the wife was tired and refused her husband in bed. As a result, she acquired a black eye. Did he think that he could achieve his desire in that way? Emotional reactions of this sort mostly take a person even further away from what he or she wants.

Emotions are like clouds. Some are beautiful and you wish to fly away with them; others are ugly and make the whole sky seem dark and dismal. When emotions overtake you, you can become unreasonable. You see nothing else and care for nothing else; right or wrong, success or failure, you want what you want! What I am pointing out is that you must not allow emotion to become the partner of desire, although they always come together. Instead, I urge you to choose the balancing function of your mind as a healthy partner for your emotions. Make your high soul the guardian of your desire.

Q: What does it mean to be spiritual?

Master Ni: Initially, it means learning to handle your emotions. It is usually easy to maintain emotional balance when nothing upsets you, but once you become upset, you speak and act very differently. Emotional reactions are often unwholesome. For example, you may feel mistreated by another and begin to punish yourself in order to make the other person feel guilty.

The maintenance of emotional health is very important in spiritual development. It is very much affected by your physical health as well as by the state of your relationships with those closest to you. Are those relationships good for you or do they pull you down? You need to identify whatever causes you to lose your balance.

Everyone is affected by your company and by the condition of your health. Therefore, in the great tradition of Tao we say that you must first correct the condition of your health, then put your emotions in order and balance. You need to clean out all old resentments. Leave no poisons within you, for they can become a disease.

It is very important to be in command of your emotions instead of reacting without control. If you have a fight with a boyfriend or girlfriend and are upset as you drive your car, you could have an accident and hurt yourself or someone else because you have lost your emotional balance. Without emotional balance, what foundation is there for spiritual achievement? Some people play a spiritual role but keep right on fighting in their daily lives; they could continue playing their role for a thousand years and never achieve the least bit of spirituality.

Since most of you are Tai Chi students, the practice of Tai Chi will guide and help your emotional energy to flow more smoothly. You will notice that when your mind is shaken, the movements of your Tai Chi are not smooth either. When you are off balance, everything you do may also be off. When you are balanced, your movements flow evenly and are as graceful as those of a heavenly being on earth.

After you've practiced Tai Chi for some time and your energy has become more steady and calm, you may begin to follow practices from the *Workbook for Spiritual Development.* Basically, you cannot meditate until you have acquired a calm mind.

Q: On the subject of emotion, I have heard that joy dissipates energy. Is it joy or the frivolous pursuit of happiness which dissipates the energy?

Master Ni: I would classify joyful or happy energy as healthy. By this I do not mean mad excitement. It ceases to be healthy when it reaches the point of excitement. When emotion becomes excitement, it has reached its peak and will go down. For example, often when we meet old friends we have not seen for a long time, we get very happy and excited. But we need to keep a balanced, peaceful mood. A peaceful mood is joyous and happy. We do not need to search for excitement.

The trouble is that most people cannot settle into peacefulness and be content; they find it boring because they do not know how to enjoy it. They would rather look for thrills and get into trouble. To a spiritually developed person, however, peacefulness is the best of times.

Q: How can you utilize this time?

Master Ni: You see, when you feel bored you are in good condition. Physically and financially, everything is in order. You just cannot contain yourself. You will never attain a truly high energetic state if as soon as you have gathered energy, you rush out to spend it on excitements which leave you low and empty. Then you must wait until your energy builds up again, and then what do you do? You cannot wait to spend it, and so the cycle repeats itself again and again.

Peacefulness is the best time to enjoy the flower and fruit that your life produces. Where there is peace, there is God. When a person can remain in peace, that is when his or her spiritual energy grows. Do not do anything to spoil such a time.

Q: You were talking about approaching Tai Chi from a centered condition. Won't the practice itself help you become more centered?

Master Ni: Yes. Under normal circumstances, when there is no pressure or disturbance, practicing Tai Chi or breathing meditation can help you form balanced attitudes. Once these attitudes are established, they will further your practice and strengthen your energy. An important thing to remember is that you foster and magnify the attitudes you focus on and concentrate with. Pay attention to these attitudes, especially while in quiet meditation. If your attitude toward meditation is too tight and you sit solemnly and stiffly, you will nourish and increase this overly serious and unpleasant aspect of your practice and this will become the sour fruit you bear. If, on the other hand, you sit with genuine joy, the world sings to you; the pores and cells of the breeze dance for you.

If you feel disturbed by anyone or anything, do not do Tai Chi or meditation, because your disturbance will attract a corresponding energy. When you are peaceful and joyful as you enter these practices, then you will embrace more of the same energy. If you do not believe me, try it. The truth never fears being tested.

When you sit to meditate, you need to sit with something in your mind that will strengthen the conception of your own spiritual being. You cannot sit empty-minded or you will turn to stone. Your goal is to bear happy, living fruit. Who needs a sour apple?

In human life, moods and attitudes are so important. They can decide your fate. If your attitude is evasive, you will dislike your work and many other things that come to you in life. In your mind you will have established a world of imprisonment. How can you enjoy such a life? On the other hand, with a positive attitude, you will embrace your work wholeheartedly and give it your best. You will also embrace the many things that come to you in life wholeheartedly.

When we were young, many of us developed a poor attitude towards the jobs and errands we were given by our parents and we started to build an unconstructive orientation toward work at an early age. As a result, many people's lives are empty and misdirected. They do not know how to find fulfillment in creative productivity; they only look forward to thrills and excitement. Many deep-rooted habits and inner reactions have their origin in childhood experiences. To understand this within ourselves, we need to contemplate and correct it.

Q: Can Tai Chi change your mood? Many people say that if they start doing Tai Chi in a bad mood, they finish in a better mood. But you say not to do it in a bad mood.

Master Ni: How bad? If it helps, there's no reason not to do it. When your mind is already troubled, you cannot work on your mind. If your body can affect the mind's condition, and the mind can respond by adjusting, then the body flows easier and the mind feels better still.

Q: Do you have any suggestions for times when we are emotionally troubled and have lost all clarity? (This question was asked by a woman.)

Master Ni: Women tend to have this sort of problem more often than men, because a woman's nervous system is more delicate. Women are also affected by their menstrual cycles. It would help all women to notice when they begin to tire; most women do not know it. It is very important. Because we are acculturated by the social demand of constantly needing or providing entertainment, women may not know when to retire and rest. But as they go on, day after day, their nervous system becomes more and more congested and anything can trigger a fight. It may not be a case of being mean or unreasonable; one may simply be tired. Even diplomats become cranky if they are always tired. That's why they cannot accomplish anything at the U.N. or other international meetings.

Q: What do you think of psychotherapy?

Master Ni: Psychotherapy can be helpful, but one still needs to work on oneself. It is important to find the right therapist, because there are many approaches that are not fruitful. You need to choose carefully. This is not spiritual achievement, but it can help you acquire a more objective view of your emotions.

Q: I've been struggling to make my spiritual and financial work the same...

Master Ni: What is the trouble? Is there a conflict between your spiritual achievement and the way you make money?

Q: I'm not getting to be around the people I want to be around.

Master Ni: Change jobs. Look for a means of earning money that makes you happy. Sometimes you may find that you are not happy in a highly paying job and you may need to take a cut in pay in order to find the right job. It is better to avoid making quick money if it cannot be enjoyed in a balanced and healthy manner.

If you become involved with bad company in your work, they can pull you into bad things. It is hard to say no to old friends and patterns. If this is the case, it is best to relocate to an area where they cannot reach you. Sever all contact and start anew.

Because of my position as a spiritual teacher, I have had occasion to counsel some so-called big fish and even some sharks. What I hear is confidential, but I will tell you this: people who are big fish in the sea of finance are not happy people. In spite of their wealth, they cannot enjoy life. Most of them slowly poison their children the same way they have poisoned themselves.

I think that everyone can find a suitable job if they are not afraid of honest, hearty work. I assure you that good hard work can bring you far greater spiritual happiness than an irresponsible job with a big salary.

Q: How do you feel about the energy around Taos?

Master Ni: It is nice for an adult of a more mature age to be here. For younger people, I believe, it would be better to experience the outside world and then come back.

Q: I've done Tai Chi for a long time. Sometimes it is better and sometimes it is worse, but it is never the same twice.

Master Ni: That is normal. When you do Tai Chi or meditation, give it your best energy. Do not scatter your energy before you practice, because then your mind, hand and foot will not follow each other well.

Q: When you talk about energy, do you mean that we get filled up with energy like a cup?

Master Ni: When you are in good physical condition, your metabolism is balanced and right and your internal secretions are in the right proportions. When everything is right, that produces energy. Health is self-generating.

If you do things in excess or are troubled, your nervous system is affected first, then the lymph system and the secretions in the body. At that point, the subtle energy does not grow. A potted flower needs to be in a place that is neither too shady nor too sunny, neither too wet nor too dry. In the right environment, the plant blooms. Personal energy is like a flowering plant; it is just less visible. If you wish to harvest the fruit, do not pick the flowers or empty the cup when you are bored. Look instead for constructive or creative enjoyments.

Q: What happens when a person's spiritual energy increases?

Master Ni: When your spiritual energy starts to become strong, you feel like you are standing on top of the world. You feel centered and happy. This stage matures to the point where you no longer care to have the world "under your foot," and you begin to see many things that others cannot. For example, you know a person well at first meeting and can even see what kinds of things have happened to him. You do not need to be a psychic.

Ninety-nine out of a hundred professional psychics are either fake or spiritually undeveloped. But we are all psychic when we have good energy. This is because when an individuals's spiritual energy is stronger, he or she is smarter, do things better, and life seems to go well. When one's spiritual energy is low, a person is clumsy and things are not quite right. In an extreme state, accidents occur.

Q: What is the best way to handle physical pain?

Master Ni: Physical pain can have various causes, so first you need to identify the cause of your pain. Some pain can be caused by viruses and sometimes your whole body can ache from emotional exhaustion alone. For such levels of pain, a warm bath and good rest are helpful. If the pain is caused by something more serious, one can be helped by acupuncture and herbs. I do not recommend hospitals or surgery in most cases.

Above all, I would like to recommend spiritual development because it is all-encompassing. You can use my books as your mirror. Check your lives against them and try to align yourself with the teachings in them. I have written a work manual for you and have given easy-to-follow guidance for how to best operate this machine of body, soul and mind. This is the purpose of my books. I hope you will find them useful in your lives.

I was happy to be with you all. It has been like meeting old friends. I hope we meet again.

An individual can be either the slave of the material sphere and spiritual underdevelopment, or a master of spiritual freedom. The pursuit of enlightenment is what enables one to attain spiritual freedom.

To end this meeting, I offer this poem from an ancient achieved one in the great tradition of Tao, the path of wholeness and naturalness.

> **If you are blocked by all the senses,**
> **you are pulled by the power of their**
> **pleasure.**
> **Sensuality becomes the master**
> **of your life**
> **in place of the true one**
> **who goes in and out the same door**
> **as the servants.**
> **The servants do not know the master,**
> **and the master mistakes the servants**
> **for the masters.**

CHAPTER SEVEN

(Special instruction to an individual who had accomplished his basic virtuous fulfillment.)

Q: In your books you have spoken about body spirits. Can you say something more about them?

Master Ni: We are composed of a number of body spirits, the complete integration of which is achieved through self-cultivation. In time, this process of integration results in the birth of a spiritual baby.

Q: Is the forming of a body spirit like conceiving a fetus then? Is this a process in which there is transformation and growth?

Master Ni: It is a process in which spiritual and sexual energies are perfectly integrated. As you well know, sexual energy has a life-producing potency. If it flows in a downward direction, it is made available for the conception of a physical child. Through self-cultivation, this downward flow becomes an upward stream that needs to be contained within and not be scattered without. In this way, it is possible to bring about a new spiritual life. This kind of spiritual life is not the same as the new life after the body is shed. When the body is shed, all essence is transferred to the new spiritual body.

Many ages ago, the ancient achieved ones knew about the existence of body spirits, but this knowledge has become lost to present societies which focus almost exclusively on the material side of life. Now it is a very special secret.

Body spirits can be troublesome. Some people can be frightened to the point of death by a ghost, even though the ghost is usually nothing more than a negative element within themselves. When a person loses his or her reign over the mind, the mind becomes chaotic and disordered and the person is considered mentally ill or disturbed. Likewise, when a person does not cultivate himself, his or her body spirits dominate and overwhelm the person in a confusing disorder. People who are deeply disturbed or psychotic are often given drugs or shock treatment, both of which harm the spirit and do nothing to resolve the true problem.

There are two main causes for such extreme disorder. One may be karmic, that is to say, the person is born with a particular problem associated with parents, grandparents, and so forth. The problem may not show up until later in life or under specific, particular circumstances. Another cause can be a conflict between the mind and the body spirits when the body spirits have direct knowledge of something while the mind attaches itself to learned information. The resulting split in consciousness between these two different ways of knowing often causes madness.

Q: Are body spirits infinite in number, like the cells of the body?

Master Ni: The number of body spirits varies from individual to individual, depending on one's cultivation. They are like money. Some people manage to have a lot; others have only a little. Some squander what they have, while others increase and multiply it. Some people have a spiritual body so large that when you enter their house you have already entered their spiritual body. Do you know that as you walk beneath the stars on a summer night, you are within a great spiritual body? All that exists in this universe is only a single body.

The accumulation of spiritual "currency" depends on one's behavior and virtue. A good person will attract energy similar to his or her own, and in this way positive energy multiplies and is increased. Similarly, a person who has extreme or negative attitudes attracts corresponding energy; thus, his or her negativity increases and becomes destructive to himself and others around him.

We have briefly discussed animal souls and spiritual souls in a single human life. The lower group of animal souls, Po, is a seven-fold organization which makes up the negative yin sphere of the soul. Po include the genetic inheritance of one's family and are identified as the "animal" part of the soul, because they are made up of blind impulses and compulsions that actualize the goals of physical existence without wisdom or understanding. Among the seven animal souls, one part is responsible for physical enjoyment, but has no ability to distinguish between what is enough and what is too much or between what is healthy and what is abusive. A strong mind is needed to regulate these blind forces relentlessly seeking nothing but their own ends. It is possible through self-cultivation to transform this denser, temporal sphere to a positive, yang state.

The second group, Hun, comprises the spiritual sphere of the soul and is made up of three parts, each having different functions. Your mind is the director conducting the activities of both spheres of your soul, and all parts need to come under its rule and obey.

Q: Does this mean that these seven animal souls are not actually negative in effect, but that their energies support life on earth?

Master Ni: Some people have very strong physical energy that can be put to positive use in the material world. However, without the guidance of the spiritual part of the soul, one's judgement and accomplishments may not be of true value. In the cultivation of Tao, the integration of Hun and Po is considered to be very important. One needs to place the animal souls beneath the guidance of the spiritual souls so that all can benefit. This brings true and significant harmony. It is not a compromise. If no integration occurs, then the spiritual souls will tend to go in one direction and the animal souls in another. This creates disintegration rather than integration. Destructive tendencies become very strong in this case.

Q: Then would you say that virtue is the use of the will to guide the animal spirits?

Master Ni: Virtue is the product of wisdom. Wisdom without virtue is like a flower without any fragrance. Virtue is not morality, but simply the correct way of living in accord with life's rules. It is your spiritual as well as physical protection. Virtue is balance. If you keep eating and drinking too much, going out every night, etc., you will harm yourself. Such behavior lacks both wisdom and balance; it violates the rules of life. Virtue is what maintains you and ensures calmness and peace. You could call it the keystone of a natural, normal, plain life.

There was a young woman who was well supported by a father who was remote and disconnected from her. She was beautiful but proud. Although she liked men, she was unable to accommodate lovers well, so in time she became emotionally disappointed in love and felt lonely and sad. One part of her animal soul gravitated toward suicide. Animal souls will transform into strong emotion and desire in this way. They only want to get or have what they want, while the spiritual souls gravitate toward independence and selfless giving. If a person's spiritual sphere is too weak, the animal souls will dominate his or her life. In this case, the young woman gave in to her desire for vengeance against her parents, teacher, lovers and society, by taking her own life. She chose to say, "I have been rejected by everyone. I have a hundred reasons to kill myself. It would be virtuous to end my life." What arrogance! Life belongs to nature. Nature gave it to us for safe-keeping; it is a tool, a vehicle for further growth. How would you feel if you saw someone whip his horse cruelly or smash a new car he had just bought? You would consider it unvirtuous behavior!

Life has been given to everyone, but very few know enough to value it. Isn't it striking that man can build vehicles that fly through space, yet he remains so ignorant of his spiritual life here on earth? He may journey to every corner of the universe and still not know himself.

Q: Is that because people cannot see the value of life?

Master Ni: Yes. It takes many years to see what life is. At the age of thirteen I thought I knew everything, because I had read all my father's books. Why should I listen to anything more my father and mother said? Fifty years later, I can see that my mother and father still knew life better than I do even now, because I have still not actualized what they taught me when I was young. It takes many years to even begin to know what life is. Is there anyone who wants to develop the ability to know?

The world is divided into two major types of culture: one which is materially based and the other which is sort of religious. Materialistic cultures tend to deny the existence of God, while religions believe that there is a God. Neither one knows for sure. They are both equally superstitious and do nothing to develop their ability to know and investigate the truth. I have outlined some methods of investigation for you in *The Workbook for Spiritual Development*, but I have not specified the order of the practices or any time requirements. You have the methods. Begin to work and find out for yourself.

Q: How should an ordinary person who recognizes that he wants to grow spiritually, but has not yet had a direct experience of the truth, proceed in this process of self-cultivation?

Master Ni: Such a person needs to develop his or her mind. If your mind is undeveloped, how can you know real worth from worthlessness? You could mistake a diamond for an ordinary stone and throw it away! In the great tradition of Tao, we have no rigid, organized standards. Everything depends on the individual's stage of development, and one is encouraged to use whatever furthers one's growth. It is alright to associate with a religion or church or philosophy, if it nurtures you in a positive way. What you must realize, however, is that if you are committed to your own spiritual growth, you cannot make a lifetime commitment to any religious or social doctrine that only serves you for a while until you outgrow it.

No one can give you the truth; only you can get the truth for and by yourself. As you move from one stepping stone to the next, do not let yourself become stranded on any one of them. Do not sacrifice or confine your life to any slogan, propaganda or belief.

Q: Once a person realizes the limitations of religion, what should he do if he lives in a small town and sincerely wishes to find proper guidance for spiritual self-development?

Master Ni: Be a good person who is natural, balanced and healthy, and educate yourself. Use libraries to gather information. Train and develop your mind to see and distinguish the true differences in things. You should bring yourself to yourself by yourself and realize that you can change everything in your life by changing yourself.

It is important to recognize that you cannot leap from the first step to the top, but must proceed step by step. The difficulties you encounter are lessons that help you to advance toward true and lasting happiness.

Q: Why is it that, although people wish for spiritual achievement, they usually find it easier to follow the animal souls? Is this because the pull of the animal nature in us is stronger?

Master Ni: On the contrary, you will find it much easier to follow the spiritual way. Do you really think it is easy to follow your desires? They complicate life to such a great extent. You have to work very hard just so you can have a new car, look nice, smell good and be amused. In the end, you pay the price of a lifetime of slavery for just a small bit of fun.

Q: Is that because it is hard for people to recognize the advantages of simplicity?

Master Ni: Yes. This is why it is so important to develop the mind. A well-developed mind can see what others miss. Once you can see something clearly, you can adjust your direction accordingly. The trouble is that people often cannot see the way things really are, because their animal nature is too dominant. The physical aspect of life overpowers them and can even bring destruction. On the other hand, if a person's spiritual energy is too dominant, the person will be useless and unable to achieve anything in the world. This is why we value balance between the spiritual and physical aspects of life.

Q: Then the object is not to deny the body?

Master Ni: To a person of Tao, the body is a gift for spiritual integration with the higher spheres. It is a chance to evolve spiritually. If used well, the human body can carry you to higher stages. There are many who do not think this way. They only think about how much pleasure they can obtain out of life; they know nothing about the purpose of self-cultivation.

If you had $500 you might spend it extravagantly and soon have nothing left, but if you put your creativity to use, you might find a way to double the amount and increase it many times over. It is no different at the spiritual level of life. Everyone comes into the world with a certain allotment of spiritual wealth. Even if it is small, it can be increased; and if it is great, it can be squandered. Life never stands still. It either grows or declines. If you do not move upward, then you move downward.

If you want achievement, you must first have understanding. There may be some who would deny the importance of understanding, but I have observed through personal experience, accomplishment follows understanding stage by stage. At first, my behavior did not measure up to my understanding, but slowly, over the years, I actualized my understanding in life. Even if you learn something, it does not mean that you have understood it. You may be able to repeat wise words, but you are no wiser than a parrot if that is all you can do.

In the first stages of self-cultivation, you need to keep a watch over the animal souls. If your mind becomes too loose, the animal souls rush up to take over, and any decision made in this state is bound to be faulty. It is very important to keep a steady reign and maintain a clear mind that can protect an upright and continuing sense of order. Our animal nature is designed to function purely within the physical realm. When it interferes in other aspects of life, it can be troublesome and inappropriate. In the same way, spiritual energies can be inappropriate if they try to operate within the physical domain. Everything has its own place.

Where do you think the notion of Satan originated? Can you see how the activity of these animal souls might take such a shape within the mind? What is temptation? Are great riches evil in themselves? Is beauty corrupt in itself? Is anything material bad in itself? How could it be? It is when the Po are out of balance and become associated with the material world that they appear to be bad.

Sin is a fabricated notion with no basis in reality. When you examine it carefully, the subconscious has no intrinsic content; but when it fills up with the activities of the animal nature, then sin is conceived. Once sin is conceived, purity is conceived. People of self-cultivation need to keep the animal souls where they belong. A pure mind and soul are simply the result of keeping things in order within oneself.

Q: In order to control the mind, don't you first have to know who you are?

Master Ni: That is true. If you do not know yourself, you can easily lose control. You need to be able to recognize that part within the mind that is objective and clear: the captain of the ship; the part of the personality which is aware of the whole and thus capable of making correct choices. The other parts of the personality - the sailors so to speak - are necessary in order to get things done in the world. Without discipline, they can take over and get you into a lot of trouble. Responsibility rests with your inner captain. Through strength of will and through developing the capacity for choice, one can ensure a safe and smooth voyage rather than let a reckless crew bring the ship to a disastrous end. The one who reaches his or her destination is the one who has developed spiritual clarity and self-discipline within.

Q: In this day and age, should I just accept that there is more to be done than one man can possibly accomplish and just do the best I can each day?

Master Ni: The word "I" is a term of convenience to distinguish one from the environment and to signify the "Captain." Apart from this relative meaning, it has no reality. The deeper aspect of the soul is linked with the source from whence you came.

    After you have experienced many lives and reached a high level of evolution, there comes a point when you feel that you have had more than your fill of the lower level of existence. You feel that you cannot, and do not even wish to, remain on the physiological or animal level any longer. You may see existence as a stormy ocean where you are helplessly tossed up and down with no hope of reaching shore. But before becoming totally achieved, one still has to deal with the negative sphere of one's own soul to one degree or another. This yin aspect of the soul is often experienced as a state of psychological inertia. It likes everything easy, trouble free and comfortable. In this state, one just does not want to bother with anything. It is important not to allow such a polarization of energies to occur nor to allow duality to establish itself within the mind.

For example, once you establish the notion of Satan, the notion of God is simultaneously present. Many a Satan will not appear demonic, but rather as a god or goddess. You may fall for it and get into trouble. Nor should you look for conceptual definitions; in spiritual cultivation, you have to know the reality of things directly. It seems like the two sides are opposing one another for supremacy. At times when you are doing better, yin aspects decrease and spiritual, yang aspects increase. For some, when the yin sphere overtakes them, the yang aspects of their nature are greatly diminished.

In order to become a divine immortal, one needs to achieve the total positive yang sphere of one's nature. Even a tiny speck of yin remaining will keep one from passing over the boundary of experience to the other side of whole yang.

If we picture pure yang spirit as the sun, we may compare our difficulties to the weather. At times the sun is obscured by clouds. A spiritual person does not allow cloudy days to affect himself or herself deeply, knowing that events will pass and the enduring sun will still be there.

Q: I have always thought that the eternal was beyond yin and yang, that yin and yang came about after the polarization of the infinite.

Master Ni: The term is, again, one of convenience. It allows us to express the distinction between the enduring and the negative spheres. In reality, achievement is totality and wholeness. It is sometimes confusing for a student to hear that the goal of achievement is wholeness, who sometimes concludes from this that wholeness must also include negativity. It does not.

Q: What is the relationship between teacher and student?

Master Ni: Well-developed teachers do not like many students around them. They certainly enjoy good students and good friends, just as one enjoys flowers in a field, but most people are not like that; their negative energy is too dominant. Such people unconsciously abuse a teacher. A good teacher, or any spiritual person, needs to withhold himself from the abusive majority of people.

Because self-cultivation is emphasized in the tradition of Tao, many people ask why a teacher is needed. I assure you, it is certainly not to release you from personal responsibility for your own development and cultivation. If you entertain the notion that a teacher can save you by simply following him, this delusionary religious attitude will be an obstacle to your development. You must realize that you have to do your own part.

Even though a youngster needs to find things out for himself, the wise guidance of good parents or teachers can keep him from unnecessary and useless trouble. It takes a long time to reach maturity, even on a mental level. A sixteen year old will declare that he is fully grown and independent. What does he know? He is helpless and vulnerable and unaware of his predicament, yet his elders can see what he is missing. So, although you may declare yourself achieved, there may be someone who sees what you have missed: someone who can subtly guide you to see the whole picture correctly, because your way of thinking and your mistakes were once his. The teacher knows the territory you are about to cover, but you are the one who must do the walking. He can only give you a map. For this reason, we respect and cherish a good teacher.

As you grow more and become happier with yourself, you cannot ignore the unhappiness around you. You begin to feel that everyone is part of you and that your achievement or enlightenment cannot be absolutely complete until others have reached their destination as well. Thus you extend yourself and help others without demanding or expecting anything in return. You take care never to dominate anyone, since each person must make his or her own decisions by free will. A spiritual teacher gives advice freely, but does not impose it. A person can take it or leave it.

An individual can be either the slave of the material sphere and spiritual underdevelopment, or a master of spiritual freedom. The pursuit of enlightenment is what enables an individual to attain spiritual freedom.

To end this meeting, I offer this poem from an ancient achieved one in the great tradition of Tao, the path of wholeness and naturalness.

The one who learns Tao
  must first know himself
  by looking into the deep mind.
He goes further and further,
  until there is no further to go.
Then, one has reached the
  far-reaching universal
  pure essence of deathless life.

CHAPTER EIGHT

Miami, Florida: July 20, 1986
(This talk was given at a Unitarian Society service in Miami, Florida.)

I am very happy to have this occasion to meet all of you. It is wonderful to meet new friends. There is not much in life that is truly enjoyable, just a few things. The first thing to enjoy is the beauty of nature. Unfortunately, it is a costly luxury these days just to get where nature is. Another thing to consider and enjoy is good food, but you must learn how to cook it without spoiling it. Then, there is the enjoyment of good friends. You will find that meeting me in person is very different from reading my books, since my spoken English is not as clear. Nevertheless, because your heart can know my heart, you can sense my meaning.

You are all in the process of looking for good information and valuable guidance, wishing to grow well and correctly. Along the way, you have received some negative, restrictive teachings that have influenced and programmed you, so you may find it difficult to open your heart.

The most beautiful of all things are people. A human being is a convergence of natural energies which is benefitted by gathering good energy and is damaged by gathering bad energy. Once you discover this, you can enjoy the beauty of any person at any time, not just in a narrow, sexual way. If you truly wish to fully witness the beauty of someone, you can do so by dissolving the restrictive attitude of seeking things for your own selfish needs. I find human beings to be the most beautiful of all living beings in this world, with horses as the second most beautiful. You might agree with me about a horse sooner than you would agree that your neighbor is beautiful. You are all so emotionally tight that you end up in conflict instead of enjoying one another. We could have such a lovely life. Instead of making nuclear weapons we could be loving each other and working together to help the world.

When you encounter difficulties in life, you immediately resort to emotionally triggered prayers, crying or yelling at the Supreme Being to help you, not realizing that this kind of approach can create even more problems for yourself. Heavy thoughts and emotions are like stones that people throw out all around themselves until they have built a tight, solid prison that encloses themselves.

The attempt to overcome difficulties by emotional means causes one to sink deeper into them. Trying to solve problems intellectually, on the other hand, causes the nervous system to tighten up so that one cannot find good solutions or be productive. It is better to relax. If you want to reach the universal spiritual energy that can facilitate the solving of your problems, you need to settle into the quietness of your own being. Only then will you open up to the full range of your potential.

You also need to reform your habits. Life can be very nice, but most people live in misery, because they have not learned how to manage themselves. Many mistakes are made because people do not know that everything would be better if they kept themselves open and lived independently within society, close to their own nature, peacefully and calmly. Instead, people anxiously look for information and solutions in bookstores, libraries and churches until they become mentally jammed up like a freeway in rush hour traffic. Inner mobility is only possible when the road is clear; you do not need to add anything, even though the modern way encourages you to.

The education that everyone receives today is most useful for making money from a career, but can you honestly say to yourself that you are content now that you have money? Fu Shi did not have money, nor did Lao Tzu or Chuang Tzu. Without spiritual development, how can you have a correct overview of your problems? How can you accurately judge the extent to which your acquired information is useful? You cannot. You need the natural development of your spiritual capacity.

More important than what any spiritually developed person can offer you is what you can do for yourself. To keep open and quiet within is most valuable, especially when you face a difficulty. At that time it is best to be by yourself. Solitude enables you to open up more easily to the natural, universal, spiritual energy that is everywhere and is ever responsive to your needs. It is the hyperactive intellectual mind that ties you in knots and causes you to feel separate from the natural, universal energy.

No matter how much you study or how many degrees you earn, they will not make you happier or more capable of solving real life problems. The intellect, in fact, tends to magnify small matters out of proportion and complicate them even further.

If you are tied into knots by the demanding tendencies of your own emotions, it is impossible to have a clear view of your involvement in a situation or with another person. By slowing down and untying the emotional knots within yourself, you will find that the outcome is happier and more pleasing than it would otherwise have been. As you change your inner attitude, your approach to specific situations also changes and happier results come in response to your energy change. If you are always worrying, you actually invite the very things you wish to avoid.

Would you like to test the truth of this principle? You can, but I would not recommend it. If you have some physical or emotional trouble, sit quietly and visualize the wholeness of your being and the health of your life. Even if you have a cyst or a tumor, try to not always think about it. Focus your mind on the knowledge that you are safe. As your mind feels better, it will guide your body to be better also. I am not suggesting that you stop receiving treatment, but I do assure you that good energy attracts good energy, believe it or not. At the very worst, you can have a happy departure from your body.

Q: Can you open someone's spiritual blockage with acupuncture?

Master Ni: It can be done. It depends on the spiritual achievement of the healer. I do not encourage this, because people would start pouring through the door of every acupuncturist seeking instant spirituality instead of working on it for themselves. Acupuncture can help some situations, but people still need to work on themselves if they wish to achieve total development.

Q: Which of your books do you recommend to a beginning student?

Master Ni: The easiest to understand, according to some of my students, are the two volumes of *Eight Thousand Years of Wisdom.*

Q: Do you have a group of students in California?

Master Ni: Yes, but I do not intentionally seek students. I just respond to people and give them advice, but they do not understand my advice until much later. Then they return, and an informal acquaintance slowly becomes a formal association.

My true wish is to help young people who want to restore their natural way of life and know more about natural truth. People, therefore, naturally gather around my work. Earlier this year I went on a lecture tour to Europe, Australia, and New Zealand and found many friends wherever I went. I believe that if people awaken to the mistake of preprogrammed education, they can find their way back to the natural truth.

Q: What formal methods of teaching do you use in California?

Master Ni: I am not like a teacher of mathematics. My way is unorganized. It is a hard job for me. When I was young, I was trained by my mother and father and by teachers who were rural, mountain people by nature. They were all so wise, but I was too young and shallow to fully appreciate them. I just wanted to grow up and have a good time. They were aware that the world would change, and they tried to teach me everything they knew. It was an important time in my personal education, but there was not enough of it. When the Communists came to mainland China, I had to leave, but wherever I go and whatever I do I make use of what my parents and teachers taught me.

In today's world of confusion, it is important for us to attain clarity of vision regarding the natural truth. The wholesale misguidance and indoctrination of people has to stop. This is why I teach my classes.

Q: Is there a difference between Eastern and Western students?

Master Ni: It is not really a question of East and West, but of good students, period. In general, my students in the East had too much love for me. They always did things for me and made it too easy to forget about this troubled world. In the West, people feel the need to struggle through difficulties and test things, so they have a different attitude toward all relationships and are more self-protective. If this attitude is applied to the relationship between a spiritual teacher and a student, the teacher finds it harder to assist the student. Mistakes cannot be seen easily or clearly when we are over-protecting ourselves. In some cases, Eastern students attempt to bend the teacher to their local culture and customs, or they over-rely on the teacher to make all decisions and advise them in their lives. In reality, students need to be fighters in their own lives and in their choice for growth.

I appreciate students who do not hold onto things tightly or refuse to grow up. Students in the East were reluctant to have me go off to teach in other parts of the world. I feel it is wasteful if people value emotional victory and do not recognize the spiritual value of suffering losses.

I would like to continue working in the West. Eventually we all have to turn the world around until West becomes East and East becomes West.

Q: Is it necessary to have a teacher to uncover the light of divine energy?

Master Ni: I believe that one needs many books and teachers. In today's world, there are many things that can poison and warp your attitudes. You build many walls, large and small, around yourself so that you cannot see the light. You need to break those walls down, piece by piece. Different aspects of this hardening may crumble in response to different teachings.

In the tradition of Tao, we recognize that you can be enlightened in a single instant, but it takes many years of work on your life to clear away the heavy accumulation of darkness and actualize this enlightenment within your own being.

If the natural spiritual light lights up in you, you still need to check with someone who is spiritually achieved to see if your light is complete or whether you are still under the influence of a worldly education. As both teacher and student, I say that a person needs many teachers. Everyone can teach you something, if you are open enough.

Q: In addition to silence and non-attachment, are there any other practices that you recommend?

Master Ni: Yes. Your daily life itself is a spiritual practice, if you do everything wholeheartedly, with sincerity, faithfulness, loyalty and high energy. There are many lures in life, and it is hard to withstand their daily pressure. Physiological needs and pleasures must be fulfilled regularly, but for the sake of expedience people give into unnatural ways of fulfilling them. There are also psychological and social diversions, not to mention the demands of family and work. You can not grow as straight and undisturbed as a mountain if your environment pushes hard against you every moment. It is therefore necessary to learn some practices that can help protect your growth. This is what we do in my tradition.

Q: Do you feel that meditation, Tai Chi and Kung Fu are beneficial to Westerners?

Master Ni: Spiritual training occurs at three levels. In actuality, a person's physical, mental and spiritual energies are interconnected and always affect one another. Reluctantly, for the sake of practical expression, we can divide these into three. But it should be known that through physical achievement one can attain spiritual achievement. Thus, you can see the value of the practices of Eight Treasures, Tai Chi Ch'uan, and Chi Gong.

As for the mind, it can be a good and faithful minister or a traitor that robs you. You reap the consequences of the way in which you manage your life. One way of eliminating the negativity of the mind and making it into an effective minister is the Wu Tao. Wu Tao is a training that allows you to develop yourself deeply and philosophically in order to eliminate unnecessary habits that hinder your development. After one is physically and mentally accomplished, one can then begin to work on the spirit. This is what I recommend for everyone in *The Workbook for Spiritual Development*. My senior students help me to teach the first and second levels, but the third level I must attend to myself.

The third level is usually a reward to those who have gone through all the training and become almost perfect in their virtue. They need only the last step to break through from the human level to experience the supernatural level. The third level is a spiritual practice that culminates in becoming a member of immortal company. I usually do not promote this level publicly. The goal of my general teachings wherever I go is to broadcast the importance of balance between physical, mental and spiritual activity in one's life. If people ever discovered the joy of a balanced life, the world would be a far happier and more peaceful place, where people could be directly in touch with natural, spiritual guidance without any interceding religion. Many things in life do not require the presence of a teacher, but in the beginning you are like a baby who cannot walk, so you need help and training.

An individual can be either a slave of the material sphere and spiritual under-development, or a master of spiritual freedom. The pursuit of enlightenment is what enables an individual to attain spiritual freedom.

To end this meeting, I offer this poem from an ancient achieved one in the great tradition of Tao, the path of wholeness and naturalness.

In the vast universal valley,
  is the eternal spirit,
  the root of universal life.
The ancient sages called it
  the Gate of All Wonders.
It shows life and death
  to the one who lives
  among the superficial
  changes in the valley.
It shows spiritual eternity
  to the one who lives connected
  with the root of the universe.

The great oneness of indistinguishability
  is the mystical origin prior to Heaven.
It is the law of itself.
It is the law of life itself.
It is the origin of all.
One who can spiritually rejoin
  the origin of all lives
  enjoys the spiritual freedom
  of universal nature.

CHAPTER NINE

Miami, Florida: July 20, 1986
(This talk was given at the open house of The Fellowship of the
Subtle Light in Miami. The meeting began with a reading from
Chapter 67 of the Tao Teh Ching by George Robinson.)

Good afternoon everyone. This morning, we discussed
universal natural energy. This afternoon I would like to go
from the great vastness of the universe to consider your
individual lives. We will begin by discussing the spiritual
light within our own lives.

Each individual is a small model of the universe and of
nature and can thus develop his or her life being to be totally
spiritualized. This may seem like too high a goal for modern
people, but if you cultivate yourself in daily life, you will
discover spiritual light growing within. Once subtle light
grows within you, it sheds light not only on your own path,
but it can help other people as well.

Today's educational systems mass produce intellectual
robots who are overdeveloped in some aspects and helplessly
deficient in others. This is an obstacle to the growth of
spiritual light within each being. In the great tradition of Tao,
which dates back at least 8,000 years, we do not encourage
people to depend on a teacher's light. Salvation comes from
within yourself, from the spiritual light within your own life
being.

People highly respect wisdom, but wisdom is the product
of experience. The creation of things like the space shuttle
comes about through a combination of spiritual and intellectual energies; however, the people involved in such creations
usually have no awareness of the spiritual qualities possessed
by man. They do not realize that, besides being able to create
such things, it is also possible to have a precognition of their
fate. Many problems in life can be seen in advance and
avoided. A person's spiritual light enables an immediate, vital
knowing that requires no past records or memories. Do you
see how important it is to guide ourselves towards the

cultivation of this inner spiritual light? With it, you have your own guidance, help and great advisor. With it, you are a beacon unto others and everything you need unto yourself. We are close to the end of the 20th century and are very proud of our intellectual achievement, but I do not see that we are any better off in the quality of our lives than those without intellectual achievement. I am not condemning intellectual achievement, but I do know that people need to develop the subtle light within themselves in order for their lives to be balanced. Otherwise, they will become more and more like intellectual robots.

Today's world is headed in a very destructive direction, which can only be corrected by the achievement of spiritual light. I believe that we would have a more pleasant and beautiful world in every way if the leaders and advisors of world affairs were to develop themselves spiritually.

Hitler, Mussolini and Tojo could have foreseen their own defeat and perhaps have refrained from waging war if they had possessed the smallest bit of spiritual light. As it was, their spiritual qualities were blocked and their intellectual superiority availed them nothing. Without the guidance of spiritual light, intellectual power can wreak havoc and bring misery, not only to individual lives, but also to the world at large.

All of you living at the intellectual and emotional level of life should begin to cultivate the spiritual aspect of yourselves. It is possible and important for each of us to develop our subtle inner light. Without it, you will always need to rely on someone or something for second-hand knowledge that often proves useless. As I have explained, the subtle light is your own spiritual nature, but it will not grow without cultivation. You need patience and perseverance, for it requires time and constancy.

If I were to overemphasize the idea of the universal, spiritual divine energy, you would develop a false concept of it as something holy and separate, high and above yourselves. What you should aim for is a balance between your own internal spiritual achievement and the universal subtle law. When this is accomplished, one attains a high spiritual freedom and lives a universal life, and may even enter the immortal realm.

Q: What is the end result of developing the inner spiritual light?

Master Ni: Very simply, there will be no mistakes in your life. We all know the role that impulse and compulsion have played throughout the last 3,000 years of human history. Without spiritual light, we doom ourselves to a future of repeated mistakes. We do not need to recreate the suffering of our ancestors; we can improve ourselves, change the pattern of our lives, and pass on a better heritage to our descendants. The only way to realize such a goal is by achieving one's own inner light. Past experience enables a person to understand things, but it is the spiritual light that saves one from making big mistakes.

Let me illustrate this point for you. Say you are at home and do not actually need to go anywhere. Your spiritual light knows something and signals you not to go, but your restlessness overrides and drowns out the delicate signal of your subtle nature. You go out and find yourself in some kind of unnecessary accident or trouble. How much trouble could we save ourselves if only we would stay open to the spiritual light?

This can be verified in your own lives. You need daily cultivation to remain calm and quiet within yourself. Why rely on others to spoon-feed you? It is far more practical to develop yourself so that you can depend on yourself.

Q: Would you explain what you mean by the law of universal energy response?

Master Ni: It is very simple. You do good, you enjoy life. You do wrong; you suffer for it. Going into it a bit deeper, you can say that what you conceive is what you attract. Belief is another matter. You may have delusionary beliefs, but they cannot come true. When you conceive certain qualities in your mind, they will come true because one kind of energy attracts more of its own kind. If you conceive nastiness within yourself, just watch and see what comes to you.

I will tell you something more. Once you develop yourself spiritually, the subtlest thought is louder than thunder, and the universal response is immediate.

In ancient times, there were many magicians. Those who were not just tricksters were empowered by only one thing: the law of energy correspondence. Today, we can influence the weather with chemicals thrown from an airplane. In China, up until two hundred years ago, the weather was influenced by human minds skilled in a particular method. Anyone with natural spiritual concentration could do it. A person of balanced spiritual energy can have an energy correspondence with all of nature. Today's people do not realize that nature is life itself; it is a whole, living being. If they knew this, how could they behave as they do?

Emotion aggravates or gives help to bacteria invading parts of the body where they do not belong. This can cause us to become ill and die. Now look at the earth. Isn't nature being invaded by human beings who insist on upsetting areas that they should not upset? Although I do not blame you, it is ultimately someone's fault. People do not respect nature, yet nature continues to respond to human energy. When a person finds proof of this in one's own life, he or she becomes much more open to the possibility of high spiritua! achievement.

The majority of people are either made into religious or political cattle by the ambition and desire for power of a few. They shove people into conditioned ways and bar them from the possibility of unhindered, natural spiritual development. How can such backward leadership be respected? The ancient developed ones knew what would affect a life being and in what manner. They recorded their knowledge and passed it on orally to their students, who could then evoke responses from nature more easily. If these practices were known today, human life and society could evolve much further instead of continuing to limp through the darkness of undevelopment and repeating its past mistakes. I wish to put you in the role of leaders. Once you have developed your own spiritual light, you can guide the world toward spiritual progress.

An individual's personal energy formation is always changing according to one's choices in living, doing and being. These changes in personal energy formation determine what comes to an individual in life. People often feel blessed when they receive a lot of money or love or anything pleasing. On the other hand, they feel mistreated by life or jinxed if things go badly. They fail to realize that the events in their lives have nothing to do with anything external, not even the stars. What comes to a person depends entirely on one's inner qualities. People who are unaware of this due to a lack of spiritual development always end up in a tight corner.

We are all well acquainted with man-made laws which can be broken or evaded, but a spiritually developed person knows that nothing can escape the subtle law. It cannot be bent, broken or evaded. If you violate it, you violate yourself, and you experience the consequence directly.

Most people rely on their intellect to view life. According to that view, it seems that one should be able to do whatever one pleases. But this view does not see the subtle law that operates behind everything. A person may see something as a benefit and consider himself a winner, not realizing that what he has seized is merely an attractive facade covering the face of the trouble.

It is difficult to explain the subtle law. You will eventually find out what it is, and that the whole universe is a network of energy. If one thing goes wrong, it affects the whole. It is like your body. I can put a needle in one point and affect several other parts of your body. It is good to know that spiritual practice is based on practical response, and it is important to know the subtle law in order to avoid making mistakes.

Q: What would you say is the most effective way of communicating with another human being?

Master Ni: It is best not to talk too much. In our daily life, quietness is eloquent. Saying nothing is the most effective communication system. Do not rely on your intellectual system. Everyone goes to school and is trained in the same way, yet each person picks up something different because everyone's intellectual structure is different. We all interpret the same words differently, so there is really very little direct verbal communication.

Q: What is the relationship between emotional energy and subtle energy?

Master Ni: A question about emotional trouble cannot be solved by an answer. It needs to be worked out through a process. Emotions are connected with physical energy. When your emotions are disturbed, you cannot see straight. Many negative things happen in families and in the world because of emotional reactions. The subtle light is connected with your spiritual energy, which is based on the peace and harmony of your emotional energy.

We all have emotions; what we need to work on is balance. There are two kinds of emotion: positive, joyful emotion which is healthy and should be released; and negative emotion which causes worry, anger, anxiety, etc., and should be diluted or weakened. Most people let themselves be ruled by the mind's first reaction to a thing or situation; this is usually an emotional response. If you have an inner spiritual light, you look at a matter clearly before acting.

All the practices developed by the ancient developed ones are as useful today as they ever were. In the great tradition of Tao, we emphasize morning and evening cultivation to help your emotions become neutral and to keep you from being easily disturbed. Once you are disturbed, you cannot see clearly or solve anything correctly. We also have methods to help the body restore and maintain its health, and regulate and help the energy flow which calms and steadies the emotions. With steadier, calmer emotions, your internal harmony is able to produce spiritual energy.

These methods also include training your mind to be accurate. Your mind is usually not accurate, because it is so critical and judgmental. You think you are right about everything, but your views are emotionally based and are therefore unobjective and distorted. I see so many people being critical. They think they are wise, but they cannot offer anything true enough to be useful.

Finally we come to spiritual training and cultivation. But you do not even know anything yet about diet. You will feed yourself anything without knowing how it affects your physical, emotional and spiritual health. How can you expect to be happy?

Q: If I don't learn the lessons I need to learn in this lifetime, will I have to repeat them in my next life?

Master Ni: You can take advantage of teachings and practices that would help you develop, or you can choose to let them pass. If you have no problems in life and nothing that you could improve, then you could leave the practices. But if you put things off, saying that you will do it in the next life, how can you be sure they will get done? You might as well do your best now. There is no chance of being or doing better in the next life unless you begin now.

Q: What is the relationship of prayer to the development of chi, clarity, work and general life according to the Taoist tradition?

Master Ni: The tradition of Tao does not include prayer as it is generally understood, because prayer is mostly an expression of emotion and desire. "Invocation" is a more appropriate term for what is practiced in the tradition of Tao. An invocation is a formalized guidance for spiritual and mental energies. When an invocation is accompanied by our own spiritual energy, it calls forth the response of corresponding energies. Without this, it is an empty religious ritual. Many people like rituals, and a good ritual, correctly performed, should be respected. But a ritual is useless unless it evokes a response from the universal divine energy or your own life being.

I have heard people say: "My prayer has been answered by this angel or that," but they do not really know the truth at the spiritual level. They are led by their own emotions into fooling themselves. Then they see some spiritual phenomenon and think, "That's it!" I say, "That's not it!"

It is important to have a correct view and approach to the spiritual world. If you take the opportunity to use a way which has proven to be effective over a long period of time, you would find out the spiritual truth for yourself.

Q: What personal experience did you have that was a catalyst to your spiritual development?

Master Ni: Many people will tell you about their experiences, but I would like for you to have your own experience. Then you will understand the subtle law and follow it voluntarily. People have so much trouble because they do not see how each of their actions is connected to the network of subtle energy. Whenever we go against the subtle law, there is an inevitable rebound from the violation, and we experience the discord that we have created.

I, or someone else, can tell you tales as pleasing as a bedtime story, but what you need is your own experience. We have many stories and accounts of the lives of masters in the great tradition of Tao. But their achievement is theirs, not yours.

I have gone to many different places with the purpose of helping people see and accomplish the possibility of their own spiritual growth. Once you are able to know universal spiritual reality, you can distinguish between mere phenomena and the reality itself. You need to achieve a communion between your internal and external being. This is totally possible.

Q: Is discomfort sometimes necessary to stimulate our attention in order to make a change?

Master Ni: Yes. Discomfort is a warning, sometimes for the physical body and sometimes for the emotions. You should reflect on the cause of any uneasiness. Once you identify the source of your trouble, correct it immediately since small troubles, if left uncorrected, become big troubles. If you are not spiritually alert, you will fail to catch problems while they are small and they will eventually overwhelm you when they become big.

Q: Can a person develop spiritual awareness through art or music?

Master Ni: Yes. Good music is an expression of good energy. When people's energy is blocked, they are unable to enjoy or appreciate good, sweet music. Someone with refined, delicate energy will always enjoy and appreciate exquisite beauty. I think that good art can be a positive way of sublimating and satisfying one's emotional life, and a good way to decide a person's spiritual quality. If art or music is used in one's spiritual cultivation, one must be careful not to allow the mind to get too abstract.

An individual can be either a slave of the material sphere and spiritual underdevelopment, or a master of spiritual freedom. The pursuit of enlightenment is what enables an individual to attain spiritual freedom.

To end this meeting, I offer this poem from an ancient achieved one in the great tradition of Tao, the path of wholeness and naturalness.

> **You look for the truth everywhere,**
> **so why not look within yourself?**
> **Look for yourself inside and out.**
> **Once you see the true self,**
> **it is strong and free,**
> **flowing with all of universal life.**
> **At this point, no devils can trouble you.**

CHAPTER TEN

St. Helena, California: October 25, 1986

Good morning everyone. It is very nice to be here with all of you. I arrived in the United States ten years ago and have spent most of that time establishing and working in a Chinese medical clinic in Los Angeles. My sons are now grown and able to assume responsibility for the clinical practice, so that gives me the opportunity to travel to new places in the world and make new friends.

You have all probably eaten at a Chinese restaurant and enjoyed new tastes, but you might also like to learn something about the way people in China cultivate and develop their essential spiritual nature. Many different kinds of temples were built in China in the course of 8,000 years. Like you, we are a melting pot of different religious and cultural influences.

There are basically two kinds of spiritual people. One kind goes to a temple to offer something in exchange for blessings, while the other seeks out the truth and support of universal, divine energies in order to develop himself. In today's world, although people are intellectually more developed and can usually get what they want without having to pray for it, a serious student will not be satisfied with material achievement alone. He or she will feel the absence of meaning in a life without spiritual direction and achievement.

If you watch small kittens, you will see that they have emotions. Even though they have feelings of anger or contentment, they are not what you could call unhappy. But when a more spiritually evolved soul takes human shape, it feels entrapped in the physical body and searches for what is missing. Serious students throughout the centuries have gone to the mountains or rural places in search of people who are spiritually achieved. A student might spend many years looking for a teacher who can help him find that missing part of himself by teaching him the practices and disciplines necessary for true spiritual development.

I watched someone chopping wood this morning and noticed that some pieces needed only one blow of the ax to split them in two. Other pieces were more stubborn, and it took several blows to break them. Once you are born, your mind begins to be shaped by educational and cultural influences that are rooted in external intellectual concepts and limited religious experience. This kind of conditioning tends to harden the mind into a narrow, confining shell. So now, just like the stubborn pieces of wood, some of you are very difficult to crack open.

The limitations of this kind of experience and education have caused many of you to separate your life-being from your true nature. Stripped of your integrity, you are left with nothing but the biological and physical demands of life and some meaningless artificial social structures. Somehow though, you sense that there is more to life than this; that there is some underlying truth behind biology and society. Even though people sense this unknown element, not everyone can see the truth of life, even when the wood is split with a single blow of the ax.

In the time before you were formed, you were happy because you were a pure spirit without any form. That phase of life is called pre-Heaven. Once you take form, you cannot know things as clearly and begin to sense that something is missing. This period is called the after-Heaven phase. Temples and churches cannot help you find what you are missing; you have to work on it yourself. Even a teacher cannot use the ax of his or her wisdom alone to break the intellectual shell in two so that the true gold of your inner essence shows. You have to work at this yourself.

A long time ago, when society was more natural, many people set out to discover if there was a truth of life beyond cultural customs and religious rituals. Anyone can learn to place incense correctly or recite some chant, but true spiritual development takes hard work, commitment and perseverance. Through the accumulated discoveries and achievements of these early spiritual pioneers, the spiritual tradition of Tao started to take form.

In today's world, a great deal of trouble and conflict stems from differences in political ideologies and religious beliefs, because everybody insists that what they believe is true. Conflict and war lead to death. Truth, however, is not a way that leads to death. If the truth depends on human beings to fight for it, it is not the truth. This is easy for anyone to see.

It is wrong to use one's shallow faith in God as an excuse or tool for social or political dominance. God is not anything that is relative to the narrow sphere of human perception. Universal spiritual energy has no name or form and is not limited by age or sex. Truth is not something that can be labeled and marketed; it is available only to those who take responsibility for their personal growth through spiritual development.

With spiritual development, you gain the capability of discernment: you know what is good and bad, just like you know at the market the difference between a fresh or a spoiled mellon. The world's problems, therefore, are a matter of spiritual undevelopment. But once people develop themselves beyond the competitive, animal stage of life, they begin to approach the deep spiritual truth. At this level, there is no more fighting or conflict.

Many people have asked me what I call God. In the great tradition of Tao, we recognize divinity by its special energy and virtue. We see the beautiful sky as a God. We recognize the good earth as a Goddess, and the tall, mysterious mountain as a God. We see a Goddess shimmering in a charming lake and a God standing strong in a beautiful tree. We recognize people who have achieved themselves as Gods or Goddesses and treat them as such. The way of distinguishing these divinities is by their special energy and virtue.

In history, some rulers have called themselves God's Divine Agent on Earth; those who knew them were not confused by what they called themselves. Spiritual development never depends on what people call themselves, but on what they do. No one can be fooled in the long run. A true divine one who embodies the universal essence of life, manifests it by the virtues of supportiveness and impartial love. This was the original way of recognizing divinity.

Before Buddhism came to China, there were two main groups. One group refused to be enslaved by the government or evil emperors. These people, who came from the tradition of Shiens, lived as hermits in the mountains and worked on their spiritual development, but they were only a minority. They were dedicated to a life of service and the achievement of physical longevity and spiritual immortality.

The other group were scholars who spent years studying for government examinations in order to attain a position in the hierarchy of government. They were ready for Buddhism when it came, because they had learned from experience that no matter how long or how faithfully they served an emperor, the emperor could always change his mind on a whim. Many of these people, therefore, found hope of escape in setting out to become a Buddha.

A few wise people who reflected on the situation recognized that a person cannot become someone or something that he or she is not. They saw that what was being called Buddha-nature was actually one's own original divine nature that exists before taking human form. According to this view, there is no need for external pursuit because the process of transformation is an internal one. So, although Buddhism originally came to China as an external religious form, certain wise masters assimilated, transformed it and eventually shifted its focus back to the untouched, pure spiritual energy that one cultivates and nurtures in one's lifetime.

People become ungrounded when they lose touch with their own true nature. They start to believe and identify themselves with everything their family and society have told them they are. Some of these things are male or female; white, yellow or black; great or sinful; rich or poor. At some point in the process of spiritual self-cultivation, however, it is necessary to put aside all preconceptions and examine who you really are and what lies beyond the superficial level of what you have been taught. People have been enculturated to identify with the physical form of the body; consequently, they suffer all the limitations that form imposes upon them.

But once you recognize that your achieved spiritual energy is beyond form, the next step is to break through the outer shell of your intellectual, conceptual mind in order to reconnect yourself with your true universal nature that is

Tao. This is true freedom which can guide you to inner peace, happiness and completeness.

Now it is time for me to stop and see if you have any questions. I will be happy to help you.

Q: I read that you studied inner alchemy as well as acupuncture. When I looked up the word alchemy, I learned that it means making something good out of something not so good. I am fascinated by that term and what you said about connecting yourself to your true nature. Is there a connection between them?

Master Ni: Yes. This is important, and I am glad you reminded me of it. Alchemy is the art of transforming base metals into precious ones. Everyone here contains their own true gold within them. It is not worth $400 or even $1,000 an ounce, it is priceless. Unfortunately, this gold is covered up by a lot of debris because people focus on superficial beliefs, lose their self-confidence and attempt to elaborate their true nature. This causes a lot of confusion. We have ways of purification which can refine the gross accumulation of untruth so that the true gold of a person's soul can shine through.

You should not allow yourself to be bothered by emotional reactions to small, momentary matters in life. Such occasions can be opportunities to further refine yourself. This is the true meaning and practice of internal alchemy. The *Workbook for Spiritual Development* can help you with the step-by-step transformation of a lump of dross into a priceless nugget of true gold.

Q: I have heard that after a Buddhist master is cremated, there can remain something that looks like purple pearls, and that the profundity of the person's spiritual achievement can be determined by counting these pearls. Is that true, or are the so-called pearls just gallstones?

Master Ni: First of all, the fact of the purple pearls is true. But it does not matter whether the person is a Buddhist or practices some other form of spiritual cultivation. If an individual who is truly achieved is cremated, there are crystals which are sometimes shaped like pearls, but they can also be shaped in many other ways. It simply means that the person had a true discipline or cultivation.

The students or sponsors of such masters often take these pearls or crystals to place in their personal shrine as something of value to worship. If the student leads a virtuous life, these crystals will increase, but if the person just regards them as souvenirs and lives a careless life, the crystals will disappear, because they are not a hundred percent materialized.

However, the purpose of self-cultivation is not just to have some crystals left after you are cremated. Cultivating the rough, crude foundation of your general personality involves three kinds of energy. These are sexual energy; mental and emotional energy; and intellectual energy and wisdom. These three energies can be transformed into spiritual energy. Someone who is spiritually achieved can die young or live to a ripe old age; he can decide to go at any time, because he has energetically built a spiritual body or established himself spiritually.

To answer your question more specifically, you need to seriously utilize the methods and principles of internal alchemy to achieve yourself. Western medicine and modern chemistry originally developed from ancient internal alchemy, but they have applied its principles to the material level only. The deepest level implies an integration of physical, mental and spiritual energy through the process of refinement. In this process you get what is called "immortal medicine." This is not something external; it is entirely internal, and the process, especially in the last stages, is not for sale but is a reward from divine achieved ones to one who fulfills his or her natural and virtuous obligations.

Q: My understanding is that traditional students of Tao in China studied with a master in a monastic situation. Here in the West we don't have that tradition. What practices would you recommend to those of us who have families and jobs? Can all of this be integrated into a spiritual path?

Master Ni: The formalized relationship and training you describe belongs to a religious situation. The Tradition of Tao of the Union of Tao and Man is not a monastery type of religion. It is people living in the regular world with decent jobs and lives who develop spiritually as the goal of their lives. This is different from evading duties. Religions embrace something shaped, formalized and fixed. The masters in the tradition of Tao usually take on decent, honest work while living as hermits from the outer world. In my family, for example, we practice traditional Chinese medicine. The practice of medicine is not the primary goal of our lives, but it is a good and useful livelihood. One needs to provide for oneself. If a person accepts donations and allows someone else to support him or her financially, such a one will not gather all the life experience needed to become a full person. Spiritual development cannot be used as an excuse to live a lazy life. Lazy living only leads to false achievement, not true achievement.

Someone who is financially dependent does not take responsibility for the direction of his or her life. It is like watching a show or a film; if you watch someone else do something, you do not have the actual experience of doing it yourself. Then, after watching the show, you think that you have done something, however, you have not achieved anything. You have only watched a movie. This way is unvirtuous and does not help one's development. It is the religion of immature people. People of virtue use self-effort to cultivate themselves on their own.

A monastery does not provide the same opportunities for growth that the world does. It is a narrow environment. To grow, you need to be in an alive world of vastness. When you go to work, nasty customers or bosses can be the grindstones that wear away some of the rough edges of your personality. This is important. Monastic life is usually an attempt at escape. Going on a retreat periodically can be beneficial, either to get a vacation from a girlfriend or boyfriend or to refresh oneself from ordinary worldly life. But we need to be able to face the changes in the everyday world and still maintain our essence.

One thing you can do while living in the world is have a weekly gathering with friends in which you discuss your life experience and use my books to guide your cultivation. Individual cultivation can be benefitted by the effort of helping each other.

Q: I would like to know what you think about the saying that "food kills us."

Master Ni: When you were children, your mother probably told you to eat everything on your plate because there are children starving in India. How can food kill you?

Overeating can kill you. But if you manage yourself well and are sensitive to your internal organs, food can nourish you. The best guideline is simply never to overeat.

I can also give you a few other guidelines. Try to avoid acidifying foods such as dairy products and ill-prepared meat. If your body becomes acidic, then your organs, your emotions, and everything acidifies and you shorten your life. Overeating is harmful because it slows down your digestion so that the food in your stomach starts to acidify, and then you become constipated. So if you do not want to end up on an operating table, do not eat junk food and do not overeat at night.

It is best to not eat, or to eat very little, after sundown. Do not go to bed on a full stomach; this will cause many problems at a later time. When you are young, your body functions well, but bad habits can cause your body to deteriorate much faster than it would normally.

If you work, you need good nutrition to maintain yourself physically. Mao, my second son, has published a book on nutrition that you might want to read.

Q: We are supposedly at the end of the Kali Yuga, which doesn't mean much to me, other than understanding and realizing that life is changing drastically for all of us. Do you see normal society as being able to survive? Do you think things are going to get much worse? How can a normal, healthy person survive these changes?

Master Ni: First of all, I want you to give up worrying. Change is always occurring, whether good or bad. The unchanging truth is your own spiritual essence. Once you understand this and make it your goal, then you must learn to cultivate it.

This situation is like a cup of wine that has been passed many times. Originally, it was just a cup of pure wine, but then someone put a lemon into it, and someone else put a pineapple and a little sugar into it, and then someone else watered it down a little, and now that it has come down to our generation it has lost its purity. We need to look for our original nature and the truth of life again. We have lost ourselves in the changes of time. But do not worry about the changes, worry about how much acid you put in yourself.

People are like eggs. An egg is a material thing; good eggs get eaten and bad eggs get thrown away. But in the right circumstances, with warmth and protection, an egg can hatch into a beautiful yellow bird. There are two ways to go: you can become a bad egg that gets thrown away, or you can decide, "I have a life inside that I need to develop," and devote yourself to internal alchemy. Even if you are a good egg, and you do not guard yourself well, anyone who likes can come along and eat you.

Beloved friends, there are two ways to live. You can live under the pressure of life or you can live above it. The choice is yours. Are you aware that if you make too much money, you will have more pressure? Why not utilize the energy of material amassment for your personal balanced life and good direction, so that you can help yourself and your fellow man by your example? It is important to be awake in life and maintain your own goal above all worldly pressures and fads.

As I see it, the flaw of capitalism is that it directs all of people's energy into making money. It even makes them believe that money is power. Once a person amasses a large amount of money, though, he or she needs to make use of it and protect it. This becomes a vicious cycle. Although wealth enables people to buy beautiful yachts and collect masterpieces of art, which is a good thing, it does not support them in going beyond their indulgence in personal fantasies. Thus they are blind to the worldly problems that are aggravated by their example of competition and false values.

Q: The first time I heard the word alchemy was in the works of Carl Jung. Are there any similarities between his work and yours?

Master Ni: Carl Jung was a very good commentator. I am grateful to him for introducing internal alchemy to the West through his commentary on The Secret of the Golden Flower, which is also called The Golden Immortal Medicine. Jung also wrote a forward to The *Book of Changes* which helped many people see beyond the conditional limits of life. Practically speaking, he was an intellectual. He was not highly developed on a spiritual level, largely because of the unfortunate cultural background of his time. But he has done an important job in bringing these ancient truths to people in the West who are broad-minded enough to accept them.

Q: Your brochure mentions the Union of Tao and Man. Earlier you said something to the effect that God is beyond gender, so why don't you call it the Union of Tao and People or the Union of Tao and Humankind?

Master Ni: You are right. Lots of women generals fight me on that. You can change it to whatever you like. In Chinese, the word for another person is not differentiated by male and female as in other languages unless a person specifically says the word "man" or "woman."

The main idea is union between Tao and ourselves. We are in a state of separation now and wish to be in union with the universal divine energy.

It is unfortunate that the English word implies a difference between men and women. It is not as simple as the Chinese character of a two-legged creature as "人".

Q: So men need to be unified with Tao, but women don't.

Master Ni: It is the English language that gives you such a misunderstanding. It is also interesting to examine the English word. Man is part of wo-man. The word woman is five letters, while the word man has only three; it is only a part of the word wo-man.

So do not worry about it. I will tell you this; most of my work is accomplished by women students. In my tradition, we worship feminine energy, we do not fight it. In today's world, natural feminine energy has been turned and twisted into competitive, fighting energy so that life is like one big rooster fight. In my tradition we value peace.

Young feminine energy is often used to symbolize the peace of motherly, feminine nature. It is hard to find a living, perfect symbol for original purity and virginity, so, as an expression of our deep appreciation of this divine energy, we have adopted the symbol of Quan Yin, the Goddess of Mercy. All the ladies who help me to accomplish my work become a part of Quan Yin, and as my main helpers they are helped and protected by Quan Yin.

We have study groups in many places. In Australia, the group is called The Fellowship of Universal Natural Truth. In Miami, it is called The Fellowship of the Subtle Light, and in other places, it is called The Fellowship of Integral Truth. We do not fight over names; we insist on the reality of perfect union.

Q: Could you say something about the relationship between internal alchemy and physical exercises such as Tai Chi and Chi Gong?

Master Ni: Yes. Tai Chi and Chi Gong build a good foundation. Once you have developed yourself so that you are above the ordinary pressures of sexual energy, then you need to learn Tai Chi and refine your energy to a still higher level. Human energy has many different levels and it is important not to concentrate only on the physical level.

There are two different kinds of Chinese martial arts. One kind is just for self defense. The other is for self control, self development, and self harmonization. The Tai Chi and

Chi Gong that I teach belong to the school of internal harmony.

I have observed many excellent masters of martial arts die young because they were heroes. All heroes die young. I would rather enjoy being ever-spring; this is what our tradition stresses. Self-defense has some value; it can give you the confidence to stand up and protect yourself against aggressive or unreasonable people. But in this tradition we do not emphasize that; you should not invite or attract such situations in the first place.

Q: In The Secret of the Golden Flower, it says that you should bring your breath up along the spine and over the top of the head when you meditate or else you will never get anywhere. Is that true?

Master Ni: That is a technical point which we can discuss in some other class or seminar. I have given you guidance on how to transform your physical and sexual energy to assist your soul energy and strengthen it. Once your energy is transformed, it will follow a certain upward route. Do not abuse your sexual energy, observe moderation, and you will have a chance to achieve yourself. If you overindulge in sex, you will lose your memory when you are old and not concentrate well even now. A person of self-cultivation values his or her own energy. It is all a matter of development; if I am on top of a hill and you are still at the foot, we would not agree on what we each see from our different perspectives. Once we stand in the same spot, there is no more argument.

Spiritual achievement comes about, step by step, through personal effort. It is not as simple as saying "I have faith in God. God will take me to Heaven." If that were true, a person could wait in the tomb for judgment day for the next ten thousand years. It is misguiding to encourage people to depend on an outside source of strength. It cripples them on a spiritual level.

Q: Would you talk about your understanding of the value of self-cultivation, independent of culture or time?

Master Ni: The value of self-cultivation is that it empowers and enables the spiritual achievement of the individual, independent of any teacher. One is thus able to be independent of cultural influences. But independence alone is not enough. We also need to correct and reform the backward, conventional religious attitudes that dominate our culture. This is the dawn of a new spiritually awakened age.

When I was traveling in the Pacific Islands earlier this year, I found myself alone on one of the islands. The isolation and quietude helped me to clearly see the spiritual responsibility on my shoulders and feel the heaviness of its weight inside me. At that moment, a kind and friendly immortal flew to me and we had the following conversation:

"Ni, Hua-Ching, can you lengthen the days you enjoy and shorten the days you tolerate?"

"No, Great Shien. I cannot lengthen the days I enjoy and shorten the days I tolerate. I do the opposite so that I can help people."

"Yet, what makes you feel heavy is different than what makes ordinary people feel that way. Do you enjoy your tolerance of these long days?"

"No, sir; I can restrain my mood from moving destructively in the direction of depression. My spiritual duty toward my inner being is to harmonize my internal condition, by keeping myself centered and balanced on the edge of each passing moment. It is also my spiritual duty to fulfill the requirements of each moment that presents itself. This is the natural obligation I have been assigned by the universal spiritual realm."

"That is why I say you should enjoy the virtue of your tolerance toward those tolerated days. Now, how would you shoulder your spiritual responsibility and accomplish the spiritual work of this age?"

"According to my spiritual conscience I will do what can be done. I will not draw back from the opportunity to guide good people in doing the work that is needed to further the spiritual integration of the world, but I will not engage in or create a struggle with outer circumstances in order to improve the world. Nor will I allow personal ambition to disturb or interfere with my capacity to give direction to the human world. I will sincerely reflect upon the correct response that can truly help others. As an educator, I will try to remove the concept of self and simply become the function of education itself. When I write or teach, I will avoid anything that could create a mass disturbance."

The heavenly being replied to me, "In order to understand and offer this help, you have had to get close to the mass of people. This closeness creates the opportunity for people to learn from you, but they might spoil that opportunity. There are not many people who genuinely wish to help the world without any personal motivation. The definition of virtuous fulfillment that is respected and honored is to do everything you can for the evolution of human consciousness and the collective spiritual development of human society, but take nothing from the world."

"In my writing I have tried to point out the direction for the spiritual efforts of people today. I feel that I cannot do enough to help some of the people I know who have the potential to carry on the spiritual duty of developing themselves. I am grateful that you have kindly pointed out that my spiritual work is only partly accomplished. The books are one part, but another part of my work should be the realization of spiritual development of all people."

"No, not at all. In your life, you have no fun. Isn't this part of one's duty in life too? What do you do for your personal pleasure? It seems like your accomplishments are something to keep your mind busy while you stay in the world. You use your work to shield your mind against the pressures and tension of modern life. Forgive me if I speak offensively. I can see it was right to do as you have done, but the work you have accomplished has been achieved under emotional strain. If you did not have the emotional pressure, you might not have accomplished anything.

"If this is true, then preaching the doctrine of being natural, spontaneous and balanced is only an ideological tool to remedy the imbalance of your own tension. You need to re-evaluate all of your teaching, especially if it was the result of responding to the challenges in your own work and life. It seems to me that you are saying that a good life is still the outcome of a correct response to miseries, troubles, problems and difficulties. Thus, by observing the underlying facts, is Satan not the mother of God? All the struggle and hard work is a problem itself. The totality is an expression of human spiritual immaturity and undevelopment. You like to pour your divine energy into this level of work, but you do not wait for people to grow tall enough to reach its fruit. At the risk of annoying you I ask, how is the truth that you have attained any different from the achievements of ordinary people? This is not Tao, it is a healing ideology, not worthy of your spiritual devotion or the devotion of others. Behind your great eloquence lies a serious problem. The problem is the pressure to cure this sick, spiritually-blocked world. Am I right? Behind your eloquence, too, lies personal stubbornness.

"You know I would not protect you if I did not say this. You must realize that the world cannot be helped; the world does not need help. The subtle law is behind everything. When things go to one extreme, it will return to balance and heal itself on its own without you. But you do not sit aside quietly, you blow on the hot soup to cool it. You take on the trouble of the world and now you are tasting its poison and that of unachieved people who poison themselves and others. It is spiritually shortsighted to devote your energy to unachieved people; you only deplete the spiritual advancement you have attained.

"You do not have to bother yourself with the world; just disappear behind the clouds in the clear blue sky. The notion of giving yourself to help the world is guided by an immature response of sympathy. You need to grow beyond this point. If you do not, you will suffer and pay the price for being overly kind. Why not enjoy the state of spiritual non-beingness? You have the high capability of enjoying the originalness of the pure, tiny spiritual center of non-being. The negligence which breaks the smallness of one's spiritual essence is not spiritual. Indulging in work that you like and making it your spiritual devotion is not spiritual. Realistically speaking, it is unreasonably ambitious.

"The human mind is too short-sighted spiritually to see the entire scope of the spiritual evolution of all mankind. How then, can we know how to help mankind? The madness that you have is that you do not have fun in your personal life. You criticize every religion you see, but people who are spiritually and emotionally crippled need the crutches of ideology. How can you dislike the crutches that cripples need? In the desert, great people are born alongside the desert rats that need a strong religion to control them. In other places, beautiful women become nuns, but when menstrual cramps come, they yearn for the comfort of God, not knowing that god in the form of ordinary men could help them. Objects that symbolize the penis and vagina are deified and worshipped in temples. There is nothing wrong with worshiping a penis and calling it Shiva or in having sex and calling it Tantra; or in referring to one's girlfriend as the Buddha's mother or her vagina as the Lotus Palace. Such religions reflect the exaggeration of people's physical and emotional concerns; they are not really spiritual. It is not necessary for all people to become spiritually mature.

"You take it all too seriously. Are you not aware of how many times the earth has changed? The land changes to become the ocean, and the ocean floor becomes the land. Why not let everything take care of itself? It is called nature, I think. Let human nature take care of the silly reformation of worldly culture and the spiritual revolution. Now, let us play a game of chess, or perhaps we could invent some other game than chess."

"No, thanks, I would like to play alone. But before you go, great friend, I must express my appreciation for your visit and for your words of gold, jade and pearl. Can I describe the essence of spiritual immortality that I have attained?

"As you know, I make an effort to point out the long history of human spiritual mistakes. Ordinary religions express defeat and twist the spiritual health of the people they reach. If any religion is worth following, it is a spiritual educational system that leads to mellowness and ripeness of mind, health and centeredness; one that nurtures the unshakableness of the spirit and enrichment of all three spheres of life, both for the individual and for society. It is one which furthers happiness in all human relations.

"The sign of a spiritually developed person is not the stamp of any artificial religious belief, but the mellowness of a mind that objectively accepts all differences and is thus in harmony with all things and all beings.

"A person of spiritual truthfulness values his or her own life as the basic substance of holiness and therefore does not neglect the reality of life by looking for or worshipping external images.

"A person of spiritual truthfulness does not lose his or her head and take sides in childish wars and confusion created by external religions.

"A person of spiritual truthfulness is one who has awakened from deceptive religious fantasies and knows that no other person or religion can take spiritual responsibility for someone else's growth.

"A person of spiritual truthfulness extends a helping hand to other people who are interested in living a healthy spiritual life.

"A person of spiritual truthfulness knows that all spiritual and social programs should continually be refined, redeveloped and reprogrammed in order to be of benefit to people. Otherwise they become dead shells that brew new hostilities. The subtle truth of universal life does not alter, but any teaching method always needs to be improved, otherwise it becomes an obstacle to human progress.

"A person of spiritual truthfulness does not place himself among conflicting spiritual practices or wars of conceptual conflict. It is a great joy to see people who live in harmony and are willing to learn from each other.

"A person of spiritual truthfulness stays alert to whether he or she is following the right direction in life. Once being sure of the correct course, that person does not allow his or her mind to wander or physical energy to scatter and does not avoid hard work.

"A person of spiritual truthfulness does not make any dualistic separation between one's life and work, between his or her psychological appreciation and spiritual goal. He or she accepts each moment of life as an opportunity for personal spiritual refinement rather than escape.

"A person of spiritual truthfulness is like a fish in the great ocean; not separate from the water, no matter whether the current is smooth or rough, warm or cold. The current is part of its life being. To be separate from the water and its current is to die.

"A person of spiritual truthfulness knows that duality of the mind and spirit happens when one's mind or spirit starts to wander away from reality. Human religions lure people away from the water of life and leave them to die like fish on the shore. True spiritual growth, however, takes place within life itself.

"A person of spiritual truthfulness may take many years to learn and experience, observe and reflect on the truth presented by different religions in order to further the maturity of his or her own spiritual growth. This is not a waste of time. It would be a waste to engage in the assertive emotions of brutal beliefs.

"A person of spiritual truthfulness knows that while life is the crown of the vast physical universe, human life is the crown of the different forms of life. Life is the substance by which the development of the universe takes place. Evolution is carried out by all lives, but especially by life with self-awareness. It is only right, therefore, to develop oneself by learning and absorbing the spiritual achievement of other beings in order to become the crown of universal development. All lives are one life in continuity. The convergence of essence and the discarding of what is unrefined is the process of subtle integration.

"A person of spiritual truthfulness concentrates on attaining the precious knowledge of how to join the physical and spiritual counterparts of life in perfect union. The simple, ordinary normalcy expressed by this perfect union is the most important thing of all. All knowledge and development sustain this great union.

"A person of spiritual truthfulness establishes the practical truth of strengthening the union of the two spheres of life by using the healthy practices of external religion to hold himself together from the outside and the high achievement of internal religion to unify all his or her spiritual elements from the inside. All spiritual practices and achievements, understood correctly, serve the unity of life. Only in the stage of darkness and immaturity is life made to fit an external or internal mold.

"A person of spiritual truthfulness knows that Heaven is the union of the two counterparts of an individual life being. By developing his or her spiritual energy to be the crown of one's life being, an individual can develop his or her life to become the crown of the physical world. Then this individual can manifest Heaven from the inside out. No longer does he look for an external God or deny the existence of universal spiritual reality. His or her life is a fulfillment of a living Heaven. Heaven is at hand, whether this person is moving or not moving, thinking or not thinking, being or not being.

"A person of spiritual truthfulness knows the value of balance. To a developed person, the completeness of life is a spiritual reality: a union of natural spiritual elements of different levels. It is the responsibility of each individual to develop the spirituality within and without himself so that both ends meet in one place. Each moment of life is the integration of two types of energy which are actually one energy with different levels and functions: one is gross and the other is refined. God is the most refined energy residing in each individual. It is the communicating energy that joins the divinity of great nature.

"A person of spiritual truthfulness puts the knowledge he or she has gathered into practice, and thus achieves unlimited development through spiritual self-cultivation. Helping people do this is the purpose of teachers of different levels. It is not up to a student to establish someone as a teacher, but the teacher who builds another human being through correct spiritual development. If a student stays with a teacher for emotional reasons, it restricts both the student and the teacher. All spiritual learners are allowed to move from one teacher to another for the purpose of further development at different stages in order to become complete and strong. All churches and temples should open their doors one hundred percent to anyone who is looking for what they need at their own stage of spiritual growth. Religion should not be reduced to an emotional tranquilizer.

"A person of spiritual truthfulness knows that an achieved teacher holds the treasure of human development which he is ready to give when someone is ready. He cannot be swayed by anyone's emotion.

"The entire world seems to be entering a new age. All spiritual beings are ready to assist the efforts of human beings. Psychic phenomena, UFO's and spiritual books such as this are all responses from the natural spiritual realm to help guide the growing baby. The kindness of Heaven is extended to everyone who recognizes it with developed eyes and works to realize it in their own life.

"If there are any truly valuable commandments in life, they are the following goals worthy to attain:

1) mellowness of mind

2) a healthy, balanced life

3) an unobstructed, undefeated spirit

4) loving people and rendering service

5) unifying the body and mind

6) the rich emotion of enjoying simple relationships and things

7) frequent self-examination of one's personal and public life

8) avoidance of obsession and extravagance

9) humility

10) constantly collecting the floating emotions that take you out of your center.

"I present this for your kind examination." When I finished speaking, the friendly immortal flew away.

Beloved friends, all methods of self-cultivation are only tools of mutual help for either an individual or a group. Please do not use them as excuses to fight, but as ways to attain spiritual growth. You will need different inspirations at different times in your life. So do not say this one is a true one and that one is not. When your appreciation has developed sufficiently to know the way, you will not lose sight of the true goal by getting caught up in any beliefs or methods.

Q: I want to ask something about sexuality. In terms of energy exchange, do prophylactics or condoms create a barrier between the man and woman during sexual activity?

Master Ni: In the natural tradition of integral spiritual development, we say that sex is an achievement that requires a lot of training. The man's achievement is to control himself and not ejaculate. If one is too weak and has not refined his sexual energy, his partner can get pregnant. Her happiness can then turn into unhappiness very quickly. A man should train himself to retain the semen and refine it to become electric warmth and chi. A woman can then use this energy to open and break through emotional blockages in her body.

I do not recommend this technique for all people. If you have not achieved yourself to this level of cultivation, you will have to be content with ordinary intercourse. The advice I give most of my students is to follow the natural patterns of sexual intercourse and not stimulate themselves by looking at pornographic movies or books. You should not have sex unless you are naturally excited by each other.

People of different ages have different sexual schedules according to their own natural physical energy. In general, I tell my friends to let the woman take the active role, because the woman knows what she needs during her cycles of ovulation and before and after menstruation. If you have sexual contact at those times, it will help the health of the woman and not harm her. If a man is impulsive, like a wild boar, it can be harmful to the woman, especially today's woman who works in an office all day long and then comes home to face sexual pressures. If a woman has sex when she is not really ready for it, all kinds of feminine problems can result. Most people, women and men, suffer from too much food and improper sex.

Q: Then would you advocate, as far as personal growth goes, that a person practice sex naturally, but that the man should work toward eventually not ejaculating?

Master Ni: No, not a hundred percent. You need to find the right partner for such a practice, but you are not achieved enough yet to know who would be the right partner. You base your relationships on attraction. Being sexy is not a requirement for this practice. I believe that, based on the knowledge that you already have, you should respond to the person at your side on the right occasions. But this should not be your main concern. Your main concern should be achieving yourself. In general, let your wife or girlfriend take the active role. If she does not invite you, then do not impose yourself. That is the right way.

Q: Is there anything in the physiological make-up of the male that parallels the menstrual cycle of the female?

Master Ni: Men have cycles too, but they are different. In general, a man of sixteen or younger will have an erection every morning. This is connected with the sun cycle, whereas a woman's sexual cycle is related to the moon. A man in his thirties might have sex once a week or once every two weeks under normal circumstances. It depends on the person's health and the level of his physical energy.

For purposes of dual cultivation, though, you need special knowledge to know who can suitably engage in such a practice. It is very hard to find the right person who can actually help you. If you find the right partner, your energy is pulled up. If it is the wrong person, the energy is pulled down. Spiritual relationships are the same as ordinary relationships in this regard, but spiritual relationships are much more sensitive. If you have an ordinary relationship with a woman, sooner or later she'll say, "Let's get married and have some children. Let's buy a house and a new car." If you can afford to do it, then do it, and after you have fulfilled all your physical obligations, then you might decide to cultivate yourself afterwards. Or you could have a family life and spiritual cultivation at the same time. Many young

Chinese people do this because their parents insist that they get married early. So they get married, but when they become older they concentrate more on their spiritual development, if it is their interest to do so.

Q: Are you considered a teacher of Taoism in mainland China and Taiwan?

Master Ni: It is what I have been dedicated to being, but universally, not specifically in one place. It could be more fun to be a football star, but that is not my direction. In general, the teaching and learning of Tao was destroyed by Communism, especially in the ten years of the so-called Cultural Revolution. It is not really accurate to say that Taoism was destroyed by Communism, because a true thing can never be destroyed. Some temples were destroyed, but Tao itself can never be destroyed. Despite a vast public health program, Communist China will never have enough doctors to effectively minister to all of the people, so many people support their health by practices like Tai Chi and Chi Gong.

How is this different from Tao or the development of the subtle essence? People just do not talk about the spiritual aspect of their practice. Through these simple practices, people still achieve themselves, no matter what anybody says or forbids.

Taiwan is a different country culturally than China. People there are very prosperous and most of them are common worshippers looking for more blessings to add their blessing of freedom, all of which they feel they can buy in one way or another. Many beautiful temples of all kinds have been built for the wealthy. If you find a teacher in such a socially mixed background as Taiwan, can you entrust your life and your spiritual growth to him?

You must develop yourself. I suggest that you gather together as a group and develop your own leadership, so that you can help each other with your personal development and knowledge. In this way the door will be opened. I can then guide you in the greater direction. But you must work out the small details for yourselves so that when you come to a different stage, you will know what you are doing and what you need to do next.

I think we will end the meeting here. It has been very nice to talk to all of you.

An individual can be either a slave of the material sphere and spiritual underdevelopment, or a master of spiritual freedom. The pursuit of enlightenment is what enables one to attain spiritual freedom.

To end this meeting, I offer this poem from an ancient achieved one in the great tradition of Tao, the path of wholeness and naturalness.

When we see the only one,
    it is the absolute.
When we divide it,
    divergence beings.
Once you reach the oneness,
    you find peace and completeness.
It was long ago that
    the awakening soul
    said grace to it.
This made later students
    misunderstand what true God is.

CHAPTER ELEVEN

New York City: November 5, 1986

Please move in closer so I do not have to shout. If I have to raise my voice, my thoughts come from a region in the brain that is rough. If I talk in a normal voice, then I can handle the delicateness of spiritual subjects and respond better to your sincere, searching minds. Shouting distorts the truth, because it only touches the emotional level. In general, it is better to avoid the rough level of emotion. If I can keep my voice down, then we will have a better spiritual connection. In other big cities in the world, I spoke to large groups of people and sometimes could not use the normal volume of my voice. I feel like a politician when I have to shout.

All of you know that the teaching of spiritual truth is an impersonal, non-opinionated matter. It is difficult to totally rely on language to effectively convey one's spiritual achievement or attainment to another person. In the first place, language is not the best means to do this, but we cannot totally abandon language either. Each language in the world has its areas of greatest suitability. English is expected to have the same good capability of any language highly suited for expressing subtle truth. With your help, maybe we will be able to find its competence in this work. English is already proven to do well in business, science and politics, and in expressing the sentiment of love songs which are so popular in this country. However, I can sing my kind of universal love to you. My kind of love is unbreakable; it can never turn out to be the blues. I ask you to join me in my kind of singing.

It is good to be with all of you here. Although I have been in this country for ten years, I have not had a chance to travel very much until now. A teacher of Tao is not someone who tries to attract masses of people. He or she responds only to those who have attained a certain level of spiritual development. In China, when people go to school to learn English, there are lots of students who start with A,B,C, but there are not so many by the time they get to X,Y,Z. Tonight, we can enjoy each other, because you have made it to X,Y,Z and are here to confirm your level of development and see what I am like. So, leave all your nervousness and conceptual ideas behind so that we can communicate on the level of truth.

I believe that a person's heart and true spiritual achievement is what is important. This is what I mean when I talk about communicating at the level of truth.

There have been many spiritual leaders from different religious backgrounds around the world who have come to this big city and attracted much attention. As for my tradition, it is probably the least attractive when it comes to clothes or language. We present only the truth that can be seen and realized in our ordinary daily lives. We work every day. We do not live life in a monastery, nor do we have any particular life-style. We just live plain, simple, ordinary lives. We face life and accept its pressures and changes.

Many people wonder whether they can truly achieve themselves in everyday life or if they should do as some ancient people did and go to a remote place to cultivate themselves. If it were necessary to isolate oneself from the rest of life, I surely would not be here in a glamorous place like this with you now. This city constantly stimulates you to pay attention to it, leaving you very little time to pay attention to yourselves. You seldom get a chance to relax your emotions and achieve what you want at a deeper level. Modern people, especially those in such crowded cities, have little time to achieve themselves spiritually. We all have to face a lot of changes every day.

We are all beings of spiritual energy, each with our own qualities and level of development. What is your spiritual condition? Does your spiritual energy support you to get up early or do you wake up dismayed and exhausted from the physical and mental burdens of the night before? Strengthening your spiritual energy is the most important thing in life, because that is the main support of your entire being. I believe you always work hard for your physical survival, but is this the goal of life? If so, then insects are the greatest masters because they are the most successful survivors, and they do not have to pay any taxes. But survival is not the point. To live a complete life at a higher level than you did before should be your goal. If you do not develop yourself spiritually, then all the hardships of your life will be for nothing. When you grow old and retire, then what will you do? You will sit around in an apartment and wait for your body to wither away. What a sad and ugly picture. At that time, you may turn to the conventional methods of un-achieved religions in order to find a psychological compensation for your empty life, but that is not spiritual truth. You are all young now; this is the best time to develop yourselves. If you practice every day, your internal transformation will begin. This is what is meant by internal alchemy: refining the true gold of your life.

To develop the essence of our being more and more each day should be our goal. In my books I encourage people toward spiritual awakening. This is why I have traveled all this way to confirm your spiritual growth and development. I am at your service. Whatever your questions, do not hesitate to ask them. I will answer you from my personal experience and learning, and from the 8,000 years of continual spiritual development that has been passed down to all of us through the great tradition of Tao. The more questions you ask, the more clearly you will understand. If I continue to stand here and talk, I will only respond to myself.

Q: What kind of meditation do you teach?

Master Ni: That is a good question. It brings us very quickly from world-wide problems to the single point of individual development. It is my fundamental belief that only when the quality of each individual's energy is improved, the world will also be improved. Social programs are usually shallow and imposing.

In general, people use the word meditation to mean looking for spiritual achievement. In our tradition, the word cultivation is used because the attainment of spiritual growth is like agriculture. In growing crops, you must choose the right seed, then you must sow it in soil that has been pre-pared in advance, and then you must pay close attention to it and give it your protection by watering it well and removing harmful insects so that it will grow strong and healthy. The word meditation sometimes means just deep thinking, but you have already become too mechanized by the intellect. You do not even taste your food or have automobile accidents, because you are too busy thinking about something else. I value thinking when it is appropriate, but most thinking is just a waste of energy.

Most people believe that meditation is just deep thinking; in learning Tao we have a kind of meditation for that. It is called Wu Tao. Wu Tao is a special gathering of several days in which the student does nothing but contemplate, "Who am I?" or "What is Life?" and similar key questions. You then present your answer or understanding to the teacher who confirms what you have reached, but does not assist it. This is only one way of training and, although it mostly deals with the conceptual level, it can lead eventually to the non-conceptual level of knowing things wholly, not just partially. It can effectively guide you to enter yourself so that you are not pulled by your nose here and there, wasting your life on one thing or another.

The main purpose of spiritual self-cultivation is the integration of all the parts of our being: our senses, our internal and external organs, and the different levels of energy such as sexual power, emotional power, intellectual power and rational power. All of these must be kept in a healthy balance. If you let one of them dominate, then your development will be partial. When you cease to be master of your life, special kinds of cultivation become necessary.

If you want to learn specific techniques of self-cultivation, the *Workbook for the Spiritual Development* can help you. I also have an assistant teacher here who can help you learn Tai Chi and some other things that can help you manage yourself better. I usually like to teach the broad principles before giving techniques to people. That way you do not lose sight of where you are going. A public talk is the right occasion to explain principles.

First you should have a good understanding of yourself, your life, the world and what you want to accomplish. For thousands of years, people who were at different levels of spiritual development have organized programs for other people to follow, and most of their teachings were just new forms of bondage for people who were less developed than themselves. Most religions are psychologically self-deceiving. They are built on a foundation of threats which enable them to gain control over people who might otherwise think for themselves and go in a different direction.

You must first develop your spiritual discernment so that you will not fool yourself any more. You can begin by reading my books so that you will have a correct understanding and good foundation for further development. With a good foundation of understanding, you will not become like spiritual cattle that are run by someone else. You will be able to say with your own achieved authority that you were born with divine energy and that you know to develop yourself further. This understanding itself is a certain kind of achievement.

The spiritual achievement I respect is not the same as an occasional good deed. Performing an occasional good deed is different than a fragrant tree that always gives off the sweet fragrance of its nature. You must first change the quality or fragrance of your personality and your being; you must completely transform yourself from sour to sweet, from low to high, if you want your spiritual future to be assured. Occasional good deeds are not enough.

Spiritual teachers of the past have taught people to become narrow and rigid and prejudiced. These low qualities are obstacles to true spiritual attainment and must be washed away. With keen discernment, you will know which of your spiritual elements to develop and which to eliminate. Decaying matter needs to be cleared away in order for new life to grow. Your own power of discernment will provide the foundation that can enable you to safely proceed on a spiritual path without downfall or wasting your time.

Q: Would you talk about the psychological problems that occur when the circulation of chi gets blocked?

Master Ni: I will try to answer this carefully, because many other friends here tonight have no knowledge of chi or the circulation of chi. Sometimes you meet a stranger and feel a very strong attraction or repulsion; that is his chi contacting yours. You see, a body is not just solid, inert matter, it produces chi. A healthy body produces healthy, harmonious chi, while a sick body has and produces disharmonious chi. Actually, chi also creates the body; it is the subtle essence of your physical being. Modern medicine has not discovered this fact; it only works with visible elements such as muscles, organs, cells, etc. It does not know that all these things combined produce the chi inside. For example, the capability of speech is a manifestation of chi. Too much talking exhausts chi. If I use too much chi, I cannot talk long, but if I use too little, then you cannot hear me.

Our bodies are like vases. What is inside the vase is chi. If the water in a vase is not fresh, the flower will decay and die. If it is kept fresh, then the flower lives longer and the vase looks beautiful. What is most important, therefore, is the chi inside the vase.

If you wake up feeling good in the morning, that means your chi is fresh and flowing smoothly. If, on the other hand, you go to bed with problems on your mind, or someone has upset you during the day, this will affect your chi. Emotion changes the flow and quality of chi. Once chi becomes stagnant inside, your mood changes. Just as I mentioned, smooth-flowing chi can make you feel great. For instance, when the chi is disturbed, it can cause your blood to become too acid. When this happens, your heart can be affected or you can have a heart attack or something similar. All because you only look at the vase and never change the water. You put a flower in it, and a week later you expect it to still be OK. It is not OK. Life is a composition of energy. If you do not cultivate your energy well, it is like not putting the notes of a piece of music in the right order. It sounds terrible. So refresh your energy all the time, especially if you have emotional problems.

You cannot repress emotions. People who try to not react when they get upset become sick. Anger is very powerful, like a big fire. When people try to hold it in, it is like driving very fast and suddenly putting on the brakes. The car makes a loud noise and might go off the highway. People here in New York must be good drivers in such an overcrowded city. Are you good drivers of your chi, though? I do not think you manage your chi with the same skill you use in driving your cars. Try not to be so angry or so dismayed or depressed. If you hold onto your emotions and stay angry for several days, this is harmful. The same is true of worry; if you do not change your water, it will stagnate and smell terrible.

Even though you do not admit your troubles, you are still attached to and entrapped by them. Why? Because your culture does not teach you to handle such things. In learning Tao, we learn to carefully watch the "vase" and the "water" and the "flower;" we do not just sit around holding onto the dead flowers and smelly water of what so-and-so did or how life circumstances are all wrong. Women who do this get breast cancer or cancer of the uterus or cervix, while the men get ulcers and heart attacks, because they do not know enough to keep their water fresh and replace the flowers.

One important benefit of learning Tao is learning to arrange and direct your emotions. It is like flower arranging. You can make a mess of a bunch of flowers or you can arrange them in a harmonious, artful order. It is also like arranging chords into a beautiful piece of music.

If emotional force were exemplified by water on earth, you would need to learn how to guide your emotions the way you would channel water away after a flood. If it is kept under the rim of the dam, then it is safe. To neglect emotional trouble is like forgetting to turn off the faucet; water will flood the house when no one is home. Anyone leaving the house should always check out water and fire, and in this day and age they should also check to see that the door is locked. These small things cannot be neglected. Nor can your emotions. We should be using our energy to help the troubled world that is full of unhealthy emotions, beliefs and spirits, not sitting in the narrow environment of our own lives, letting a flood of emotion submerge us.

We have come together tonight to review some problems of the world. People basically have good energy that can be used to help their own life condition and that of others too. By using your energy to improve the world rather than holding onto stagnant emotions, the golden age of humanity can be brought about.

This is how chi relates to your health and the health of society. Even if your purpose in life is to make lots of money, I do not think you will enjoy it if you cannot handle your chi well. Learning to manage your chi is the most important thing you can do for yourself.

Q: I think problems are created when people try to impose calmness upon themselves. The Chinese seem more reserved than other cultures. Is this a culturally imposed quality?

Master Ni: Calmness is something that cannot be imposed, either on oneself or someone else. If you try to, it is false. True calmness is a sign of spiritual achievement. In general, if one is not overly impulsive, he might be overly cautious; if not hasty, then procrastinating. I wish I had more time to be a student of calmness myself.

People who achieve internal growth are naturally calm. All my work is aimed at helping people grow internally. The durability of life comes from within, not from some dogmatic teaching. When a Tai Chi teacher tells you to slow down, relax and gather energy inwardly, he is pointing out that your health and strength are built from the inside out. You need to slow down your nervous system, but not the speed of movement that outer circumstances require. If you are relaxed, you can face a tense situation more effectively. If a friend tells you to calm down in a tense situation, can you? No. The external circumstance imposes itself on you. But if you slow down your breathing, then you will become calm. This is because your breathing can affect your chi. Mind control alone cannot work. If you have mental or emotional problems, a good simple mantra will be helpful for a while, but if you overuse it your mind can become dull and lose its healthy sensitivity. You could even become a vegetable. When the mind borrows something external to impose on itself, it eventually becomes numb. It is a way of refusing the nature of life.

This is the training of Tao. It does not offer escape, it offers the consistent path of enduring life. If these principles are not part of your life, it is impossible to live for very long.

In the unnoticeable tradition of Tao, people fulfill their lives through good daily habits. Teachers of Tao pay close attention to and give suggestions on matters of every day life. For instance, staying up and getting up late interferes with the natural rhythm of the bowels and causes constipation. We say, "A day of constipation is a bad day." Then again, the more excitement there is in your life, the more you need strong drugs to calm you down. You need to carefully study the nature of all life and learn what works and what does not. Then you should make the necessary changes so that your daily habits follow the natural way of life. These will eventually become instinctive and natural.

All commandments should come from the deepest sphere of natural life. This is the first commandment of students of Tao. Your mind has been abused by too many unreasonable orders imposed by external forces such as parents and teachers who were also victims of an external, forceful culture. Society, government, school, etc., all command your obedience without helping your wisdom grow, thus you develop the habit of needing to be controlled or threatened before you will change yourself. So, now if a teacher gently tells you to do something, you do not listen; you only pay attention when a policeman tells you something. This is a degradation of the human spirit. That is why there are so many nuclear weapons. We think the Russians are threatening us and they think we are threatening them, so we all live up to that threat and are heavily taxed for its sake. This is the motivation behind most important political activities.

All the troubles in the world can be traced to your parents using threats to control you. If we continue this bad habit, is there any hope for humanity? No. Do you think our modern world is any better off than before? No. Our scientific and material achievements may be greater, but they are superficial changes. In reality, the basic role of humanity is the same. If our international relations, our personal and family relationships are still based on threats, what hope is there? You tell your wife you will divorce her if she does not do what you want or your boss threatens to fire you if you do not work harder. Would you work as hard if you knew you would not get fired? Everything you do is an expression of your dignity. Where is your dignity?

Please change yourself. Do not rely on force to put you under its command. If something is right for you, then do it. Develop your own wisdom by seriously learning Tao. You do not need people watching over you all the time to make sure you do something as small as getting up earlier or not reading the newspaper during breakfast or not smoking. Is it too plain? Is it not exciting enough? Can you command yourself not to do these things? Once you change these little things, then we can discuss higher learning.

People who teach lofty ideologies promise that you will become something else tomorrow. We are interested in you as you are today. Change yourself; do not take any threats. If your parents or any other authority abuse you, it is because they are also victims of an externalizing, forceful culture. Their lives have been hard; the flower of their wisdom has been poisoned. Forgive them, but do not accept any more threats. Help them understand the common, fundamental problem of society and invite them to work together for change.

This question was valuable. Thank you.

Q: How should we use the I Ching?

Master Ni: In your daily lives, I believe you need a good friend at your side who can help you see things at a deeper level and reveal the changeability of the situation. That good friend could be the *I Ching* whose guidance reveals the laws of change. I recommend my version of it which is called *The Book of Changes and the Unchanging Truth.* I put a lot of work into it so that it would be of value to you. Consulting psychics can be useful, but the *I Ching* is very convenient and can accurately reflect and develop your own capability, like a mirror. Do not use it only for divining purposes; learn the principles of life and use it to improve your general attitude toward different situations. If you do use it for divination, then do not get excited when you get a good line. Your fortune could change in a moment. Likewise, do not be dismayed if you get a bad line; it is just a warning. A true friend will always tell you if you are about to do something wrong. My personal version not only gives you the light of ancient achieved wisdom, but also the universal, natural truth behind everything.

A sound mind is the language of nature itself. The subtle essence of the mind is called Shen, which can be interpreted as "spirit." Generally, people subject themselves to external programs which destroy their good mental and spiritual energy. If you seriously use the *I Ching* as your tool, then you should withdraw from any activity that does not support the eternal principles of harmony, objectivity and balance in your life. Power comes with concentration. It is the unchangeable foundation that lies within your own life being.

Q: What is a life reading? Can I do it for myself?

Master Ni: No. You need someone to do it for you. I do not like to do it too much, because when I do I must open my spiritual eyes wide to see the problem and offer a suggestion. It can be draining. When you consult the *I Ching*, you do the same thing to some extent, but the problem with the *I Ching* is that it reflects your mind and if your mind is in turmoil, you cannot be helped. This is why it is better to consult a sincere *I Ching* practitioner who can be more objective.

Q: Exactly what do you do when you give a life reading?

Master Ni: We have several ways to go about it. One method examines the five elements of your personal energy. This system can reveal what your imbalances are, what you need, what direction you should follow, what lifestyle you should adopt, and what life cycles occur at different times in your life. It also reveals the important events in your life and possible difficulties. If you study this system deeply, you will be able manage your life much better. It can also be very useful in developing your spiritual gifts.

A few years ago, I began to study the difference between Western astrology and the Five Element system. Someday I hope to be able to express our ideas in terms of Western astrology. I mean to put our essence in your container. I have not had time to do it yet, but some day I hope to get together with some good astrologers to re-organize and unify both systems.

Most of you have had your charts done, but they are not as accurate as the ancient way. A person's characteristic tendencies can be right, but the cycles of the person's life are not clear in Western astrology. It is too generalized and makes life too narrow. Among people of the same astrological background, why will one be stupid and another wise? Why is one forward and another shy? This missing "something" is the composition of elements and cycles. I would like to make the whole system more serviceable by combining both.

Q: Do you plan to write a book then on Chinese astrology?

Master Ni: If I do, my idea is to use your astrology to teach the ancient system. I would need good Western experts to help me with this project.

Spiritually achieved people always like to manage their own destiny, because they like to take responsibility for themselves. Such a book could be useful to them. A person's life can be fruitless without understanding his or her own destiny. For my own personal use, I only use it to offer guidance to someone.

Q: What circumstances should be present before becoming sexually involved with another person?

Master Ni: First of all you must decide to be responsible and not harm anyone. Then I recommend that you develop your spiritual discernment so that you can know whether the time is right and whether someone is the right partner for you. You often let the best person go and get involved with someone else because you are pushed by desire instead of following your spiritual light. Everyone has desire, but the choice of entering a relationship should not be made on the basis of desire alone. Usually, harm goes hand in hand with passion. If there is no harm done to either side and you both benefit by a healthy relationship, then it is a good opportunity for both people.

Q: Is there a Chinese numerology system similar to ours in the West?

Master Ni: Yes. One way of using the *I Ching* is as a system of numerology. There are other numerology systems too. Right now I am working on big problems first. When everyone in the world is happy and spiritually evolved, I will spend some time on numbers.

Q: When you do Tai Chi, what should be going on in your body?

Master Ni: The movement of chi. Tai Chi is only a form. The purpose of doing Tai Chi is to harmonize your being. We are all troubled by over-using our minds. It is very hard to slow down the mind, so we use body movements to pull back the wanderings of the mind. When your mind merges with the body's movement, we call that an internal marriage. But you always divorce your husband or your wife, and similarly, your minds always wander away from your bodies, so you have no harmony. There is no magic about this. Tai Chi is just a way for the mind to reconnect itself with the body. Can you do it?

Our bodies have many points, just like the sky has many stars. When the stars move in harmony, the sky is beautiful and peaceful. It is the same with the body. The earth is always reshaping itself. When it does so in a quick, violent way, such as an earthquake or a volcano, we call it disorder. So it is with the body also. You must learn to harmonize yourself internally and externally. This is why I call the Tai Chi I teach The School of Internal Harmony.

Q: Do you feel there is any special significance to you and other teachers coming here from the East?

Master Ni: Yes. For over two thousand years the Western mind has been blocked by conventional religions. People do not know what is true from what is untrue; they only know to dedicate themselves to blind faith.

Many problems today are still related to religious conflict. This morning we went to the Cloisters where I saw a lot of beautiful statues with no heads. They tell me that the Muslims tried to destroy the statues because they were Christian images. This is not a thing of the past; it is still going on today. Christians even fight among themselves. No one is developing themselves spiritually, they only argue about whose artificial theology is right.

The Western mind has been dominated by this kind of thinking for two thousand years. Now that things are loosening up a bit, there is great deal of confusion. People no longer believe in the old ways, but they have lost all sense of morality and spiritual responsibility. Unfortunately, they have never looked deeply within themselves for their own divinity. How many people in India or China have looked inside themselves for the Divine? Probably the same two percent that have done so in the West. Everyone looks outside and tries to force themselves to be divine, but it cannot be done. If they would look within and attain something, they would get an external correspondence, just as you did by coming here tonight. It is only because you have reached your own divine energy that you can recognize mine. Otherwise, you would go somewhere else. New York has lots of places to go.

Communism is not really something new if we look back in history prior to the establishment of private ownership. The early leaders of modern communism learned from the historical example of the church. In place of a worldwide theocracy, they offered a new socio-economic trend and the rulership of the party. Neither the church nor communism has reached the maturity of human wisdom. Both still persecute those whose beliefs differ from their own, and God and the Party are interchangeable conceptual tools for social dominance. Neither system is based on objective truth. Communism is just the angry response of intellectuals who are expressing their dissatisfaction with religion by substituting a new kind of dictatorship. This can only lead people into a new age of darkness.

Communism is not so much an ideological problem as it is simply a radical approach. As such, it is an error rather than a solution to the problem. It is a great thing for people to make a joint effort to bring human society to a new epoch, but you need to develop society's understanding before trying to enforce a new and different vision on them.

In the old Catholic world, there were some monks and nuns who actually achieved themselves spiritually. Their achievement did not come about through their attachment to dogmatic doctrine, but through their courage and special inspiration that rose above the suffocating, conventional religious practice. They had to cultivate themselves naturally, or they would not have been able to achieve themselves. Fast and easy sacrifices cannot replace the maturity of understanding. Real progress is made when an individual or society is open and courageous enough to turn away from dogmatism and look for a new light.

What I emphasize is that all individuals, especially social leaders, should work toward spiritual maturity. What does such maturity look like? Such a person is able to see one's own and others' mistakes and how to correct them without making emotional judgments and without using his or her knowledge for personal or political benefit. Nor does he yield to conventional obstacles such as social prejudice or approval. Who can do this? Only someone of spiritual development.

The problem of the world, as I see it, is that ambitious leaders have pushed their immature ideas drawn from hasty conclusions onto people. What we face is the force of that conventional, established immaturity.

I have been lecturing and writing for many years now, but I do not consider myself someone of high stature. Nor do I consider myself a strong spiritual leader, although I have spiritual friends everywhere. I would, with great pride and happiness, be happy to assist a correctly organized society in the direction described in my book, *The Uncharted Voyage Toward the Subtle Light*: a world of cooperation and progress. That is the true intention of my reaching out as I have and as I continue to do.

If there is any significance in my coming here, it is to confirm the direction you are following. You agree with me because we have a similar understanding that unfolds as we talk. Although the negative force in the world is strong, by working together, you and I can give birth to the positive. Only after you start to live positively and virtuously will negative influences decline. These are meaningful times for all of us.

Q: What can be done about human aggression? What is its source?

Master Ni: This is a good description of New Yorkers. Aggression comes from unrecognized tension.   It is a bad habit from childhood.   When you were a child and you had brothers and sisters, there was only so much food, clothing and love from your parents.   If you did not feel secure, you became aggressive.   Also, your parents were aggressive with you and so encouraged those tendencies.

As I mentioned before, threats are a form of aggression. Be thankful we are all here where we can reflect upon how harmful aggression is.   Do you think the people in the Middle East understand the evil of aggression?   They think it is necessary for their survival.   Christians and Muslims both come from that harsh area.   That is why they are so aggressive as religions.   People in that area work mostly with cattle and sheep, lowly animals that constantly need control, so the religions that developed there naturally emphasized laws and other morality-controlling devices.   God is just the shadow of an executioner in people's lives, and whether one is good or bad, one is always waiting for the executioner's decision on the outcome of one's life.

Aggression can also be caused by jealousy.   The whole world hates America.   Why?   Jealousy mostly.   Communism caused the leveling of wealth due to jealousy.   Hitler was an "achieved" student of Judaism, but he destroyed the Jews because of jealousy.   All that trouble because of jealousy and oppression.   Two thousand years ago, if religions had encouraged people to develop naturally, can you imagine where the world would be today?   I also believe that if religious leaders had developed themselves naturally all this time, they would be much more advanced spiritually, and they would not have incurred the hostility of the intellectuals who started communism and developed nuclear weapons.   Our healthy strength can still be used for good purposes.   This is the work before us now.

As I mentioned, a fragrant tree gives off a sweet fragrance from its own nature. It does not need to be threatened. Likewise, you do good because you are a good person. You must change your own childish, aggressive habits. The price you pay for them in these days of nuclear weapons is too high. You cannot change aggressiveness with aggressive methods. Change will only come about through understanding the need for change.

Q: Do you think there is a good and an evil spirit fighting for supremacy over the world, and is the evil spirit winning? What do you plan to do about it? What can Taoism do to help the world?

Master Ni: Instead of a good or evil spirit fighting over supremacy in the world, I prefer to use the words "yin" and "yang" to express past and present situations.   When yin energy grows, yang energy diminishes; and when yang energy grows stronger, yin energy starts to decline. This theory can apply to a person, family, nation, company, community, the entire world or anything. The human world is a battlefield of starry energy.   Undeveloped spirits all take turns injecting their good or bad influences into human affairs.

Your question shows the depth of universal spiritual reality. Extremes are brought about by the lower sphere of starry spirits which send souls into the human world for further refinement.   Instead of refining themselves, they become lost in worldly events. Rescue comes from the higher sphere of starry spirits symbolized by the Big Dipper and the North Star, which is where the teaching of Tao originated. It sets up the axis for human rightful spiritualization.   If universal life wins, we win; if it loses, then we lose. The truth of eternal life never loses in any battle though. It is above winning or losing.

Divine qualities are expressed by the sincere efforts of good people in the world, and their influence can help turn the world in a different direction. If I were to come here, like spiritual teachers of ancient times, and perform magic to attract your faith in me, nothing would really come of it. Your minds would only be attracted to the magic as a kind of entertainment, or it might make you feel threatened to be good. But what does that contribute to your true spiritual growth? You become emotionally stirred up, but in reality nothing spiritual happens. Also, if you hear of another teacher who can do other tricks, then you will have a conflict over which master is the most powerful.

I think you all understand that the different stages of civilization are like the stages of individual life. When you are a child, you need a certain kind of teaching and guidance, but if you continue to receive the same guidance when you get older, you will never mature properly. Today's people no longer need that, nor will they develop further if they continue to get bedtime stories and magic shows from religious leaders. It is time to move on to more mature things. True God does not perform small magic. True God makes no threats. True God may live in your neighborhood without your noticing it.

By examining your lives, you can change yourselves from within. This change will spread then from you to everyone in the world. This will be your magic and the true salvation for all. I would very much enjoy seeing this.

Q: It seems that your kind of cultivation generates a gentle kind of energy. How can soft energy get through to gross, troubled people?

Master Ni: You are right. It is soft and there are no threats. Just like herbal medicine, some people will not respond to it unless I use a very strong formula. It depends on what kind of poison you are treating. In the old days, a teacher had more control over a student. If he was good, then you were good; if he was bad, then you were bad. But today, people are so strong-minded that they will try to destroy a teacher or demand that he teach them in a certain way. By holding fixed images in their minds about how a spiritual teacher should be, they become very unreceptive. It is better to come together in this way and help each other by studying the material I give on paper. You can consider the person or the book as a friend or a teacher if you want to. If you are sincere, either way works.

I do not demand that you give up your life to follow me. That is not the way today. If your energy is light and sufficient, you will be inspired by my books. There are many secrets there. I hide nothing. You just need to increase your awareness. In many places I show the way to the great treasure, but you are so busy searching everywhere that you cannot see it. I have drawn the map for your personal achievement and virtuous fulfillment in great detail. If you read my books carefully, I will come back to give you further training.

Do not doubt that the soft can win over the gross. Most soft and gentle of all is the universal subtle law. It is always the winner, even when it appears to you to be the loser. I win you by my friendly energy. In history, you have witnessed many rough and gross leaders and fighters, but the victories they enjoy only hastens them to their tombs. Check out what I have said here to you and to other people at various times. The truth is indestructible. True winners cannot be seen.

The nature of worldly events were illustrated by Master Chuang Tzu thus: in the field, the grasshopper stands ready to catch the cicada. Behind the strong grasshopper is a little yellow bird who is ready to catch the grasshopper. Behind the tree, a child with a sling shot quietly aims at the bird. Everyone is someone else's target.

So who is the real winner? Behind you there stands a subtle force that holds you in its palm. What do you call it? Chance? Opportunity? I call it, "Do not childishly believe in muscle alone."

The secret of survival is not totally dependent on the balance of nature. Even the weakest cicada can survive without depending on a grasshopper to discover the bird which stands behind it. Human survival depends on spiritual fitness. The old religions are no longer fit for the present stage of human development. Mankind needs to look for new spiritual fitness. I do not promote co-existence; I promote the harmonious existence of all people. China cannot survive unless she finds her spiritual fitness, nor can the United States, the Soviet Union or any other country. Only by your own wisdom can you see and follow the guidance of Tao that is the spiritual fitness of each generation. Only by adopting the guidance of Tao can the world find the wisdom to guide its further steps to endless survival. Saving the world starts with saving yourself. Come along and learn the harmonious way of life for all people. Do not focus on troubles alone. See the way things can work. Come along. Do not drink the stale water of narrowness, jealousy and prejudice that is leftover from past generations. Let us drink fresh water from the fountain of all-embracing eternal life. Thank you.

An individual can be either the slave of the material sphere and spiritual underdevelopment, or a master of spiritual freedom. The pursuit of enlightenment is what enables one to attain spiritual freedom.

To end this meeting, I offer this poem from an ancient achieved one in the great tradition of Tao, the path of wholeness and naturalness.

**You do not see the subtle truth
    that is so close to your life.
Once you learn to give up the
    self-opinionated mind,
The subtle truth will embrace you.**

**Give up the attachment to ignorance;
Give up conceptual partiality,
And all stubbornness will dissolve.
Then the entire universe
    will express the naturalness
    of the subtle law.
The responsive center of your life
    is like a crystal bowl;
If you keep it empty of everything
    except your original spiritual energy,
You can unite with the ageless
    life of nature.**

CHAPTER TWELVE

Malibu, California: Saturday, December 27, 1986
(First day of a two-day Class on Spiritual
Development and Methods of Self-Cultivation)

First I would like to tell you something about what we are
going to do in these two days. I hope to show you how to
guide your energy, and then how to conduct your energy in
one specific way from among the many valuable techniques
that are available. In addition, I will tell you how to use
things like fire and water in order to purify and sanctify your
body in particular circumstances; how to protect yourself and
your surroundings by your own spiritual practice; and how to
develop your personal spiritual energy by utilizing the natural
energy of the sun and the moon.

I want to begin by acquainting you with some of the
achievements of the ancient developed ones and helping you
understand some of your attitudes. People today are basically
no different than people of ancient times; they have just
developed in a different direction. We should examine the
details of modern life that have caused us to lose sight of the
wholeness of life. When people mistake some part of life for
the whole, it is usually due to conceptual attitudes which
emphasize differences.

There are two main directions that personal development
tends to follow: one is solar in nature and the other is lunar.
Most world religions, such as Christianity, Islam, Hinduism,
etc. create followers who become fervent believers in teachings
which guide people's energy towards external projections.
With this type of conceptual foundation, people are guided to
such extremes such as martyrdom or so-called "holy" wars as
if they were drunk on strong liquor. This is a solar cultural
tendency, carried to excess.

The other direction is intellectual development, which
falls into the lunar type. By contrast with the sun, which
gives you warmth and is sometimes too hot, the moon is cool,
reflecting energy. Solar energy tends to be fiery energy, while
lunar energy is more watery. "Sun" types are enthusiastic

promoters; "moon" types are skeptics, questioners and examiners. The different qualities of these two sources of light underlie the entire conceptual development of human society and have become equally influential as organized religion and scientific technology. As you might expect, intellectually developed people usually disdain the solar attitude of looking at the big picture and neglecting the details. The solar type of mind, on the other hand, rejects the lunar approach that is over-meticulous about each and every detail, complaining that it blocks one's vision of life as a whole.

Basically, we manage our lives with our intellectual mind; how much material benefit we can accumulate depends today on how intellectually achieved we are. But a happy life does not depend solely upon intellectual strength. Nor can happiness be known by the intellectual mind.

If we were to make happiness the goal of life, then which do you think would be the better attitude to have: solar or lunar? I do not believe it is difficult for anyone to see the necessity of having both, but in real life, the battle between the two can very seldom be resolved.

When the natural, ancient developed ones discovered these two types of human nature over five thousand years ago, they saw that the two tendencies were both functions of the mind itself and that a healthy mind is not dominated by either. The integral truth, and its consolidated knowledge and skills that we learn and that I teach, are not the achievement of a one-sided mind. Any half-sided achievement leads to extremes, and extremes do not support the integration of the body, mind and spirit in a direction of universally high life.

If happiness means material gain or emotional expansion, it usually brings mixed results. So first of all, we need to set up a healthy goal for life: what kind of life are we going to have? I do not think anyone wants a terribly unhappy life. We all appreciate happiness, but how can true happiness be achieved in life? First you need to have the correct understanding of life. To achieve this, deeply, one must master both the lunar and solar tendencies in oneself, because happiness comes from the harmonious foundation and re-union of both.

The integral truth and its associated practices require devotion and spiritual-centeredness. It is something you do for your own benefit. Then, when you are achieved, you might wish to extend the benefit of your cultivation to others as well, but the warmth of your devotion comes from spiritual achievement, not impulsive religious fervor.

The teaching of Tao does not demand martyrdom. As a student of Tao, you do need devotion to the universal natural truth, but you should still question things and demand the truth. A teacher of truth does not demand your devotion; he can see for himself whether you are devoted or not. He can also see the direction and further development of your present understanding. With a good attitude on both the student's and the teacher's part, the great task of learning and teaching the truth can be accomplished.

If a teacher is going to do a good job, he must be a living example of internal and external harmony. A good student must know that what he is looking for is the reality of internal and external harmony in his or her life, not just a verbal description of something.

There is no fight involved in learning the truth, nor does it involve any emotional extreme. Anyone with extreme emotion will have problems, the source of which could be personal or a twisted religious education. If the solar tendencies of a person's mind are strongly developed, then the lunar qualities are usually suppressed by the person's fervent, but blind, religious impulses. One who develops only lunar qualities, on the other hand, is intellectually strong and may not have the slightest interest in spiritual development. If you are devoted to any single direction in life, then your mind naturally builds resistance to something else. In learning Tao, one is devoted to the truth of total development rather than to establishing one narrow focus.

People who have not achieved the integral truth have tried to combine things together in an attempt to save their splitting hearts. Like many people in the East, they worship all kinds of gods and prophets: the more the better. This is not true spiritual achievement. They have not found the spiritual essence behind all differences. The integral truth is above all conceptual differences of the mind.

Once you know that all religions are creations of the mind, you might say, "OK. If that's the case, then we will find the creator and worship that." But, if the creator is your mind, do you think an unachieved mind is worthy of worship? Then again, you might think that you should worship the good work of the mind, so you worship the work and ignore the mind, the creator. But who is the one that decides whether it is the work or the manifesting mind that is good or bad, high or low? There must be something higher than the material you examine.

Sooner or later one begins to realize that the scope of the mind is inexhaustible. The inexhaustible mind is the achieved mind; the limited mind is the unachieved mind. You might like to know how to achieve an inexhaustible mind. If you start out on your own, it would be like attempting to build an airplane without referring to the experience and achievement made since the Wright brothers. You could spend your whole life trying to work something out that could have been learned very quickly and perhaps developed further. The same is true in spiritual development. Many people attempt to find the way without inquiring into the truth that was achieved long ago.

Sometimes our minds have good ideas and other times they cause us trouble. Problems arise when the mind goes one way or the other, either with solar or lunar tendencies. That is the nature of the mind. If your creator has this kind of nature, how can it qualify as God? If the mind is not qualified to be God, then how can its creations be respected as God? Neither ordinary religious conceptions nor intellectual knowledge can be regarded as God. At this level, all dispute is useless. We need to look deeply into the core of life.

This energy is the first thing that is important to know. The second is to learn the art of confirming that you are safely on the path of your good life with the support of that energy.

Now you should ask your questions, because it is not just a matter of knowing the truth, but also of understanding. I do not want you to fasten yourselves onto words and concepts rather than the non-verbal truth itself.

Q: Do solar and lunar energy try to draw us toward them? Is there an attempt by the sun or the moon to dominate, and is that why we feel a conflict between the two?

Master Ni: Nature is certainly not lifeless, but it has no preferences. Nature is big life; mankind is small life. In order to live "supernaturally," the mind should know the nature of the universe as well as the internal nature of its own being. Otherwise, people would be too strongly affected by the natural physical environment and thus be limited by the mechanical level of life.

Since nature has three levels, when it gives birth to life, its offspring has three levels also. As the saying goes, "like father, like son." Thus, all lives, especially a species like mankind, are endowed with the other two subtle levels of energy: mind and spirit. The mind can manage the mechanical sphere of nature, both internally and externally, but a more subtle level of energy, generally called "Shen," is the supreme essence of one's being. If one achieves harmony among all three spheres, Shen will guide the use of the mind.

One's personal nature is formed by past lives, family environment and individual tendencies which make one either a lunar or a solar type. In order to be healthy, you need a balance between both sides. The balance between your personal energy and that of society is God.

Q: Is there any correspondence between solar/lunar consciousness and right/left brain functioning?

Master Ni: Yes, and this is why we need complete, not one-sided, development. The ancient masters saw long ago that when the two halves of the brain cooperate, they form a powerful whole. Some of the practices they taught can help balance the two sides of the brain. The balanced, re-integrated energy which takes birth in the brain is "God," but you cannot locate this God in any physical organ in the flesh-and-blood body.

Q: What you said about solar and lunar energy reminded me of changes in my own psychological moods. Sometimes I feel very male and aggressive and strong, physically and psychologically. Other times I feel very passive inside.

Master Ni: This is basically true of everybody. In general, men are solar types and women are lunar, but we all have both tendencies and therefore need to adjust ourselves in life. There is a story about a famous poet that illustrates this. A young poet had graduated from Cambridge University and was teaching in a university in his country about forty years ago. He fell in love with a very attractive woman and began writing love poems to her. He was very happy when he finally got her to agree to meet him for a date, but once they were alone together all he did was murmur poems by Keats and Shelley to his undressed, waiting beauty. The whole night passed without his ever taking any action toward the physical Goddess before him. It was his solar energy that got him the date with the woman, but his lunar energy spoiled it. I heard afterwards that she married a common soldier rather than the talented, poetic professor.

Q: *What is it that is beyond the mind that can see the mind?*

Master Ni: This is an important question. If you cannot see your solar or lunar tendencies and correct them immediately, then how can you balance yourself? There is definitely something above the mind itself. That subtle self is the one which holds the reins; the mind is just the horse. You need to be a strong, wise rider. I do not know what to call this super-energy without personifying it and entrapping us in the same conceptual pitfalls of past religions by over-decorating reality until it is impossible to see the truth.

Q: *Is this what is referred to as the "superior man" in the I Ching?*

Master Ni: The fifth line generally exemplifies the high subtle essence in each individual which is sometimes called the soul. It is better to say "spiritual energy," because most people do not understand that the soul of an individual is actually a group of unified spiritual entities that depend on individual achievement through spiritual self-cultivation. What is called

God, or universal self-nature, is simply the spiritual energy of the entire universe. In teaching Tao, we use both of these terms.

Q: Are solar and lunar tendencies indicated in a person's astrological birth chart? Do they have to do with the place of the sun and the moon in the chart?

Master Ni: Astrology is a generalization of personality.   I would like to set it aside for now. It is safe to say that each person is a mixture of both tendencies.   No one is a hundred percent one type or the other.   You only have tendencies which can guide you in a certain direction.

Q: I just want to add my observation, as a doctor of Oriental medicine, that there is a basic tendency in human beings to polarize mentally, physically, politically and socially.

Master Ni: This is very true. Over-polarization can happen in all aspects of human life if there is not a higher directing energy from one's spiritual center. The question is, what is that center or function which can harmonize the two functions of the brain? No bodily organ can do it. In the learning of Tao, there are spiritual organs called "spiritual checkpoints" in the body. By working on and developing them, they can be made a powerful means of attaining different spiritual capabilities, balance and harmony within one's being. This requires specific guidance in the spiritual practice of self-cultivation.   For instance, the posture of the body and the position of the hands and fingers can cause a response between personal and natural spiritual energy. The basic postures are recommended in *The Workbook for Spiritual Development*.

Placing the thumbs together, face to face, can link the energy of both sides of the brain. If they are held too low, they can draw your energy and attention down to the sexual center, so keep them above the navel.

Keep your spine straight. The spine is like a stalk of bamboo, made up of sections which are empty inside. It is the channel through which your personal spiritual energy is transported after having successfully broken through different sections. If you cannot do that, then how can you say that the spiritual achievement of a free soul is accomplished? No one can walk through walls, but your spiritual energy, after concentration and fortification, can pass through walls of any density. The practice of the orbit circulation of spiritual energy can build your spiritual capability. Can you physically break a wall? No you cannot, but your spiritual energy can enter even a stone. Can you fly? No, but your spirit can fly. Can you enter the flames of a fire and not be burned? Your spirit cannot be burned by fire or drowned in water. The question is, how do you realize these capabilities?

Religious believers accept emotional control by an external authority, but this is no proof of spiritual truth. In learning Tao, your own spiritual practice is what takes you to heaven, not a superficial commitment or emotional connection. Your personal achievement is the proof. The training we do in the shrine is not done for the sake of external show, but for the purpose of attuning ourselves with heavenly energy. The spiritually achieved ones who live millions of light years away can sense our energy as easily as if they were standing next to us. It is important, therefore, for us to refine and purify our energy as well as offer our devotion and respect to our own beings.

At a general level, your energy responds to the energy around you. When you see a handsome boy or pretty girl, you respond at a physical level. Once your physical energy is refined, it can be transferred to higher level than you ever expected. But how can you find the path of spiritual wholeness if you are engaged in the process of self-splitting and separation, and if every thought, sensation and impulse you have distracts you from the very thing you are trying to achieve? What can you do?

This brings us back to solar and lunar energy. Solar-mindedness leads to development of social religions in a healthy, positive sense, while lunar-mindedness leads the mind to create science of a serviceable nature. Each, therefore, contributes to human life in some way, but neither is beneficial if it becomes extreme. People should thus develop their spiritual center, which is above both the solar and the lunar tendencies. This is the only thing that can keep them from becoming extreme.

Wisdom and clarity are capabilities of a mature mind which also includes common sense and sophistication in human relationships. Intellectual maturity and the art of using the mind expresses a person's spiritual growth. This is not the same thing as the growth of personal spiritual energy which is the unfolding of a group of refined and unified souls within an individual.

When people do something extra to make their life fuller or happier, they actually create the opposite result. For instance, around a hundred years ago Chinese women still bound their feet. This custom started because in the Tang Dynasty (618-918 A.D.) there was a great beauty, Queen Yong Yu-Wan, who walked so gracefully that her body swayed in a most beautiful manner. The fact was that her legs were too weak to carry her, so she had to walk in a peculiar way that was like the soft sway of weeping willow branches hanging over the surface of a lake swept by the warm spring breezes. Other women tried to imitate her way of walking by binding their feet, because when your feet are restrained, you walk very softly and gracefully. This custom lasted for almost a thousand years until the establishment of the Republic of China by Dr. Sun Yat-Sen.

Now women buy high-heeled shoes which also make their bodies move very gracefully, but they are not good for the brain or the bone structure. People always seem to care more about looking beautiful than about being healthy.

Once I saw a country girl in Taiwan who had come to the city for sightseeing. As she got off the train and started walking across the tracks in her brand new high heels, she caught her heel in between the tracks and broke it off. That saddened her greatly, because one heel was gone and one was still high. I happened to be nearby, so I told her to take off her shoes and walk naturally on her bare feet, because they were just as attractive as the shoes. She took my advice and got lots of attention.

The world has developed many unnatural things and customs that create stress for us. The thing to do is undo unnatural customs and habits so that you can have a healthy body and normal life again.

In the teaching of Tao we say there are three kinds of healers. The first kind can help you avoid becoming sick; the second kind can treat you when you are sick; and third kind kills you, without your ever noticing it. That saying can be applied to social and religious leaders too.

(Noon Break)

A natural life is one that is lived for itself, not for show. People who have emotional fantasies often live to show off. They are not qualified to be celebrities, but they do something special or create some kind of trouble to attract the kind of attention they want. If your life is for show, you cannot live honestly; you live for shallow emotional drives, not for your true self. When you live in a social mode and mold made by others, you deviate from the truthfulness of your own nature. If you are unable to say no because you need to be socially agreeable, you pull down your spiritual level and tax your health just to participate in a show. Therefore, people of spiritual centeredness do not mingle with any crowd. They either live alone or become recluses. But in such cases, the world loses a true teacher, and the recluses lose the opportunity of practicing kindness and sympathy toward many lost ones.

Can a student of Tao be an artist, politician, soldier, lawyer or policeman without losing his or her spiritual integrity? Yes, because when people are aware of what they are doing, the joy of achievement comes from their own nature, not from a superficial desire to please others. In any walk of life, one or two people will do and enjoy more naturally than others and will thus be able to achieve a higher degree of accomplishment.

Beware of the word "nature." We have lived in the world and learned worldly ways, which are almost second nature to us now. If we suddenly come in contact with universal nature, we feel like it is something new that we have to learn all over again. People must find their true nature before they can undo the unnaturalness they have accumulated throughout their lives and lifetimes. Only then is it possible to restore the original health of a natural life.

People lose their true nature by becoming interested in things they do not really want and by living according to unnatural social fantasies and expectations. It is important to know the boundaries of your true nature and how much compromise and adjustment can reasonably be made to the unnatural structure of modern society. If the price is too high, if it affects the natural health of your three dimensions, I would suggest you withdraw from it.

In ancient China, people would offer their guests a big cup of wine and toast "Bottoms up!" as they filled their cups again and again. You could not refuse or they would feel like you were not being whole-hearted. Here in the United States, no one offers wine that way, but people drink by themselves, bottoming-up not just cups but whole bottles. Invisible social pressures are much stronger now than the happy mood of well-meaning friends. People who try to escape into alcohol or drugs or self-cheating religions are destroyed. You must hold to a plain and honest life and follow your true nature without compromising yourself internally or externally to unnatural, harmful influences.

The negative extremes of psychologically cheating religions have not been totally cleaned up. You need to put all those immature cultural creations in their place without letting them warp your true nature any further. In a holiday season such as this, it is okay to give and receive gifts from your beloved ones. In fact, if Jesus did not have a birthday, we would not have had this holiday to meet each other for a constructive purpose. Even though Christmas is not his real birthday, a sage can be born on any good day. All religious customs should be flexible.

The essence of Jesus' teaching is forgiveness. As students of natural spiritual development, let us recognize this as a day of forgiveness. The correct application of this day is to dissolve the hatred or resentment in your mind and heart toward things or people that you do not like. Do not let Christmas be just another commercial holiday, but remember it as a day of spiritual forgiveness and remember that in the past there was a sage who fulfilled the essence of his great teaching.

More deeply, when you think of Jesus' great teaching of forgiveness, remember that you only need to forgive people if they make trouble. If they did not make trouble, why would you need to forgive them? This teaching is secondary to the teaching of spiritual originality, but it is useful for people who have developed in an unhealthy direction. When you understand this, you can appreciate Jesus' work without waiting for people to harm you so that you can forgive them.

Jesus taught in response to a certain stage in the development of Jewish culture. At that time, the Jews were enslaved by the Romans and expected a messiah who would save them. Jesus was the one to respond to the historic call, but he came to do the job religiously, not practically. Thus the Jewish "nation" was not saved by him or his teachings. The enemies of his teachings were the religious nobles of his society, the Pharisees, who are still in power today. As Jesus' teachings became widespread in other regions of the world they became popular among people who sympathized with his sacrifice. An emotional tie was made, but the religious revolution died. It is like Buddhism, which was a revolution of its mother religion, Hinduism. Thus, when Buddhism is taught, Hinduism is explained and taught too. When the rough base is understood and accepted, higher achievement is blocked. Thus the true humanistic essence of Jesus' teaching has been blocked and unseen.

I have some friends who visited Kashmir where they saw two tombs. One tomb was that of Moses and the other was Jesus'. The tomb keepers they interviewed were descendants of Jesus. I believe this discovery is true. No one needs to play such a trick on people's minds. To me, it is not a question of whether it is really Moses or Jesus in the tomb. The respectful facts are that they fulfilled the work required of them at the time they lived. I think they both courageously did what needed to be done in their lives.

People who are spiritually undeveloped usually want to see special things. They like wonders more than they trust the normalcy of nature. Moses and Jesus, therefore, had to do something to make themselves accepted by the common people who are blind to the true miracles that are performed in everyday life. Small magic can satisfy the emotional fantasy of a small group of people. Big magic, at the level of God, happens in everyday, honest efforts that go unnoticed by most people.

The magic that is reliable in all circumstances of life is the great magic, not small miracles. If you can change water to wine, it is no big deal. It is a big deal, though, if you can remove wine and drugs and false psychological beliefs from the minds of the majority of the population. People did magic a long time ago, and they still do it today. Small minds enjoy such achievements, because they cannot see or appreciate the great magic of honest results in the events of their daily lives. I worship the person who works honestly and efficiently to support his own life. Students of continual spiritual development should worship perseverance in spiritual self-development instead of some emotional fantasy of forever-postponed salvation.

The learning of Tao nurtures one's own simple essence with the simple essence of the universe which is the same in everyone. It is what supports a good, honest life in each individual being. This great endowment is abused by the cunning mind which brings about divergence. Embracing the simple essence is the only truthful guidance. The practice is simple, the "religion" is simple, but a teacher needs to spend a lot of energy to teach the religion of one universal life in a day and age when dualistic religions are so widespread. When Buddhism came to China, wise teachers utilized it to teach the indescribably simple essence, but once its religious shell was adopted, the true teaching was blocked. To teach the unequivocal truth of oneness, no conceptual creation should be adopted.

I have mentioned ancient spiritual development a lot today. Do you ever wonder why people suddenly became wise five thousand years ago? Why them? Why five thousand years ago? At that time, no dualistic religion existed to confuse them. It was easier for people to grow in a healthy way when there were no unnatural obstacles. Also, human life was assisted by higher natural spiritual energy at that time. Great sages like the Yellow Emperor, Niao and Yu were all different spiritual energies that came from the stars and took human form by entering the womb of a woman on earth. These beings had great mental and spiritual capacity. The skill of natural spiritual development is not new. It is a continuation of what these heavenly beings gave to mankind. Why did humanity gradually become foolish and deviate from the truth? Energy-wise, it could be compared to a cup of wine that has been passed from one person to another. When the first person drinks a little bit, he puts some water in the cup to fill it up again, and so on down the line. By the time it gets to the last person, it is all water. People become spiritually blocked, physically weakened and mentally confused by their own deviation from the simple truth of spiritual reality.

In the beginning, many people greatly benefitted by the advice and direction they received from the starry beings that were born into human life as great sages. The teaching of Tao started when the natural balance and harmony in people's lives started to decline.

It is not necessary to deny that people were originally lower animals, but without spiritual evolution, there is no physical evolution. Otherwise a monkey stays a monkey and a gorilla stays a gorilla. Why didn't they ever transform into human beings? When a new specimen appears, it is due to the intervention of some new energy. I am not going to tell you a Sunday school story so that you will believe my description; that is not my concern. The original teaching of Tao came from those great sages. Usually anyone who has broken through the obstacles in human life has been helped by energy from the stars. When the spiritual condition of any life is low, no advancement can be brought about without help from a spiritual source.

We have been handed the last cup of diluted wine. Our development is not enough to handle simple things, so we need self-cultivation; we need to renew ourselves. We need to reconnect with our starry sources, the spiritual source of the vast universe.

In ancient times, people believed that Heaven was in the sky, the home of the stars. Although men build spacecraft that can fly to the stars and the planets now, they cannot see the subtle intervention from the stars. All of us are recognized by our physical body, but above that we are endowed with spiritual energy which comes from the subtle origin that is unseen, because it is blocked by our modern way of life. Heaven is the stem of all lives. The high essence is emitted through the stem of universal life. Bananas have a stem, oranges and apples have stems; the stem takes energy from the tree on which the fruit grows. The stem is called "Ti" in Chinese. The word "Ti", 帝 has two parts: ㇒ㇵ and 帝, to compose one Chinese character. With the grassy head, "蒂"

Ti means stem. Without the grassy head, it means God. So " 帝," Ti, means God, and "茼 ," Ti, means stem.

The word Ti or God comes from the concept of a stem. God, or the spiritual energy in an individual life, is the stem of a stem. We call this stem God, but it is only one connection, it is not the entire source. Once the connection is broken, God does not exist any more for the person. With no God in them, they come back as animals.

You do not have a visible stem, but you do have a spiritual stem. You have a spiritual individuality that can hook up with the big spiritual computer of the universe. This big computer is the subtle origin, but most people are not hooked up with it yet. My work is to hook you up with the subtle origin of all life. The part that you can be hooked up with is Ti or God in your life. A good life cannot be without a source; it will wither if separated or cut off from its origin. When people go against the spiritual nature of oneness, against the real God, they punish themselves by being cut off from the source of natural life. They dry themselves up.

If people strengthen and develop themselves through a good connection with their spiritual origin, their lives will be prosperous and they will enjoy health, happiness and longevity. Their lives will unfold beautifully. If they live for the pursuit of more and more money or fame, without working on their connection with the spiritual origin, then the more they do, the more they weaken their lives until their stem is completely cut and their life is that of a zombie without a soul.

On the border of Wu Nan province in southern China, a long time ago, when a traveler died it was hard to hire someone to carry the body back to the family or the hometown, so there was a professional magician who turned the corpses into zombies and made them walk home. The route that was used for the small army of zombies at night was clearly marked so that no living people would come across their path. There were also special hotels for them to rest in during the daytime. This custom continued up until fifty years ago when bad people began using the zombies to smuggle opium.

You know, you can still find many zombies in the streets today. You do not need to go back fifty years ago to Wu Nan province to peek at them through cracked doors. Zombies are just people whose souls are gone.

I am going to teach you how to renew your spiritual connection with the subtle origin. The "magic" of spiritual cultivation is true, and it works. This magic can support you through many different stages of growth. If it is not learned from a true teacher, you could really waste your time. You may think you achieved it by yourself, but actually it is the growing of your spiritual energy. You cannot make a breakthrough unless you have developed your spiritual energy. Your highest development will raise you to the level of a God. I do not feel entirely comfortable using the word God, because in your customary thinking it implies some kind of rulership. I would rather translate it as the "Divine One," because to be divine is to be virtuous, as I define it. Also, all divinity is one universal, virtuous energy. God is a word that has been narrowly used. Divine One has not. All Divine Ones are just beings who have attained more universal divine energy than ordinary people have. A Divine One is simply a person who can express universal divine energy purely in his or her life.

Q: Is forgiveness the same thing as the Eastern practice of letting go?

Master Ni: I am not sure which interpretation or what context you mean, but if your personal understanding makes a connection between what I teach and something you have learned before, that is fine. It is my personal impression that both are psychological tools which are useful to people who have emotional difficulties.

Q: Some people say that Jesus traveled to Tibet and China to be spiritually educated when he was young. Do you think that is true?

Master Ni: The discovery of the tombs I mentioned in Kashmir would seem to suggest this. You can see that the task of Jesus and Moses was not simple. The way in which they worked must have had a master mind behind it.

Q: You said that the essence of Jesus' teaching was forgiveness. What about love?

Master Ni: I believe that love became the later emphasis of some of his disciples when they began to form new communities and needed guidance for relationships between different individuals and the various communities. Jesus concentrated primarily on attacking the Pharisees.

Love is a good thing, but it is very easy to misinterpret. For example, do you love them enough to discipline them? If not, then how can you talk about love? You are just indulging in immature sentimentality. Real love that is associated with helping the development of another individual in all respects. Does your love fulfill that? How do I express my love toward young ones? I point out what they do right and what they do wrong. Parents often try to express their love with money. There is a lot more that could be said about how to express love. It needs a seminar of its own.

Q: What did you mean by "Divine One" earlier?

Master Ni: A person cannot become divine all alone; it takes joint energy to make you divine. I sit here as a teacher talking about things that are divine, but if you do not recognize things with a divine nature, how can you become divine? This is the conceptual level of understanding. If you could break through your conceptual separation, you would reach the conjoint divine energy of oneness.

If you extend your belief or faith to a dominant character or God, then you reject the divine energy itself and stay at the relative level. People in the same church believe in the same definition of God, but in another religion people believe in a different concept of God, so they fight over their differences. In the religious world today, God is only a name for disguised ego, racism, nationalism and narrow self-interest. Communism is one of God's new names. Like other gods, it is nothing more than a cruel ruling machine that rips off human nature. I am also annoyed by people who use the name of God to knock on the door of each house. Their god has never respected peace. I think there are some wolves beneath the skins of these sheep.

My work is to help individuals find their own God and the God of all people. To do this, I need to correct the historic misconception of God. For instance, I have changed clothes three times today, but I am still the same person inside the clothes. If you can see through the changes, you can see there is only one of me, not three separate people. The Divine One is the same; God changes clothes every Spring, Summer, Autumn, and Winter. I recommend that you do not use the word God, because different people hold different definitions and are willing to fight over them. I can teach you the single essence of the Divine One. Always reach for the true heart of God, not the wrappings.

You cannot cut the Divine One up. If you put a narrow definition on it, it is not the Divine One itself, it is something you created so that it would be easier to see. I have tried to clarify the false concept of God as a warlike deity and show people the truth of God as a universal source of harmony.

Where I come from in China, each village has its own god. In one of the villages there is a dragon boat festival on the fifth day of the fifth month each year, and each boat that participates has its own deity that helps the boat during the race. Sometimes, if a boat is in an unfavorable position, it will attack a nearby boat and even kill its occupants because of the anger of the different gods. The universal divine energy is far above such villagers' gods. Nobody needs to fight for the true God.

At the spiritual level, there are differences in how people cultivate themselves, but there is no limitation to personal development. Once you are developed, you are as good as any god. This potential is natural and beyond all conceptual limitations.

I refer to the oneness, to the subtle origin, to Tao, to the integral truth. They all express the same truth of nondescribable individuality: one path, one nature and one universal life. I have worked hard to help you understand these things, but please do not mistake my language for the truth itself. When I point at the moon, you should look at the moon, not my finger. Do not get caught up in my words; look for what they point to.

Q: Are Tao and divinity synonymous?

Master Ni: Tao means the source, the initial, fresh, pure energy of the universe and all life. It represents the unspoiled, integral nature of human beings and the universe. Integralness expresses itself in completeness and absoluteness. Sometimes Tao means the whole, universal divine nature, while divinity is Tao expressed. We refer to things differently on different occasions, though in deep reality they are united. I function as a teacher, healer, writer, father and lover at different times, but I am still one being in reality. Most simply, Tao is the source and divinity is the offspring. From divinity we learn to respect Tao. From Tao we come to know the universal connection of divinity. One is many, many are one. All my doubt was dissolved when I reached Tao. I hope it will be the same for you.

(Class takes a break)

In our last discussion, I explained divinity. True divinity is the universal, pure and simple essence of nature at a non-personified level. It is the deepest subtle essence of all things. There can be experiences of personified response from the non-personified sphere of the universe, but the image or being who is seen and contacted is just an expression of divine energy responding to the conceptual form of a particular human mind. The image, personified as a god or goddess, cannot be held as concrete fact. This is the source of original misunderstanding about spiritual reality.

People try to understand, but it is hard to admit one's own roughness. We are not objective or quiet enough to know the subtle spiritual network of the universe. We are too open to the philosophical influence of others and the narrow conceptual structures of our culture. A gentle, neutral mind naturally hooks itself up with the spiritual network of the deep sphere of the physical world. We waste time learning religious and intellectual information that is of little real use in our lives and neglect the value of simple objectivity. The so-called Tao, the so-called integral truth, is not mystical. Many people think it is, but it is perfectly clear and obvious to an unspoiled mind. It is only unclear and hidden to a mind that is buried in heaps of cultural and religious spoilage.

When mankind was young, many things were done without its knowledge, and people grew without ever giving a thought to anyone else. Spiritual matters are very subtle; they are never solid and controllable as general religions would have you think. Religion tries to color the true divine nature of the universe with its own childish imagination. The real spiritual sphere is a blank. You color it by yourself. It depends on one's development whether one colors the book beautifully or not. There is no need for conflict over the different ways of coloring it. If you worry over how other people color it, you will never reach the divine source of the universe, because you can never attain nature itself by holding onto the coloring book. I would like to show you the original book of no color. By correcting the misconceptions of divinity that different religions have created, I hope to show you the truth that there is a true spiritual origin of all lives.

If you understand things correctly, you can do better in your life. Patiently studying my books can help you understand how to develop correctly.

Now let us turn our attention to some practical methods of cultivation. How much we can do will depend on the time and your understanding.

You all know that we live on earth, but earth is not a single entity in the universe. To start with, we have the sun and the moon and the first five planets of the solar system: Mars, Venus, Mercury, Saturn and Jupiter. These are all very influential in human life. We utilize their energy and acknowledge them as the seven days of the week. There is a hidden spiritual practice behind this that was known to the ancient sages. I believe most of you are already familiar with the so-called "Five Elements" which correspond to the first five planets: metal with Venus, fire with Mars, earth with Saturn, wood with Jupiter, and water with Mercury.

The first five planets have corresponding energies in our bodies also. Mercury, for instance, is the water system or kidneys; Venus corresponds with the lungs or breathing system, which is metal energy; Jupiter corresponds with the liver, the gall bladder, and the nervous system, or wood energy; Mars corresponds to the heart and mind which are fire energy. Saturn is not liked very much by conventional astrologers in the West, but its natural energy corresponds with the stomach and spleen as the stabilizing energy symbolized by earth. The heavy quality that is associated with Saturn is a misconception of its nature. Spiritually, it represents balanced energy.

In realizing a wholesome life of Tao, we use the five elements to develop many important practices. To understand the correspondence of energy in this simple but abstract system, I would like to give you a few examples. Some of them are very interesting. Joy and laughter correspond to fire, while anger and shouting correspond to wood and a nervous burst of energy. Fear is related to water energy, while reminiscence and sighing are connected with the hurting energy of metal.

There are also color correspondences such as red with fire, green with wood, black with water, white with metal, and yellow with earth. These things are helpful to know when you are cultivating your own internal harmony.

Our solar system has ten planets in all: five belonging to yang energy and five to yin. Yang energy is represented by the sun, while yin is represented by the moon, but all ten planets affect us.

Now let us talk about how to utilize the energy of the sun and moon. We know that one of the best social welfare systems in the world today exists in Sweden, but Sweden also has a very high rate of suicide. Why is this? It is because their winters are too long and they do not get enough sun.

If you lived in a place without sunshine for six months, don't you think you would get depressed? If a mature woman was isolated and never saw a strong man, her life would have no light or warmth. It is important for people to have solar energy within and without. People commonly utilize the sunshine by going to the beach and baking themselves. Sometimes they overdo it and get freckles or even sunburn to the extent that they develop skin cancer. So this is not the way to do it. I want to show you how, in the great teaching of Tao, all people, but particularly women without men or men without women, can utilize the great energy of the sun and moon to balance themselves.

Men sometimes have lowered sexual energy and suffer impotence because of the tension caused by intellectual or emotional struggles in their life. Impotence is a kind of weakness. Every morning, when the sun rises, you should stand in a place with good air, face the East and breathe in the solar energy. Swallow it and send it to the lower Tan Tien, the place just below the navel. Even if it is cloudy, you can still do the practice. The sun is still there. By your spiritual development, you can make the sun energy come to you through the clouds.

Q: Can you do this indoors?

Master Ni: Yes, if it is too damp or cold outside. Men who suffer from sexual weakness can use this practice to cure themselves. By doing this thirty times every morning, a man's strength can be restored within one to nine months. Nine swallows is the minimum practice. Thirty times qualifies you as a person of Tao who lives on more than just physical food alone.

How about women, now? Women are often not satisfied with their husbands, so they need a true husband who is always available. This is not a husband that will cause your first husband any jealousy, though, because it is the sun. At the most, a woman should breathe in the solar energy only nine times, otherwise she will become too manly. You need to balance yourself so that whether you have a man or not, you will not be unsatisfied or crave a man. You suffer without a man, but you suffer once you have one too. It is better to have the sun as your great husband and your other husband as refreshment. You will also increase your vitality in this way. This is the secret of men and women's practice.

Q: What if you are satisfied without a husband?

Master Ni: Then there is no problem. You can use natural energy to supplement your general vitality. A woman who is happy without a man, though, is not natural. It is true that you can never be 100% satisfied with any man, but there must be some disappointment to make a woman turn away from men. You need to look for help from the great husband and father, the sun.

Although I have given you this information, I wish you would not share it with other people before they improve their own virtue and discipline. If your virtuous condition is not improved, it does not matter what capability you have or how many practices you know, you will only make trouble for yourself and those around you. That is not right. I do not teach people that way.

One thing I would like to point out on this occasion is the connection between taking in the sun and moon energy and your sexual strength. I do not promote the general sexual arts which are publicized as the indulgent, so-called "Tao of Sex." That is just part of Chinese culture, like Chinese cooking. It is for fun. I have given detailed guidance in the second volume of *Eight Thousand Years of Wisdom* and other books on this subject.

Q: When you say swallow the breath, do you mean swallow like swallowing a drink of water?

Master Ni: Right. You should be relaxed and do it very gently. Do not be nervous.

Q: Should you look directly into the sun when you do this?

Master Ni: No. You need to close your eyes. You should face the sun in the early morning, around sunrise. If your vision and nervous system are strong enough, you can open your eyes a little. That would be safe. Do not stare at the sun, though. There are harmful rays. By your spiritual energy, you can take the good rays from the sun and breathe them in.

Q: After you swallow the breath, do you hold it?

Master Ni: After you swallow it, you should send it down to the lower Tan Tien, the area two to three inches below the navel. Then you relax and breathe in again. Be careful not to swallow the outdoor air if the weather is foggy.

Q: Is it still thirty times for men and nine for women in the summer?

Master Ni: Anytime, summer or winter, with sunshine or without.

Q: I don't get up at sunrise. Can I do it later?

Master Ni: It is not quite as good, but you can still do it as long as it is before noon. If you are not up by sunrise, though, you disrupt the natural flow of energy in your body, so you should try to get up earlier.

If you live with someone, your companion must have the same understanding of life and the nature of the universe and spiritual cultivation, otherwise the relationship will cause difficulty in your life. You do not need to make your companion follow you, but it is necessary that you do not follow someone who is less developed than you.

Q: My biggest problem in doing spiritual practices is that I have had to give up a lot of friends. I start feeling their bad influence and don't want to be affected by it.

Master Ni: This is not the real problem. The problem is whether you have the strength to give up the crowd. If you have that strength, you are spiritually strong and you will find corresponding friends at your own level someday. If you stay with the old flock, you can never move on. If you are with a flock of crows, you are one of the crows. If you are in the company of phoenix, you are one of the phoenix. The choice is yours. Life is flexible.

Q: I have a problem with re-entry in the mornings when I first wake up. Generally, I wake up angry. Is it okay to do these practices when I feel that way?

Master Ni: That is a common problem for many people. Energy conducting exercises are helpful in this kind of situation. You might be interested in learning the Eight Treasures or Tai Chi or Chi Gong or some meditation arts. In this seminar, I will teach you another practice to build the natural flow of your energy cycle and help you become more balanced. Then you should be able to do this kind of practice in the early morning. One of the most important things is a good daily schedule. Go to bed early and get up early. If possible, sleep alone, and do not do anything that would disturb your energy during the day.

Q: Can you do this before sunrise? I am always on a bus just when the sun is rising, and by the time I get to work it's already up.

Master Ni: It is okay to do it on the bus, if the area you are traveling through does not have bad air.

Q: I still don't understand whether you swallow the air or the energy.

Master Ni: It is not a matter of understanding. Your achievement comes from practice. In the beginning you still do not recognize your spiritual power, so you do not really know how it can happen. Once you are hooked up, then your spiritual energy can pass through the clouds and take the energy directly.

Q: Is this just breathing air down into the Tan Tien?

Master Ni: No. You breathe in the energy and use the movement of swallowing to help it.

Q: Should you do this standing or sitting?

Master Ni: Standing is better, unless you are driving or riding. It is better to do it in a relaxed manner. It is not as comfortable in a car or a bus as in your own yard or garden somewhere.

Q: What if you live in a mountainous place where the sun doesn't come up until 9 o'clock?

Master Ni: You should climb the mountain! If you are not crazy, you cannot learn Tao. That's what people say. You must be crazy about your spiritual cultivation; then achievement might come.

Q: I'm still not clear on the swallowing part. It's not like swallowing saliva?

Master Ni: It is different; it is your mind or your spirit that makes it happen. Without the mind, nothing happens. That is important. This is why you need single-mindedness for spiritual practice.

If you cannot feel the sun's warmth, then as a special practice you can do it twice: once at 6 a.m. and again at 9 a.m. or 10:00 or 11:00 if the air is right and you do not open your eyes. Then you can feel the warmth and swallow that. Do not ever do this practice after the sun has passed the midpoint of the day, though. Anytime before noon is okay, as long as the air is good.

The sun represents your soul energy. This practice, therefore, strengthens your soul energy. This is the knowledge of the deeper sphere.

Q: Should we visualize negative energy leaving our body as we breathe out?

Master Ni: No, not in this practice. When you first get up in the morning, you should exhale the black energy and breathe in white energy. After doing this for a few minutes, you can start to do your regular spiritual practice. This is a good thing to do before doing the sun exercise, if you do not have another regular practice that you do. You can also do it when you have a real physical problem.

While this practice will strengthen your energy, you should be careful not to spend more than you make, sexually. If you make ten dollars, then do not spend fifteen. It is better to spend less and save more.

Now, quiet down for a little while. In a moment we will go further into a technique which can bring you a great deal of benefit.

We mentioned the seven heavenly bodies in the beginning of this talk. We have covered two: the sun and the moon. If your minds are still fresh, I will cover the rest now.

What affects your everyday life most is your emotional and sexual balance. Is this true or not? How to manage yourself as an independent, developed being is the question here. Do you know how? The only solutions in the world so far have been religious ones, but I do not think they can really solve the problem. If God chased Adam and Eve out of the

Garden of Eden, who should take responsibility for having made them different in the first place? It is our responsibility to fix the problem that rough craftsmanship left us.

Every day you should spend from twenty minutes to two hours harmonizing and adjusting your internal energy. If you can balance your emotions, you will have no anger or sadness and will not be easily excited. So listen well and I will teach you another practice. In doing this Five Energies meditation, it does not matter what position you sit in, but it is important that you are not disturbed during the time that you do it. So unhook your telephone.

As you sit, you correspond a specific color to certain internal organs. Begin with the heart and visualize red chi or a soft red cloud that is transformed from your heart and watch it carefully with your internal vision. After a few minutes, watch the red cloud move to the area of the stomach and then gradually change to become yellow. This is a pure mental practice; you need to do it until there is no "me," only clouds. From the stomach, the cloud moves up to the region of the lungs, expands to cover both lungs and becomes white. Then, after a while, the white cloud sinks down to the kidneys and bladder where it becomes dark, like the water of the North Sea, deep, dark blue with a little gray in it. This cloud surrounds all your water organs and then moves up to the liver area just to the right of your spleen and gall bladder. When it comes to this region, it changes from blue-black to green. From here, you can begin the cycle over again by moving the green cloud to the heart where it becomes red, and so forth.

Do this cultivation calmly and gently, following the order I have given you. Do not change the order. Water gives birth to wood energy which gives birth to fire; fire gives birth to earth, and earth gives birth to metal; metal gives birth to water and the cycle repeats itself. By your visualization, you burn away negative energy, and your internal movements harmonize your sexual energy beautifully. People are made of living energy. Someday the physical house of your soul will die, but these five clouds will be your new home that can carry you flying. The minimum goal of this practice is to fortify your energy and balance yourself.

Q: How do you bring the practice to a close?

Master Ni: Gently. Be gentle when you do it; be gentle when you stop it. After several circulations, you should take a break or stop. If you have done the circulation for two hours, then slow down before you bring it to a close. Collect your energy back to its original order. Just calm down. You do not need to use strength to do it. Use your gentle mind.

The second stage of the Five Cloud Meditation is to sit quietly and visualize the center between the nipples or the area one half inch above the navel. I recommend that women use the point between the nipples.

Q: Is it better to do this practice in the morning or evening?

Master Ni: Both times are okay, but do not do it when your stomach is full. You should also be emotionally peaceful.

Q: Do you visualize any particular color when you finish?

Master Ni: No color. In order to stop the practice, you move the energy away from the internal eye.

Q: Does it matter which color you end with?

Master Ni: It should be according to the health of your organs. If you do not have a particularly weak organ, then any organ is all right.

This is one of many good cultivations. It is as if I had given each of you $500,000. Now you will go out with it and we shall see how much each of you can make from it. I would like to see all of you prosper.

Let's stop here for today.

An individual can be either the slave of the material sphere and spiritual underdevelopment, or a master of spiritual freedom. The pursuit of enlightenment is what enables one to attain spiritual freedom.

To end this meeting, I offer this poem from an ancient achieved one in the great tradition of Tao, the path of wholeness and naturalness.

If you ask where the true self is,
   where your true life comes from,
Do not stay in the sandcastles
   of your mind's conceptions.
For long lifetimes, you have been caged
   and shadowed by self-created clouds.
Once your true eye is open,
   you will see the true self clearly.

CHAPTER THIRTEEN

Malibu, California: Sunday, December 28, 1986
(Second Day of the Class on Spiritual Development
and Methods of Self-Cultivation)

There was a recluse in the time of the Han Dynasty (206 B.C.-219 A.D.), who achieved himself with the practice I taught you yesterday. He lived for about two to four hundred years in the high mountains of a particular region, but he would occasionally ride down on a buffalo to render his services to the people living in the valley. People knew him as The Buffalo Rider, but his true name was Fong Churng-Da.

Many good practices have been developed in this great tradition. In this class, I will only introduce the method that was passed down from Master Fong. In the future, I will teach other practices from different masters.

All of the ancient masters were hooked up with the starry energy that used to be called Heaven: just the sky with all its starry beings. Each star, you see, is a big being with its own beautiful energy formation which cannot be seen with the naked eye, no matter what device you use. Different stars have different spirits. Once a human being achieves himself enough to ascend to Heaven, in reality he joins a new life on the stars. All gods are starry beings, and the real God is the unity of the spirits from the stars.

An achieved human being can relate with spiritual beings from different stars, but ordinary souls can never do that. Most past religious leaders knew very little about the spiritual realm, because they were not yet developed enough to communicate with the stars where spirits actually come from. So they created a conceptual God instead of continuing to search for the actual spiritual truth. This is what divides general religion from true spiritual achievement.

A person of Tao is dedicated to working for the well-being of all human beings. Generation after generation of great masters have fulfilled this virtuous self-obligation. By their teaching and writing they have formed the great tradition of Tao.

The Gentle Path of Spiritual Progress   163

The picture we have here of Master Fong Churng-Da shows a beautiful being riding on the back of a buffalo. Before reaching spiritual achievement, all people are half-animal and are thus controlled and pulled down by the lower animal half of their being. They live at the command of their animal nature; their buffalo nature rides on them, whereas an achieved person rides the buffalo.

So the question is whether you are riding the buffalo or whether the buffalo is riding you. Sometimes you make a lot of unnecessary mistakes and it is easy to see the animal part of your nature that causes the trouble. If you understand this, you can put things in the right perspective. This is the first level of achievement.

In the upper right corner of the picture of Master Fong there is a poem that says

> "Worldly people are fighting
>   for something unworthy,
>   but they stubbornly
>   push forward just the same.
> Impulsively attacking some target,
>   their whole lives
>   are unproductive journeys of struggle.
>
> Look at this fellow
>   who enjoys peace and freedom,
>   freely roaming in all directions.
> No matter whether he goes
>   into the world or out of it,
>   he is an extraordinarily happy being.
>
> When you look at him, remember
>   be a buffalo rider.
> Do not let the buffalo
>   of your animal nature ride on you."

The speed at which a starry spirit can travel is much faster than the speed of light, so its response can be direct and immediate. A person who knows how can thus make an emergency call when something goes wrong. Just like a gentle earthquake, the spirit will be at your side asking what it has been called for.

Besides starry spirits, there are human immortals who have achieved themselves by their association with the starry spirits. No one can achieve himself highly without help from the spiritual energy of nature. This is why I mentioned that God is not a single being, but the conjoined, united spiritual energy of divine ones. It is not a matter of who does better. It is a matter of who develops and enlarges one's own personality. One soldier alone cannot be a general; you need an army. It is the same in the spiritual world. There are a lot of spiritual entities. It is a matter of how, by virtue and spiritual practice, you attract and gather the spiritual power that can give you the united spiritual strength to perform your life and work.

Great achievement of anything is a convergence of power. It is not an individual accomplishment, even in a person of genius. Exceptional mental capacity does not come from a single, normal brain function. It is inspired. Most geniuses are strange people, and they attract certain levels of corresponding spiritual energy which enable them to be used as tools for making discoveries in human knowledge.

Some of you who practice Tai Chi Ch'uan know that it is not a single muscle or nerve or one particular internal organ or especially your mind that makes a move. Everything comes together in one unit as you move. When I sit here and talk about something, it is not just a matter of my mouth moving. My muscles are supported by many levels of physical, mental and spiritual energy coming together to do the job. Although a strong leader may be able to make many people accept him as a hero, such a person can never accomplish results alone. Thus, people of Tao respect not only the strong leader, but also those who help such a leader behind the scenes. Many people of Tao, in fact, become great advisors, because they do not like show. The greatest are not always those who are in the limelight; they are often the invisible helpers behind the person.

Here in Los Angeles, if a producer or director finds a beautiful young woman and wishes to make her a star, he will have to invest lots of money to make her famous. The fame is really superficial if someone is pulling the strings behind the young woman. Yes, she may be a good actress, but how she attains her outward fame is a matter of joint management, not her own single-handed effort. People usually see only what stands out and do not honor what lies behind it.

Yesterday we discussed how to use color to move the five kinds of energy in an internal exercise. This practice can help alter your destiny. People have different natural cycles which can be organized according to the five different phases of energy. Sometimes you do better in life and other times you do poorly. When your cycle is high, you enjoy your life more than when you are having difficulties in a low cycle. To harmonize the flow of your life, do not become excited by the high points or depressed by the low ones. Always remember, the high is built by the low. You should respect the times when you are in a low cycle, the times when you are a nobody. Do not struggle to be somebody, because you will only be somebody when other people say you are somebody. "Somebody" is built on the moments when you are nobody. This guidance is not the same as ordinary teachings that only look for high respect and exaltation and do not value the low. When you look up to the high, spiritually and emotionally you are low. When you respect the low, spiritually and emotionally you are high.

When people have a low cycle, they think of it in an emotional way and feel terrible. They want to die or kill themselves. They feel boring, unattractive and uninteresting. They receive no attention or respect from anyone, and they do not love themselves either. They do not realize that their low cycle can make them wise. Life is built up by each uninteresting moment, not just by excitement. Your destiny is that way too.

How did Master Fong Churng-Da live so long in the mountains? By taking in solar and lunar energy and the energy of the first five planets. If a person lives more than two hundred years, he or she will experience many, many cycles, both high and low. Even those of you here who are in your thirties, forties and fifties - not too many of you are over sixty - have already experienced many cycles in the short time of your own lives. How have you managed? Not very well, I'm afraid. You are like a drowning person who gets a breath of air now and then before sinking beneath the waves again. You cannot manage your life and you do not know where you are going or when the water is going to push you up or drag you down.

Someone like Master Fong does not teach methods alone, but life itself. It does not matter what kind of cycle you have. By internal harmonization, you can harmonize all situations and cycles.

You can do the internal practice of the Five Elements for fifteen or twenty minutes or up to two hours. Yesterday I told you how to stop and come back to a normal energy condition. Today I will give you two more important details of this practice. First, when you start this cultivation you should see the five different colored clouds descending from a high clear sky into your body. Then there are two ways to proceed. One is by natural inspiration: take whatever color you start with naturally, and stop whenever you naturally feel ready to stop. The second way is to start and stop with a particular organ that you know is weak. Usually, you know your weak areas from information someone else gives you, but it is possible to know a trouble spot by your own developed spiritual discernment.

We have talked mostly about solar energy. Now, if you are interested, we will talk about the moon's energy.

The sun's energy is connected with masculine energy, and the moon's is connected with female energy. In general, the body of both men and women is mostly water, which is strongly affected by the moon's energy. In the Fall, around the 8th lunar month, the ocean tides are strongest, because lunar energy attraction is stronger at that time. In ancient times, women's menstrual cycles began with the full moon, because when feminine energy is at its fullest it causes the blood vessels in the uterus to compensate for the increased pressure of the body's energy flow at that time by releasing some of the blood. If the regularity of this natural balance is blocked, emotional and physical stress and illness can occur. In today's society, with so many unnatural influences, most women's cycles no longer follow the phases of the moon. Some have no pattern of regularity at all.

The moon not only affects women's energy, it also affects all people's mental energy very much. The moon is your mind. People who are born near the time of the full moon are brighter, as a rule, than people born on the night of the new moon. If those born on the new moon do not have support from other energy sources, such as good spiritual inheritance, they will not be as smart. In general, intelligence is connected with the moon. You should not have sex, therefore, on a night with no moonlight, because if you conceive a child at that time, the baby's mind will not develop well. Actually, I do not recommend sex during either the full moon or no moon. As a special, beneficial practice, you could sit and do your quiet cultivation during the full moon, but not a meditation that involves deep thinking. In general, the full moon is very disturbing to the peace of the internal liquid of your body, but by cultivating non-mental activity at this time, you can do better.

Now I need to tell you how to use the moon's cycle to help your cultivation. You can take lunar energy in the same way as solar energy. You should begin at the time of the new moon and go until five days after the full moon. After that, the moon's energy is not strong any more.

If a woman knows how to utilize lunar energy, she will become very full of feminine energy and be very attractive. It is important to know how to guard and protect your good energy once you have gathered it, because other people and beings like to come around and take it. If you do not know how to guard yourself, then your energy can be destroyed and will need to be built up again. Ladies of Tao know how to make themselves young, even in old age, by increasing their energy without letting anyone take it away. Not only do men try to take this energy, but also spirits and human ghosts.

Ordinary houses have a spiritual house guardian, but you can be attacked by ghosts if you stay in motels or other public places, especially if you are a single person. If you have good energy, you need to take care of it.

To take in the moon's energy, you face the moon when it is just rising, gently breathe in the lunar energy and swallow it. If you do this faithfully for three years, your face will have a light. Natural energy can be accumulated and grow, so that when your body fails, you will have an energy house built from the natural energy you have gathered, along with your personal refined energy. You can then move into the subtle sphere of life as a heavenly being of light.

Q: How many times are you supposed to swallow the lunar energy?

Master Ni: Men should do it six times, and women should do it thirty times. If a woman is already too manly, she should utilize the lunar energy more. Even if a man is not very masculine, he can still do this practice along with the solar cultivation.

Q: Is it okay to remove your clothes while doing these practices?

Master Ni: I do not recommend it. If you remove your clothes, you will attract spirits which are particularly active in the full moonlight.

In ancient times, in my tradition, it was not just the student who looked for the teacher. The teacher also looked for the right student, because while the teacher affects the student, the student also affects the teacher. As a student, it is up to you to purify yourself of your old ghosts.

This is a good time to talk about some simple spiritual practices such as setting up a personal altar and using fire purifications and offerings for natural protection.

First we will talk about incense. Different fragrances and materials have different levels of use. The fragrance you use can attract different kinds of spiritual energy, so it is important to use only the best. Do not use the chemical substances that are commonly marketed; they are not a good offering to the high spirits. The best incense is made from a fragrant wood that sinks in water. In Chinese it is called Chern Shiang. In English it is hgaru wood or lignaloes. It is not as strongly scented as ordinary, cheap incense.

There is also an incense made from the black cypress tree that has a powerful fragrance, but is not stimulating. It has good energy and is called the "Saliva of the Dragon."

If you do not use incense, it is all right, but if you use it, then use the best.

Some of you here are doctors and healers, and some of you are ordinary family people or you live alone. Always keep some incense in your room for patients or friends who have bad energy that you can feel and are affected by, especially if they have infectious diseases. Burning some incense can purify the bad energy that continues to float around the room after the person has left. This can save you lots of trouble. You can also hold a piece of yellow or white paper and burn it to purify the room.

Sometimes when you have sex or menstruation, there may be some odor afterwards. You can burn paper and circle your body with it for this too.

Q: Aside from its therapeutic value, can moxa help purify bad energy too?

Master Ni: Yes. There are also other herbs for fire purification. You just light them and let the burning herb fumigate the house. It is said that this can chase ghosts away if you use chang zhu or atractylodis lancea from Mao mountain.

Q: Is it good to do this as a precautionary measure if you live in a house with other people?

Master Ni: It should be done whether you move into a new house or an old one. Be careful, though, that you do not burn your house down. Fire needs to be used responsibly.

Also, do not offend other people whose energy is still unrefined. You should be tactful. If you burn it right after you have sex, your lady friends might get upset if they think you are trying to burn their bad energy away, so you'd better use water. After washing yourself, you can visualize being totally burned by fire. That is beneficial. Or you can visualize a bright star shining on your whole body and penetrating all of your internal organs.

These are general guidelines for using water and fire. Now we can go into purification and protection a little more deeply. You can express your spiritual authority or sovereignty over something by simply drawing the Tai Chi symbol with your hand in the air. This is done with your personal energy. By hooking yourself up with the natural spiritual realm through your personal cultivation every day, you attain a certain degree of spiritual authority, at least over your own life.

Use the middle finger of the right or left hand, which is connected to your heart and mind, to draw the Tai Chi circle thus

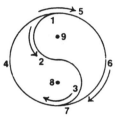

In general, energy moves upward from below. When you do this practice, however, the sovereignty or authority comes from Heaven, so you guide the energy to come to the circle from above. With single-mindedness you can utilize this circle to decree your spiritual connection with the natural spiritual realm. You can also make this symbol over your meal to purify and sanctify the food.

Q: Can you do this for your family when you prepare the food?

Master Ni: I think it is enough to attain spiritual authority over your own life at this stage. Moreover, once you have sanctified your food, you should finish everything on your plate or else throw it out. It should not be left for anyone else or for animals to eat. Only you should eat your spiritual energy from Heaven; no one else can claim it.

If you have a new piece of furniture or clothing or bedding, you need to do this too. If you are physically or emotionally uncomfortable, you can use your spiritual sovereignty over your own body to cure your trouble. If you were to expand your spiritual authority before you were wholly achieved, it would only stir up challenges that you could not handle, so I humbly recommend spiritual self-cultivation to you, but nothing beyond that. Anything else is your own responsibility.

Q: Can you do this practice mentally?

Master Ni: Yes. That is actually higher. The reason I recommend you do it with your hand is that the body is more concrete. Once you get used to doing it physically, you will find that your whole body responds. Then you will come to the level where your personal energy responds when you do it with only your mind.

There was a great master of spiritual self-cultivation who practiced his spiritual cultivation on the beach. By drawing a Tai Chi circle in the sand around himself, he could not be washed away by the changing tides. He could also make a circle around another person and that person would be protected from any hostile attack as long as he stayed inside the circle. I do not recommend you try this though. First make yourself responsive to your own spiritual authority. When you can truly help yourself, you are an achieved master who can help other people and perform spiritual protection and healing for them by your energy conductance.

Your personal health is connected with many things such as your thoughts, understanding and knowledge of life. If these go wrong, something is greatly disturbed as a result. So you need to dissolve all mistaken ideas and beliefs that aggravate your emotions. Do not let yourself be misguided in an unhealthy direction. It is important to learn a healthy philosophy. Without that, it is hard to attain personal well-being. Once you have achieved it, it is your responsibility to promote the well-being of the entire society. This is the main teaching of this very old and ageless tradition.

I will continue now to explain how to practice your spiritual sovereignty. Your life stem is your personal god that hooks you up with the spiritual energy of great nature. In practical everyday life, you may have a weak organ, such as the lungs or intestines, etc. for which you can use the practice of Five Color Clouds to guide energy from the spiritual realm to cure yourself. If you can make your old problem go away by your own spiritual practice, this is wonderful. As your spiritual authority over your life being grows stronger, you can protect yourself from intruders or troublesome energy in new environments. You can simply make the Tai Chi circle around either the room or the bed and ghosts cannot trouble you when you sleep. Women need to do this especially, but men sometimes have trouble, too, because there are also lots of women ghosts around. We have mentioned that natural spirits do not have any gender, but human ghosts still have a sense of gender because of their mental heaviness and attachment.

Q: What about divine immortals? Supposedly there are male and female immortals. How can they still have gender if they have achieved union with Tao?

Master Ni: If their achievement is genuine they can remain invisible or appear as any gender, age or form of life, or just as an inanimate object. They can pop in and out in a split second.

Q: I was involved with a group of students who were encouraged to demonstrate the power of their practice to other people. Someone brought a cancer patient to me and it changed my energy and caused me a lot of trouble. Is there anything I can do to clean it up?

Master Ni: It sounds like the story of a young exorcist who tried to catch a ghost that was too big for him. Great masters of exorcism perform their practice through their own body. After cultivation, the body is an achieved, unified kingdom of many spirits. If such a master decides to punish a troublesome ghost, he summons the ghost into his own trained body where the strong spiritual soldiers of the body collectively kill the ghost. If you do this, you must be strong enough to handle and kill the ghost. Otherwise, you just invite bad energy into yourself.

There are two things you should remember well. One is not to be too ambitious to treat a patient that you cannot help. (Sometimes it is hard for you to refuse because of your profession or social custom, but if accepting would cause you trouble, do not do it.) The second is to remember that there are different levels of religions and ghosts and that you need to make yourself stronger by your own self-cultivation and good spiritual discipline in your life in order to meet this challenge.

If you are a serious student of Tao, you should have a room for your personal cultivation with your own altar or shrine. In the center, the image of the three highest Heavens which were printed on the covers of my books should be displayed to the positive and negative spiritual world to express your own spiritual direction. In the room where you treat patients or accept visitors, there should also be a spiritual altar with the following ten Chinese characters hung high on the wall. These should be written vertically, as they are here, in one line. They can be translated as "The Highest Divinity of Universal Response." It is the most powerful protection in the entire spiritual world.

九天應元雷聲普化天尊

I first introduced this invocation in my class on How to Cure a Broken Heart and some students have had very good experiences with it. These ten characters can be read and repeated ten times in the morning to enhance your positive spiritual power. They are pronounced Chiu Tien, Yen Yuan, Rei Sheng, Pu Hua, Tien Tsun. I give it to you for your spiritual benefit. Be serious when you use them, not scattered.

(Break)

Do not join a tradition lightly, no matter how old or popular it is. Different religions have ghosts of all levels associated with them. When you join a particular spiritual group, it is like joining a club. It gives the spirits of that tradition a chance to participate in your body. Unfortunately, you do not know this beforehand.

A few years ago, a Christian group that started in San Francisco moved to New Guinea. They had collected mummies for some reason, but immortality above the ground (in a tomb) is absolutely different than the immortality I talk about. Ancient Chinese and Egyptian practices are different, and the results are also different. The science of immortality has different levels. By collecting these old mummies, the group brought themselves a lot of trouble because they were not truly spiritually achieved and did not know how to guard themselves from the underground influence. Their spiritual practice was Christian, they had never made any actual step-by-step spiritual progress, and all they had were their beliefs in blood energy. That was what the ghosts liked to suck. Eventually the ghosts of the mummies instilled a drive in these people to kill themselves. A lot of people think this happened for political reasons, but politics were not at all to blame for the murder.

All religions and spiritual traditions represent different stages of human development. There is a religion in some big cities today that worships a half-cat, half-human idol and advocates sex with animals. The existence and popularity of such religions point out the deep need for spiritual education and the kind of knowledge that cannot be learned from teachers in schools or from parents. Once you go to the wrong school of spiritual learning, you become a victim of its invisible spiritual connections. The only true spiritual achievement I have discovered is the starry energy, whether high or low.

All of you should first pursue the well being of your body, mind and spirit. Then, based on that, you can go further in spiritual development. Do not practice what you learn on other people; you will only invite their troubles to yourself. And do not fall prey to colorful trappings that seem holy. It is better for you to stay in peace, reading and studying, until you are mature enough to know a teacher who can truly assist you rather than rush into becoming the student of someone who will use you to assist him.

For example, at the beginning you might have thought it was a good idea to join the People's Church and go to New Guinea, because you were dissatisfied with your society and wanted to move away to a new life. If you had placed your trust in a spiritual leader who understood all of your psychological problems, you would probably have seen their underlying problems too late and ended up dying with the very people you thought were going to save you. Forget about old practices that keep you from growing, no matter what they are. Learn something new that assists your growth.

Q: If I forget about my old practice and go with the new one, will the old problems eventually go away?

Master Ni: Yes, depending on how serious you are in your new practice and whether you really let go of the old practice. If you subtly keep your old connections, though, you will never be rid of them.

Q: Should students of Tao have pets?

Master Ni: I do not approve of pets, myself, unless they are useful in some way. Pets make you emotionally dependent. If your pet is spiritually undeveloped, it will come back to emotionally possess you. Many people who have pets even sleep in the same bed with them. When the people fall asleep, the soul of the animal rides on their nervous system.

If the person's mind is not refined, he will see the animal as a human being rather than what it really is. Why invite this kind of trouble? You do not need it. It is not safe, spiritually or emotionally.

I recommend my kind of pet. Would you like to know what they are? Everything I do is my pet. All the practices that are supported by my spiritual strength are my fun. A person of Tao does not appreciate empty talk; talk is conceptual. It is too rough. A person of Tao prefers doing and being. My work is my pet. I hope you can enjoy such pets and help yourself and other people in the right circumstances.

I have some small pets too. Would you like to know what they are? A few months ago, Mao, my second son, took me to Sequoia National Forest and I found some small stones there. When I brought them back, I put them in a crystal jar with some water, and now I am going to grow them. It might take a million years, but I do not need to ask my friends to look after them when I go out of town. Sometimes I add fresh water to them. It is great fun. It gives me great delight.

Q: What about keeping fish in an aquarium? Is that okay?

Master Ni: There is an ancient practice called geomancy. If your house is not aligned well with the earth's magnetic field, it can affect your energy and your life very much. You can put an aquarium in some part of the house and if the energy is detrimental, the fish will die instead of you. If it is good, they will live and so will you. Should you replace the fish or the house?

Q: I sometimes consult the I Ching about patients I have. Is this a good thing to do?

Master Ni: Yes. As a young doctor, you need to learn to touch people at different levels. Also, do not be anxious to take on a job that is too much for you. When people are too demanding and try to force you to give them special attention, just manage the situation better or refer them to someone else.

Q: Are crystals useful for protection?

Master Ni: There is a special knowledge about what kinds and shapes of crystal or stone or metal are helpful to different people. For the most part, I think we need to protect ourselves by our own spiritual practice. If you have a big diamond or something else so valuable that you need to protect it, then that goes beyond the spiritual purpose you got it for in the first place.

Q: Is there a special technique for calling on the Star of Help if you have trouble sleeping at night?

Master Ni: Do you like people to visit you at night when you have gone to bed? Why would you call on a spirit to visit you then? Starry beings are so energetic that if they responded to your call, you would not sleep the whole night. I made this mistake myself when I was young and ambitious to know all the spiritual secrets and connections. It caused me lots of sleepless nights.

If you are attacked by ghosts and have nightmares, you can lie there in bed and visualize the sixth star of the Big Dipper which is a double star. Then you can be spiritually helped by that connection.

When someone is spiritually achieved, he can sit on the clouds and fly along. This is not just a Sunday school story. The truth is, once you become a spiritual being, your energy is so light that you can ride on a cloud with no difficulty at all. You are too heavy to do that now.

(Break)

To start this afternoon, I want to introduce my pets to you (holds up a jar with pebbles). You should not think that everything a student or master of Tao does must have great significance.

People need watery energy if their own energy is too fast or fiery. This kind of practice is very simple. You can do it for yourself.

In China there is an island very close to my hometown. There is a cave on this island where many people go to look into a bottomless hole to see a vision. When they see a good vision, they are happy. When the vision is not good, they are disturbed. Once a young soldier saw a vision of himself floating dead in the ocean. He became very angry at the vision and took his rifle and shot at the image, saying that the whole thing was a trick. Only a few hours later, when the soldier took a boat back to the army barracks, he was struck by a bullet and fell dead into the water where his body floated, just as it had in the vision.

What was special about that cave was a light beam that could guide people's energy to see spiritual visions. It is not hard for people to see what is going to happen to them, but it is hard to avoid having things they see happen. I teach you how to help yourself in everyday life. The practices I have given you are simple. You can all use water or fire energy or a piece of stone or metal or a flower to help balancing your life. Water simply represents the element of water, fire the element of fire, stone the element of earth, metal the element of metal, and flowers the element of wood. You can develop this knowledge further by further intellectual development that is integrated with your spiritual cultivation. Take it step-by-step.

Modern people go to school and memorize all kinds of information, but when it comes to the matter of their own lives that knowledge is so far removed from real life that it is totally useless. The burden of it is too heavy for the amount of good it does.

Q: On the solar and lunar breathing, can you do it more or less than thirty or six times, or does it have to be exactly that number?

Master Ni: It is flexible. If you do not have a teacher, do what seems reasonable according to your own achievement. If you have a teacher, you could save yourself some trouble and follow his or her guidance.

Master Fong's practice is different from self-hypnotic measures to slow down the mind and act as pain killers.

Master Fong's way is to make your mind very sensitive and fortified, not numb and weak. His way will make you spiritually and rationally strong by developing your soul energy. Once you are connected with the subtle origin, your spiritual power is much stronger. You need to practice, though. I have taught you how to exercise your spiritual authority. Now I will teach you how to confirm your spiritual growth and spiritual authority.

You should do your practice in a quiet room, with the door locked, so that no one will disturb you. It is preferable to do it early in the day.

Put your right hand into the sword position and put your left hand in the thunder position. The sword position ismade by extending the index finger andmiddle finger together while holding the other two fingers with the thumb. The thunder position is made by curling the ring finger over the middle finger, and then curling the index finger over the ring and middle fingers. The little finger curls over the ring finger and the thumb supports the middle finger. By writing the following four characters, you can guide your spiritual energy and make it stronger, and you can also confirm your spiritual authority. You can also visualize these characters to help you enter a state of quietude when you start to do meditation.

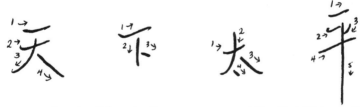

These can be used for similar purposes as the Tai Chi symbol, but they are much stronger in effect. This is the secret code of the Great Dipper and the North Star. It is the natural strength of people on earth and has great authority over all spirits and spiritual energies. These are common words, but very few people know their secret. Translated they mean "There is peace under Heaven." Subtly, they mean that peace is within your control and within your spiritual sovereignty.

The order of the words is exact. Once you enter the quietness of your body, mind and spirit, then draw the characters in the air with your right hand in the sword position. The general response of this practice is peace and quiet. The whole world quiets down with you. You should practice them and keep practicing. You need to concentrate with your eyes wide open. This practice can subtly effect change in people and circumstances.

I hope you learn this well. It can be very useful. This practice exercises your spiritual energy mostly. The practice of the Five Clouds is for harmonizing and fortifying your internal spiritual energy. These characters are your spiritual dedication and the application of what you have cultivated. Do not do this practice in disturbed surroundings or in front of people. The cultivation comes with practice.

If a living being loses the universal principles of balance and harmony, you are authorized to assist them with those principles you have learned, but you are not authorized to perform your personal practice in public. The shortcoming of young students is that they learn something through their ears and it goes right out their mouths before they have even had a chance to learn it well. Keep these things to yourself as your personal spiritual assets.

(Break)

Q: Would you please give us some guidance in sexual practices?

Master Ni: Movies, TV, newspapers and magazines are all geared to stimulate people, but they only drain your energy. Sex should only happen as a result of the natural movement of your energy. For women, the time just before and after menstruation and just before ovulation are the best times to do it.

My teaching in this is to help you achieve independence. If you do not have a good companion, I do not encourage you to seek out someone who is not fit for you and who could cause you a lot of trouble if you became attached to them. The companion you choose reflects your level of life. If you are paired with someone, it should not be out of social custom or emotional pressure, but personal happiness and mutual assistance.

Men need to become strong and have yang or male energy to bring a good spiritual and material life to the family or to the small team of man and wife. You should not force a woman to become your sexual victim. Although they have a deficit in their spiritual bank account, many men have too much sex in order to emotionally conquer someone or release themselves. If you have a suitable companion, you should only have sex when the cycle is right. Do not spend your sexual energy extravagantly or you will someday find yourself filing spiritual bankruptcy because of the high interest on your emotional credit card. If you do not have someone, then please learn the practices in this class and my books to support your single life in a healthy, balanced way.

The thoughts in your mind can also cause your energy to sink. Men think of women and women think of men, but this kind of longing and anxiety is a troublesome thing. It can be the raw material for your higher achievement. If you do not have the longing for the opposite sex, that is great, because your life will be much simpler. There are two kinds of non-longing, though. One is due to balanced energy, and one is from lack of energy. The first would be the case between a spiritual couple, while the second is the case with people who are too weak or old. If you do have the longing, please wait for the right time and the right person.

All individuals have yin and yang. The upper half of the body is yang, and the lower half is yin. The front of the body is yin and the back is yang. Inhaling is yang, exhaling is yin. There are two kinds of energy inside of us as well. In fact, there are many kinds. We need to unite all categories and have internal intercourse. This is the teaching of the Eight Immortals who achieved themselves by means of internal intercourse and the refinement of their Immortal Medicine. We will not go deeply into the subject at this time, but you should value your individual life as the precious foundation for all spiritual achievement.

Sexual intercourse needs the right time and right energy in order to be beneficial. If your energy is low, you shouldn't do it, especially if you are sick. Give it up in that case.

When I was younger, I studied the biographies of many great masters, and carefully observed whether they had sexual activity or not, especially those who lived over a hundred years. I would say that the majority had sexual contact in the early stage of their life, but gave it up in their later years and lived alone. They hooked up with nature (with the sun, the moon, the stars and the earth) and thus achieved longevity.

We mentioned education earlier. You spend such a long time going to school. Then you work for a long, long time just to bring a little fruit into your life, and then it's time to die. It is such a great loss when you finally reach mental and emotional maturity, but lose your body's strength.

It is better to find the right sexual partner if you can, but if you cannot, then maintain your good energy and do not waste it. Remember the immortal masters of the past who achieved themselves spiritually with or without external assistance from man or woman. You can research this matter for yourself. Statistically, the majority of spiritually achieved people do not bother with family or sexual life.

Q: If you're doing the solar practice and building up your yang energy and it increases your sexual energy, how can you control or uplift it?

Master Ni: The internal movement of the five corresponding energies will help you with that, because it balances your energy. It also helps you emotionally, depending on how you utilize it. You are young and handsome. If you decide to look for physical pleasure from sex, you still have a chance to do it. Serious cultivation, though, should not start too late in life. The reason there were more achieved masters in ancient times than there are today is that today we have too much freedom and it tempts us to become scattered.

If you live somewhere that is cold in the winter, it is better not to have sex. You need to store up your sexual energy in the winter. During the warm season, after spring, you could have two or three ejaculations at your age. But, if you were over sixty, you should not have an ejaculation. This is all possible to achieve.

You should set aside a time each year to study good books on spiritual cultivation. When you concentrate, you won't be bothered by other things.

Q: Is there any special advice for women after menopause? I want to know specifically about life after menopause.

Master Ni: Menopause is a difficult situation. I suggest herbs and acupuncture and emotional relaxation. Is the problem that you do want sex or do not want it?

Q: I don't feel the need for it any more.

Master Ni: After forty, women's sexual activity should cease or be reduced in order to start working on personal energy transformation. You still have around ten years to achieve yourself. If it is after menopause, the cultivation is different. Once the physical function of giving eggs is lost during menopause, the process of spiritual transformation in the body is difficult. If it is not too late, one might learn the process of adopting a spiritual energy or working for a different achievement.

In general, whatever age you are, you need good company. Not necessarily sexual friends, but friends who can support you emotionally. That is more than sexual companionship, because sexual companions do not always support you emotionally. Harmony is an achievement, not a gift.

You have reached the stage where you do not need sex, but you do need a friend. It is very important to have male energy to make you feel supported and not left out of the world because of your age. You need to build your spiritual strength by your cultivation before this happens.

Q: How can you protect yourself against people who are negative?

Master Ni: You need to look and see what you are willing to tolerate. If something goes beyond that, then step back. If you live in the same house with negative people, you need to create a mental territory in which you exercise yourself. You should first of all practice prudence in your life and avoid situations that will be negative.

Q: Is there a particular hand position that should be used in the practice of the Five Element Clouds?

Master Ni: You can refer to the examples given in *The Workbook for Spiritual Development.*

Q: You also said that the clouds descend into the body. How do they enter the body? Through the head?

Master Ni: Yes.   You can see it and feel it by your body's response.

Q: Should we follow the clouds with our eyes as we look into ourselves?

Master Ni: Right.

Q: In the sexual practice for men, is the goal to have orgasm without ejaculation, or neither?

A. If you have an orgasm, you must have an ejaculation. If you feel it happening, you should not block it. It cannot be controlled if you have been without sex for a long time.

Learning the principles of Tao in regard to mental, physical or emotional trouble helps you maintain peace and quietude so that your spiritual energy can handle matters without relying on emotional struggle or active thoughts to find a way out of situations. The important practice is to sit down calmly and not look for help from any outside source. Just look for help from the natural practice of calmness and quietude. There is no higher doctrine or discipline than this. Some people say that prayer works for them. That is a tool, not the goal. People with psychological troubles often look for psychological substitutes instead of working on the existing trouble.

When I lived in Taiwan two people with hepatitis consulted me, and I recommended that they take herbs and maintain a peaceful life to cure the illness. One of them proceeded to take the herbs, but the other was involved in a Christian group and turned instead to emotional prayer, hoping for a miracle. The person who stayed quiet and took the herbs lived, but the one who emotionally chased after a miracle cure did not. This is just one such example that I have personally observed in my life. If a person will just first slow down his or her mind, he or she can always find the best way to total recovery. No matter how long they struggle with the problem, they cannot dissolve it by either mental or emotional efforts. The best solution is to simply keep quiet. It is hard to do, but it is powerful. Your disturbed mind itself is the trouble. The best medicine is a calm, quiet mind.

Q: Will you ever teach more about the five elements and their application through the ten stems and twelve branches?

Master Ni: This knowledge has many, many practical applications in life, in spiritual practice, in medical practice, in astrology and so forth. I hope to do more with it later. There are many practices to learn, but the most important is to keep your mind concentrated and gently concentrate on this spot when I open your channel.

Finally, I have something very important to say now. This practice that I recommend is connected with the natural environment we live in. It is practical and supportive. On one level, human life is formed by all kinds of natural physical energies, and we are one among many beings of universal nature. All physical beings are transforming. No one stops transforming for even a single second. With or without your knowledge, the transformation process constantly and subtly keeps going on.

Spiritual immortality does not rely on the material plane, but it is nurtured by it. You see, the whole material sphere is not reliable. All living beings must die. All the stars and planets and heavenly systems are aging. They too will die. Some religions, if not overly superstitious about the power of the stars, then pick up this observation as the conclusion of life and being. But the great tradition of Tao does not stop here. As the ancient developed ones saw and experienced, there is a power of life-giving that always makes life come back again. Someday the old sun will die, but there will be a new one born somewhere else. When the earth or the moon dies, a new earth and a new moon will appear somewhere. It has happened, and it will happen again. Life energy is unobstructable, as the immortal ones teach. Life is not obstructed by death; it always comes back. It is important to understand this universal fact.

We learn through the obstructable foundation and basic structure of the body, but we cultivate and integrate the unobstructable sphere of subtle energy. In other words, the physical sphere is destructible, but the subtle essence always rebuilds a new world and gives a new life. This subtle essence of the universe is what the ancient developed ones called Tao, the origin of all things, the origin of all new life, the subtle essence of the physical universe. Tao forms itself. It gives birth to all lives, and all lives and beings are Tao.

To be a student of Tao, the main thing that you learn is the unobstructable spirit. As human beings, we struggle a lot with the restraints of the physical sphere of life. The wise ones untie themselves physically, psychologically and spiritually in order to reach something more subtle and more fundamental. They can thus enjoy the unobstructable happiness of being. We call this kind of achievement absolute freedom. This freedom was especially emphasized by Master Chuang Tzu.

It is important to us, as students of Tao, to learn, maintain, nurture and embrace the unobstructable essence of life. This universal subtle essence is not the same thing as self-sense. It is not the conceptual ego with structures of race, nationality, religion, politics, gender discrimination, age, education, social position, or anything else. It is important, at the end of this seminar, to point out this direction for all of us. Your participation in this seminar does not mean that you have learned something to practice. From the practice, you will learn something much more important, something much higher and more subtle than your conceptual ability to grasp. That something is Tao, the root of the universe, the root of you and me. We cannot afford to live a way of life that goes against it.

An individual can be either the slave of the material sphere and spiritual underdevelopment, or a master of spiritual freedom. The pursuit of enlightenment is what enables one to attain spiritual freedom.

To end this meeting, I offer this poem from an ancient achieved one in the great tradition of Tao, the path of wholeness and naturalness.

> Once a motivation from the darkness
>   of your mind begins,
> Your spiritual self moves aside.
> Once your spiritual self moves aside,
>   bandits and robbers start to
>   make the center of your life
>   into a den of animals.
> Once the house becomes disordered
>   by those infernal beasts,
> There is no more mastership over it.
> Life then gradually slips back
>   to the level of seaweed.

CHAPTER FOURTEEN

Malibu, California: January 1, 1987
(A talk given to a small group of students.)

Q: It seems to me that most devotional religious practices come from Western culture, while most practices that actually improve one's physical, mental and spiritual condition, come from the East. Do the tendencies of the Eastern and Western hemispheres of the earth parallel the right and the left sides of the brain? Do the people of each hemisphere use the corresponding part of their brain more and thus have a tendency to develop one kind of spiritual practice more than the other? I have also wondered whether the two approaches actually complement each other rather than conflict, and whether religion and spiritual practice should go together rather than be separate.

Master Ni: This is a very good question. Intellectual achievement and religious development are affected by the two hemispheres of the brain, but I would be cautious about putting them into such generalized categories. All religions originally came from the East, but as they moved Westward they began to be used more and more as a social and political tools, especially toward the end of the Roman Empire when Christianity became a "state" religion. Going back even earlier, though, Moses' teachings were based on social regulations rather than individual spiritual achievement. Islam is fundamentally the same. It is not hard to see that Mohammed was inspired by Jesus and the Jewish prophets. He actually wrote the Koran in Ching Hai, a Western border province of China. At that time he was the leader of a small caravan. He was also a strong, handsome young man with talent and intelligence who had gained social and financial strength by marrying a rich widow. He became very knowledgeable from his travels by paying close attention to religious matters as he traveled back and forth along the Silk Route of the East and Middle East. He put all this raw material together into the first new religious movement in his region since Moses.

To answer your question, though, we need to consider the difference between social religious codes and personal spiritual practice. Religions such as Judaism, Christianity and Islam are based on social discipline and codes of behavior. If you do not share their beliefs, they will attack you until you surrender, and once you do join them, your devotion must be absolute. You must keep their law or be punished.

On the other hand, the practices of yoga, Zen Buddhism, Tibetan Buddhism, and the tradition of Tao are matters of objective fact rather than expressions of subjective emotion.

Speaking of emotion, human beings have three kinds of pulls (sexual at the lower end and spiritual at the top, with a social pull in the middle) and each person responds to these pulls differently. Some become very physical and sexual, while others become spiritual and develop religions. Religion is a human phenomenon. I do not think you would have much success if you tried to start a religion for foxes or wolves. They already have a religion: eating, fighting and sex.

What is the difference, though, between a religion and learning Tao? General religion, and even philosophical ideology, is based on subjective emotion, whereas the learning of Tao is objective. It could be called the "science of life," because it is based on accumulated facts of physical, mental and spiritual reality. Without those facts, there is no cultivation. You need the special knowledge of subtle things like chi that can help you improve your physical condition by the practice of Tai Chi or Chi Gong. Most religious practices, on the other hand are either emotional releases or methods of mind-control. Like carrots on a stick, they keep you headed in one direction, but they do not develop you. You must know and understand all kinds of spiritual practices so that you can know which ones actually help your spiritual development. This is why we call the practices of the learning of Tao the "science of life." They are based on true development and achievement. You can hardly say that you are attaining Tao if you are only following your emotions or looking for substitutes for your psychological problems.

Some people are users of the science of life and some are researchers and helpers in the science of life. One will develop something, another will promote that person's discoveries so that they can be used by many people, and yet another will work on explaining the discoveries so that they are closer to modern conceptions and can be more easily accepted as a particular type of science. Whether you are a user or developer or experimenter in the science of life, you are qualified to say that you are one who embraces Tao.

Even in the science of life, you still need devotion. Without it you cannot achieve anything, but pure devotion is different than emotional, religious devotion. Social religions impose an image that you must follow and believe in. Human beings are not cattle that can be branded as this religion's or that.

The devotion to a social religion is only an attempt to escape from too much sexual or social activity and from the trouble it can cause. The three kinds of pulls I mentioned earlier are the motivating forces in everyone. It is important to distinguish which force you are managed by in the after-Heaven stage of life. If you understand your own personal tendencies, you can see things objectively and not mistake an emotional carrot for the true spiritual goal.

Q: Are yoga and Tibetan Buddhism the same kind of practice as the practice of Tao?

Master Ni: No. They are very different. Tibetan Buddhism is an application of psychological principles, just as Christian Science is today. In their practice, if you want to become rich, there are rituals and mantras to learn, and the Buddha of Richness to worship. If you want to become socially powerful, there are rituals and mantras for that, and the Buddha of Power to worship. If you want sexual satisfaction, there are other rituals, mantras, and religious practices for this purpose. Whatever your psychological need happens to be, there is something that can meet that need. This is like a spiritual department store. The application of the science of psychology is helpful at this level of life, but it should not be mistaken for true spiritual development.

In yoga they artificially beautify the natural system of chakras with visual images of the body's natural spiritual functions. Yoga is a general name for all kinds of spiritual practices in Hindu culture. A teacher can develop almost any kind of yoga and find followers for it. For example, masturbation has been organized as a yogic practice with esoteric religious sanctions. This one is called Pali Yoga. A Western psychologist who was deeply involved with this particular sect made a psychological, therapeutic program out of it and even taught her own twelve-year-old daughter to do it. The result was that the child's physical development was permanently damaged.

The most popular and beneficial yoga is Hatha Yoga. It is one of the first ancient energy conducting exercises, like Tai Chi and Chi Gong which go back to the time of Pan Tzu whose energy conducting exercises are the basic foundation of this type of physical movement. Pan Tzu was a minister of Emperor Nido (2357 - 2258 B.C.) and was still alive at the time of Emperor Jo, (1154 - 1121 B.C.). Pan Tzu specialized in a number of things such as sexual practice and discipline, diet, cooking and energy conducting exercises.

During the Tang Dynasty (618-906 B.C.), Tantric Buddhism was essentially a re-programmed spiritual practice of Tao dating from the Jen Dynasty (265-419 B.C.). This practice is now considered part of esoteric Buddhism and is still preserved in Japan.

Readers of Joseph Needham's *The Science and Civilization of China* can find many useful things in the modern world that were initiated in the cradle of Tao. Many renewed and reprogrammed old inventions have returned to China as "new" things. Cultural integration is a natural force, and I am happy to see global cultural integration developing more widely and deeply.

The pure spiritual practice of Tao can be appreciated when you are familiar with and understand all kinds of practice. Then you can see what is more realistic and practical and belongs to the science of life.

Q: Do you mean to say that no one in the world is truly achieved except those who practice the tradition of Tao?

Master Ni: No, no. There are many highly achieved people from different cultural backgrounds, but they have all given up their cultural and religious contamination and are thus realistic and have true vision. Tao means to return to natural originalness. If this were not true, Sakyamuni would have continued to follow Hinduism and not have started a new religion. His new direction might not be totally right, but at least he made attempts to move away from the old forces.

Spiritually, it is important to understand and achieve the goal of learning Tao. In the beginning there are five goals: happiness, longevity, wealth, health, and natural death. (The last of the Five Blessings means that when a fruit is ripe, it naturally falls from the stem. Ordinary people are killed by the kind of life they lead. They do not die a natural death. Death is not the right word to describe the exuviation, or molting, of an achieved immortal. It should be called a transformation from one stage of life to another.) Practices have been developed to enable people to attain these goals. If you cannot achieve these five things, then whatever else you do cannot be called the science of life.

Five thousand years ago the Yellow Emperor in China became tired of attaining satisfaction in life. After being Emperor for sixty years he turned the country over to his ministers and went off to find the great masters who lived in the high mountains. He was the first important student of Tao, and the spiritual stature of the old culture was established by him and his direct heirs. Later, Emperor Niao came to the throne. It was the custom at that time in China for an Emperor who had made a very great accomplishment to go to Wah Mountain and offer a prayer to Heaven for what he had accomplished. Then the heavenly beings would decide his credit or responsibility. According to ceremonial custom, the officiating minister said to Emperor Niao, "May Heaven bless you with a happy life." Generally people are very grateful for such a blessing, but the Emperor said, "No, thank you!" Then came, "May Heaven bless you with longevity." "No, thank you!" was the Emperor's polite reply. The third blessing was, "May Heaven bless you with great vitality and many sons," to which the Emperor replied again, "No, thank you!"

So many people seek these blessings, but they were not what the Emperor was looking for. He had already reigned a hundred years. He had achieved longevity and happiness and a big family. He did not need any verbal blessings. In the

West, religious leaders sell people blessings which are nothing but superstitious, verbal nonsense. I think this puts people back at the level of at least three thousand years ago. Maybe more. The Emperor Niao did not look for more personal blessings. He looked for ways to bring blessings to others.

Now I would like to talk about something really important that may be good for all of you to know. There are four fruits of spiritual cultivation. I want to talk to you about what kind of fruit is correct. The first fruit is spiritual immortality. This is what we need to pursue in our cultivation. Virtuous fulfillment is the main pillar of that helps you achieve immortality and ascend to Heaven.

The second fruit is the general level of immortal spirit that continues to live in a human body. There are two ways for such spirits to live another human life. One way is through blood relationship which gives them a natural right to ride on the body of someone whose energy is the same as theirs, and the other way is by association through spiritual practice. The practice you do can cause spirits who have done that same practice to come and live in your body. All parts of your body have different ghosts or spirits that have perched on you in one of these two ways.

When we talk about immortality, the second kind does not represent total spiritual achievement, because such spirits cannot live independently. They still rely on flesh and blood life energy and they secretly borrow another person's house. You could call such spirits "guest spirits." They are either guests by relation or they are uninvited guests who sneak onto you. In the practice of Tao it is important to purify yourself so that you are not pulled down by either.

Q: *How do you get rid of them?*

Master Ni: By your practice itself. Your practice makes your personal spiritual energy purer and stronger, so that you are protected against such intruders.

Q: *Is it like a person comes into your house in regular life?*

Master Ni: No. They come to occupy your "house" without any intention of paying rent or assisting your life in any way.

They just come to make a mess or destroy you. You could become such a spiritual parasite after your physical life has ended, if your achievement is incomplete. These nasty guests continue their sense of life vicariously through others. There are two ways to rid yourself of such guests. One is by your own practice and the other is through exorcism.

The third fruit is when you have not accomplished your cultivation or achieved yourself, but your soul has attained a little bit of ability. In this situation you chose a mother and are born again. Earlier I mentioned spirits throwing themselves into the red aura around a couple that is having sex. That is the level of a totally unaccomplished soul as opposed to a soul with a little bit of ability who can chose who they wish to be born to. Even if you are able to choose your birth, though, it is dangerous, because in the forty weeks that you spend in the womb, you could lose all your achievement. Especially at the conceptual level of intellectual achievement.

Q: Isn't true achievement always part of you?

Master Ni: A person who has reached true achievement would not take that kind of life. They would have achieved independent spiritual immortality. This kind of life comes from the desire to participate in worldly life again. This soul has attained a certain degree of achievement, but it cannot live independently. It still likes flesh life, so it comes to the womb of a woman again to ride on the white light of the fertilized egg. In the forty weeks in the womb you can be badly influenced. This is ordinary fruit, not good fruit.

There is one exception. When a spirit who has a spiritual mission wishes (or is sent) to be born again, he is protected and will not lose the good quality of his mind and spirit in the mother's womb. Someone who has only achieved a little bit cannot attain the spiritual independence of divine immortality, so they are born again to have a chance to accomplish it.

The fourth fruit is a kind of theft. When someone's body fails because of disease or old age, the person's soul looks for another "house." When this happens, the result is usually madness because of the conflict between the original spirit and the intruding spirit. It is like two women living in a small house with one lover.

Of the four fruits, only the first one is right. The third fruit is correct for a spiritual leader or teacher who comes back to society for the purpose of redirecting misguided people. The other fruits are not considered true fruits of self-cultivation; you need to understand this.

I will talk a little more about the first fruit, because it is important. We do not usually talk about it, because once you bring the subject up there is so much discussion about the conceptual aspects of it. In learning Tao it is said that men can become pregnant and that women can become pregnant without having a man. This kind of pregnancy is referred to as a "Red Baby" or spiritual baby. It is totally different than ordinary conception. Ordinary conception involves a flesh baby. What I am talking about is a spiritual birth. You integrate all of your spiritual energy.

You must understand that religious stories are personified universal spiritual energy, and personification is the work of the mind. A piece of spiritual energy can be any way at all, it does not have to be in human shape. It can be a star or just a tiny particle. If a spirit has a human shape of only a few inches, it is a very high authority indeed; they are usually very tiny. Anything that can respond to the human mind is spiritual energy, and if you have the same vibration, you can cause it to respond to you. The entire universe is just like a human being. At the spiritual level, therefore, there is no separation.

When a tiny spirit rides on the human nervous system, it affects the energy formation in the body. If this happens when you are sleeping, then you dream of this person or that as you respond to the visiting spirit in your nervous system. The people in dreams are not the true form of the energy affecting you, just as your body and mine are not our true forms, but the forms we got through our mother and father on the earth. In reality, spiritual essence is just a piece of energy. Religions that set up gods through the process of mental personification characterize universal divine energy as a human so that people can understand and relate to it.

The way to attain spiritual immortality is through the process of subtle pregnancy. It is therefore important to protect yourself from scattering your energy in too much sex or food or entertainment. You need to gather your spiritual energy at the right spiritual subtle orifices. There are three centers in our body: a sexual center, a social or mental center, and a spiritual center in your head. Spiritual pregnancy is the accumulation of spiritual energy through an important spiritual channel in your head, by which it is sent down to the lower Tan Tien as spiritual nutrition for further development. In Chinese this is called the "Holy Womb" or "Holy Pregnancy."

There are two ways to accomplish a Holy Pregnancy. One is to stop having sex and transform your sexual energy to enhance your spiritual energy. (In reality, an intercourse or convergence of your body's subtle energy occurs at different levels.) Through your head you can see the golden light. Then you gather the golden light and send it down to the Holy Womb. Then you need to take time with the spiritual baby. Once you have a spiritual baby, you are almost like a pregnant woman. You need to take care of yourself very well. Do not watch disturbing things on television or at the movies. Do not do anything to twist the image in your mind. It is much easier to have a miscarriage or other problem in a spiritual pregnancy than in a physical one, because ordinary flesh is much more solid than spiritual energy. Spiritual energy is much more flexible and impressionable. So you must control yourself well.

There is another way to accomplish a Holy Pregnancy if you cannot gather your personal spiritual energy. There are many spiritual entities or particles in the universe that are born of the combined energies of the sun, moon, water and earth. You can adopt one of these spiritual entities by inviting it to your spiritual organ, sending it down to the Holy Womb, and building up your energy. Since you are going to die, you bring everything to the adopted baby. It is not your seed, but it is a seed of the universe, of nature, just like you yourself. Eventually, you transfer your personal nature and energy to the Holy Womb.

A person who has achieved spiritual immortality is a personified spiritual entity. Since they have human experience, they know human problems and tricks. This is not like natural spirits who have no human experience. Many geniuses were born as a spiritual particle of nature, but once they are born into the world, they only have a special talent for one thing or another and do not adapt easily to human society. They usually cause themselves a lot of trouble. Spiritual endowment is separated by a paper-thin wall between genius on the one side and crazy people on the other. One is confused and the other has very good spiritual energy, but neither of them adapts well to worldly life, and they are usually mistreated by people. There is a fine line between healthy spiritual achievement and craziness.

The true spiritually achieved one respects the natural spiritual world without having to personify it with a white or purple robe or a gold crown. That is junk. It is really childish. It is not true. Religions fight each other over the conceptual level of life. Once you formalize God with a certain shape and color and robe, you fight over what is in your mind as opposed to what is in someone else's mind. At the true spiritual level, conceptual vision is both all right and all wrong, until you reach the subtle essence.

It is important, therefore, to know and see the entire universe as one being. The organs of a spiritually achieved person develop their own spiritual energy and spiritual entities, but they all make up one complete spiritual being. It is the same in the universe. You and I are supported by the same universal spiritual energy; the whole thing is God. There is no separate "God" in the realm of integral truth.

Q: Are there lots of universes, like there are lots of people?

Master Ni: Yes. An individual human being is a universe. The universe is an individual human being. All individuals are many universes. Many universes are different energy entities of the multi-universal one life. In all the different universes there are stars and starry beings. I like to mention the stars, because stars produce spiritual energy and natural spiritual beings at the human level.

Q: The only thing I didn't understand clearly is when you adopt a piece of energy. Do you just invite the energy to come in?

Master Ni: No. First you need to achieve spiritual authority. You need to guide them in the door. They are wild. They do not have any sense of time in their life. You need this piece of energy to be your horse so you can ride on it somewhere, so you need to make a corral to coax it into.

I need to talk a little more about the subject of devotion. We talked about the science of life and objectivity.   What should you be devoted to? Without a second thought, I would say it should be the goal of attaining spiritual achievement. No amount of information or practice can accomplish this goal without your devotion. You should also remember to respect the past achievement of other masters. For example, if some set out to make an airplane today, it would be foolish to start from scratch like the Wright brothers. One person's lifetime is too short. If the person studied everything that had been accomplished up until now and used his ability to continue developing what he had learned, his achievement would be much greater than if he started from the very beginning.

The most important guidance in the teaching of Tao is: A person of Tao takes the entire multi-universe as his own personal life and makes his own life that of the multiuniverse. Outwardly, one should dedicate one's life to the one universal life.   Inwardly, one should be responsible for fulfilling the universal self-nature in one's own life by engaging in self-cultivation.   One's achievement thus comes about through subtle universal integration. This is the life of a person of Tao. This is the work of a person of Tao. This is this the religion of a person of Tao. This is this the truth of endless and boundless accomplishment of a person of Tao.

After Emperor Niao (2357-2258 B.C.), social and religious leaders in other regions used threats to establish themselves. The social systems that they created were thus based on exploiting the human emotion of fear and attracting people's dependence. By using threats, you get what you want. The whole culture of human society has been totally distorted since then. This is the basis of religion. This is the basis of communism. This is the basis of the nuclear arms race. This is the basis of insurance and most other individual life activities as well.

What we can learn from the teaching of Emperor Niao is that without fear you are naturally blessed with a happy life, longevity, vitality and reproductive energy.   I wish that everyone may be blessed in this way.

To learn Tao is to learn to live without fear. To learn Tao is to be saved from making mistakes. If an individual or society lives without fear, they experience no internal conflict. This is why spiritual cultivation and discipline is the effective channel of self-development. When you fear your own or someone else's dissipation, you need to develop discernment that can sort out which emotions are healthy and creative and which are unhealthy and destructive. The path of universal subtle integration is the way for an individual human being as well as society to untangle the psychological complications of life. This is the path of universal natural life.

An individual can be either the slave of the material sphere and spiritual underdevelopment or a master of spiritual freedom. The pursuit of enlightenment is what enables one to attain spiritual freedom.

To end this meeting, I offer this poem from an ancient achieved one in the great tradition of Tao, the path of wholeness and naturalness.

> **Can you give up precious things**
>   **to look for your true self?**
> **It is not that you cannot find it.**
> **You are blocked away from it.**
> **Once you find it,**
>   **you find true preciousness.**
> **You can see the whiteness of the snow**
>   **covering your court.**
> **There is the top of the Heavens.**
> **The one who cannot see it and cannot find it**
>   **has the soul of a lower animal.**

CHAPTER FIFTEEN

Malibu, California: January 5, 1987
Instruction to students

Q: Would you tell us how the ancient achieved ones became immortal?

Master Ni: Normally, this question is not answered, but because of your virtuous fulfillment, I will give you an overview. Hopefully, the answer will also benefit many other people. As you know, the learning of Tao is not dogmatic. Nor is it ideological. Many people consider it mysticism, because it contains secret formulas that are not given to the general public, but I call it a science because it consists of many things that can be studied, practiced and proven through individual experience. In truth, it is a science.

What is your definition of science? I will give you mine so that you can see whether it fits the ordinary definition or not. The craftsman who makes pianos uses wood and steel and his musical skill, and the knowledge of how to make a piano is a science. You understand that pianos are made for the purpose of music, but the craftsmen who make pianos are not concert pianists. Playing the piano is an art that takes years and years of refinement and practice. Art makes the craftsman's work useful.

I have called the practice of Tao the "science of life," but it is also the art of life. It is like a piece of bamboo in which several holes have been made. When it is played by an achieved flute player, beautiful melodies come from it. It is just a piece of ordinary bamboo, and the mechanical process is very simple: you just make a few holes, and the rest comes from the talent and achievement of the flute player. Life is like the raw material of the bamboo. The music you produce depends on how you cultivate and achieve yourself. This is provable. You may call it mysticism if you like, but I call it the science and art of life.

All religious practice could be called the art of life, but not the science of life, because nothing except psychological satisfaction can be obtained from religious teachings and discipline. Religion is unprovable. It is not objective and so cannot be considered a science. Colorful clothes, beads, chanting, rituals and so forth could be called the art of life to some extent. How to bow, how to burn incense, etc., is a personal kind of practice that involves aesthetic appreciation, but the psychological effects that produce good feelings only last while you do the practice. Afterwards, there is no real profit or result except the emotional satisfaction of faith. This is very different than the practice of Tao which can bring you health, strength, and spiritual capability. It is a science which involves spiritual survival and the achievement of immortality. True spiritual immortality is a result of personal spiritual cultivation. That is to say, your own efforts are what make it happen. Your virtue must also be high and complete. Human beings are jealous, and so are spiritual beings. You will not accomplish yourself unless you have great virtuous fulfillment and transform all jealousy into friendly energy which can help you with what you wish to accomplish.

Real spiritual immortality occurs through spiritual conception. I do not mean a conceptual thought, but the actual conception of a new being. Spiritual conception can happen to either a man or a woman. It is the flower and fruit of transformed sexual energy which becomes higher subtle energy. You must use the principle of convergence to gather your energy and endow this piece of conception with your personal life. After refinement, we call the sexual energy of each individual the Immortal Medicine. This Immortal Medicine becomes the seed to which you slowly transfer your personality. At the beginning, it is a piece of refined sexual, mental, and spiritual energy combined. This piece of energy moves down to the prostate gland and then up through the spinal column all the way to the top of the head. The equivalent gland in women is documented in a popular but not scientific book called The G Spot. In acupuncture, the female prostate gland is called Wei Yin, the meeting point of yin energy. In Chi Gong practice it is called Yin Chou, the point of strong yin energy. Both names do not discriminate between a male or female body; the point is the same for both. There are three important checkpoints that you need to practically break through before reaching the top. Then the seed comes down the front of the head to the mouth and into the "Yellow Court" one half inch above the navel, where the spiritual baby is conceived. The conception process is very practical. Imagination and visualization can support it, but the main thing is the internal intercourse between different yin and yang energies within your life being.

The life energy in the head is called yang, while the life energy in the area below the navel is called yin. Sometimes we use different terms and refer to the energy in the head as "fire" and the energy in the kidneys as "water." These two kinds of energy must interact internally and become an integrated whole.

If the water energy sinks and the fire energy rises up, then there is a real problem of disintegration and the person becomes very weak. If the two energies interchange (the water energy moving upward and the fire energy moving downward) then they start to interact, like water boiling on a stove. If you put the water under the fire, nothing will happen. The right order is the water on top of the fire. Then the liquid energy becomes vaporized by its intercourse with the fire energy. This is the first step in the transformation of your internal liquid energy into vaporized chi inside your body. When the water in the body becomes chi, it can then be transported to any part of the body. With concentration and integration, it produces power.

If your goal is to achieve spiritual immortality, then you need to further refine the energy that is produced from the intercourse between the head and sexual energies (fire and water). This essence is the immortal seed to which you transplant the best part of your personality. You make the best version of yourself by taking all of your essence and converging it into a higher being that does not have to rely on physical existence. Such a person can live in the universe everlastingly.

In ancient times, in the terminology of internal alchemy, they called the head the pot and called the lower belly the stove, referring to breathing as the bellows that started the fire. Mental conception is the fire itself. Your life-being is the laboratory in which your new life is produced. The process has internal and external results at the same time. The internal fruit is externalized in vast outer space. It is a very scientific process once you actually do it. This is just a general introduction to this vast subject.

How many people achieve such spiritual immortality? About twenty-five percent of those who follow the correct spiritual practice. In spiritual achievement, the champions are few. The most reliable method is to do half yourself and borrow the other half from external energy. The first half is the process of refinement. This is hard enough to accomplish in itself, because your sexual desires and mental burdens are so exhausting. So the first thing you must do is refine your own energy to become the seeds you need. The second part is to nurture the growth of the seed. This is much easier than the first part for people who have spent most of their energy in worldly life. They can conceive the baby, but they cannot refine their energy sufficiently to produce the seed. If you are unable to accomplish the first part, then you must invite or adopt a pure, natural spirit into your spiritual organ and give all of your energy to it, like a woman who conceives a child from a sperm bank. The hard part of spiritual fertilization is coaxing a natural spirit into becoming the future spiritual you.

Spiritual immortality can be achieved by your own totally self-reliant cultivation and a lifetime of devotion. It also can be achieved by adopting a natural spirit to whom you transfer your energy and entire personality, but not your darkness or jealousy. The adoption process is not quicker or easier than independent conception, and it is not that you lack something. Your earlier life just did not provide sufficient opportunity for the necessary cultivation to accomplish the job with total independence.

Spiritual immortality is something other than union with Tao, conceptually. When you begin, there is still a "self." Then you dissolve the self (the lower life being) and unite with the selfless, deathless Tao. The purpose of this whole process is to offer your after-Heaven beingness to actualize Heaven in a new deathless life through gathering subtle essence internally and then expressing it externally as a spiritual being. There is no great mystery. It is merely by proceeding through a good after-Heaven life that the spiritual reality of oneness inwardly and outwardly reappears. I do not mean that you clean up your beingness and give it to Heaven as a good tool. You become Heaven when you purify yourself. You do not need to give up the physical, mechanical process of life in order to realize Tao; your physical being is dissolved when your self-cultivation is totally achieved and fulfilled.

Let me come back to the level of students. It is interesting, as a student of Tao, to go through all the real experience of detailed guidance and practice and find out for yourself what the science of life truly is.

Once I had a patient who was a beautiful singer. She purchased a house that had belonged to an old widow who had recently passed away. Before moving in, my patient went to look the house over. When she checked out the basement she discovered that one whole wall was covered with flies. The sight of it made her hair stand on end. She had never seen such big flies - almost the size of a finger. She called someone to fumigate the basement and get rid of them, but the next morning when she and a friend went over there before the fumigation started, all the flies were gone. She looked for some outlet, but there was none, and there weren't any dead ones on the floor either. In her amazement she asked me what kind of phenomena this was. I did not explain it to her carefully, because it was not necessary to scare her. She only needed a peaceful house to live in.

The old widow was not spiritually achieved, so when she passed away her energy scattered. (At other times, I have described body spirits.) That scattered spiritual energy was seen by the young woman as flies. It was not an illusion or a transformation. It was the raw material of the old woman's unrefined energy. When this touched the nervous system of another unachieved person, it appeared as flies to the person's sense of sight. The flies were the viewer's own interpretation, not the exactness of fact.

This is an illustration of the disintegration of personal energy. If you are not achieved, this would be the natural result. It could be worse.

Achieved beings are very different. They can gather all their energy into a very tiny spiritual entity and can also express themselves in many places at once. When I was young, I went to visit a mountain to look for an achieved master. When I got there, the peak of the mountain was covered with white cranes. Since they were not afraid of me, I came very close, because I liked them. When I tried to hold onto the leg of one crane, all the cranes immediately disappeared and became a beautiful human being in front of me. From that experience I saw all Western theology - monotheism, polytheism and atheism - as a laughing matter. To a spiritually achieved person, one is many and many is one. To be is not to be; not to be is to be with absolute freedom. There is no way to put such beings under anyone's control. It is interesting to discover how the mind tries to make everything concrete while life itself holds the secret and mysticism of the entire world.

I will now use this information to supplement what I mean by saying that to learn Tao is to learn the science of life. Two cooks can use exactly the same materials and produce very different results. Art is not based on material alone. Tao is also religion, philosophy and mysticism. You cannot use one general concept to understand its greatness.

Q: What is the relationship between spiritual energy, the heart and the mind?

Master Ni: People have often approached me asking for spare change as I walked along Ocean Avenue in Santa Monica. The first reaction comes from your heart energy to help the person, but then your mind says that these people are lazy and irresponsible. They ask for money because they do not bother to support themselves, and they use the money to buy wine instead of food.

Individuals could be divided into two broad categories: sun types, whose heart energy is stronger, and moon types, whose mental energy is dominant. Sun types are more strongly motivated by personal desire, whereas moon types are cool and reflecting, with different ideas and opinions. In most circumstances, both kinds of energy are active in the same mind and play "to be or not to be," "to do or not to do," always putting you in the middle. Most people have experienced this condition of the mind with its dual nature of solar and lunar energy.

There is a higher, spiritual energy that is above the solar and lunar type of mind. If a person is predominately solar or lunar minded, it will result in some trouble and mistakes. It is important, therefore, to know how to balance the two sides. The balance that develops contains your spiritual energy or soul and is what can give you the right guidance at the right moment. It all depends on how developed you are. A spiritually undeveloped person is spiritually weak. If they do not listen to their heart, then they listen to their mind, but they never listen to their own spirit. People of mind energy usually take advantage of people of heart energy.

What about a wino's heart and mind and soul? That kind of person is so self-abandoned that there is nothing left any more. All three parts are weak. He cannot be called a person of any energy.

Individual spiritual strength is matter-of-fact, but people refuse to recognize it as such because they tend to be one-sided. If they are heart-oriented, they seldom question anything or think about the result of what they do. If they are mind-oriented, they doubt everything other than their own personal interests. When a person extends his cold mind energy, there is usually a conflict between one cold mind and another. The mind brings war and the heart brings the mistake of haste. The true god is above and impartial to the energy of both the mind and the heart. It can therefore guide you to a safe, happy life if you will only realize the spiritual function in yourself and in every individual.

Most people cannot see the normal function and value of spiritual energy, because of religious education in the world today. It is important for each person who suffers from worldly life to look for God within himself as the unified strength of his life. Now let's use your own experience to take this discussion further.

Q: Several years ago, I had an experience of what I believe to be God helping to direct my life by providing me with something I needed. Being dissatisfied with the life I was leading with my husband, I decided to leave him. I had no money, but a friend graciously gave me lodging for a while in her small apartment. Soon I obtained a part-time job which gave me the resources to rent a tiny apartment of my own and buy some food. My spare time was spent doing psychological work on myself to clear up negative feelings about my past, and as part of this work, I wrote a letter. But I was so broke I didn't have a postage stamp or the money to buy one. I wondered how I would mail this important letter. The next day, as I was crossing a street, I looked down and found the postage stamp I needed on the ground. Was this an example of spiritual forces leading me in my life?

Master Ni: Your personal experience is valuable. Many people who have experiences like the one you have described could prove the existence of spiritual energy, but unfortunately they attribute such things to their mental and emotional image of a dominant God who rules over everyone's life. You should understand that it is God who guides you back to yourself, but you did not notice that as clearly as you did the postage stamp that you needed. The reason is that the guidance given to you from your spiritual center is hard to notice: much harder than a postage stamp. So you appreciate the stamp more than the true god that guided you back to yourself and started you on a new direction in life. Many religious believers bear witness to what they call "God," but they do not know where this spiritual energy comes from.

In learning Tao, we would rather not emotionally exaggerate spiritual energy. We recognize that each individual has spiritual energy which is connected with the spiritual energy of the entire universe. It doesn't mean that there is an inner God and an outer God. I means there is one nature: the spiritual energy of the universe, of the natural world, and of each individual. We use the term "self-nature" to describe your deep personal spiritual essence. Once you discover it, you may think it is something external, because you are not spiritually achieved yet. In reality self-nature or universal nature are one and the same.

Self-nature does not mean self-centeredness. It is universal. Because we are born as individual entities, we develop our minds to serve ourselves, thus cutting off our connection with the universal self-nature which is the true God. Godly energy is universal spiritual energy. We cannot narrowly, selfishly restrict the universal self-nature to some church or religion. It is universal. Many methods and ways of faith can guide people to recognize their spiritual energy, but people are endowed with that energy by nature, originally, in the first place. If people think it is something outside themselves and worship it as an external spiritual being, this is a total misconception.

It is especially important in today's world for people to heal their fragmented visions of universal spiritual reality. It is also important, not only to talk about the universal spiritual nature, but to know how it applies to our individual lives.

As I described earlier, the way in which one treats others comes from different ideas that have different origins. How is a person to distinguish which idea comes from solar energy and which is lunar? What is more important and much more subtle is your spiritual energy, your personal divine nature. This personal God is not really personal at all, but it still guides you to balance, safety, and harmony. If this spiritual energy is distorted by your moon type of mind, it can bring about conflicts. If distorted by your sun type of mind, it will bring about wasteful sacrifice. It is important, therefore, to look for the God within and see whether your life activities are directed by that or by a solar or lunar oriented mind. Do not be a follower of extremes in your life.

Q: Is spiritual energy the feeling I have when I go out in nature or when I see the woods and the open sky?

Master Ni: Strong attraction can pull you away from true spiritual energy. Many young people lose themselves in the colorful activities of this "dusty world." Once you are close to nature, you come back to yourself and look for balance inside. Your eyes become eyes again, your ears become ears again, your nostrils become nostrils again, your mouth becomes your mouth again when you are in nature.

In the city, your ear is not your ear. It is too full of noise. Your eye is not your eye; it is full of too much color. Your nostril is not your nostril; it is full of smog and smells. Your mouth is not your mouth; it is full of chewing gum and bad words. When you come back to nature, it is not hard to practice, if you get rid of all the unhealthy stuff you are full of. Most people are like dolls with nothing inside.

Q: Do spirits look after people sometimes? Sometimes I do the right thing at the right time, but I didn't really know that it was the right thing ahead of time. The thought just comes into my mind to do it and, after I do it, I find out it was exactly the right thing to do.

Also, I had an interesting experience with someone last week. When I called him on the telephone, he had just tried to call me, but there was no answer. My telephone had not rung, and there was no busy signal either. We decided to test it. He called me right back, but my phone still did not ring. Since the phone worked perfectly before and has ever since, could it have been spirits playing tricks on us?

Master Ni: To answer the first part of your question, good thoughts receive the help of good spirits. Bad motivation receives the help of evil spirits. One helps you ascend to Heaven while the other helps you descend to Hell. You are in the middle to cast your thought and receive the right response. Therefore, it is important to be right and prudent when you cast a small thought in the beginning. Thoughts are more powerful than knowledge at this stage of development. It becomes more powerful than your own unassisted thought.

In answer to the second part of your question, it was not spirits, but the projection of your two minds. The energy hit the telephone at the same time and made the telephone die off for a while. People do not see the subtle power they possess. They would rather use emotional force or segmented intellectual force. If one's subtle energy is channeled correctly, one can doubtlessly achieve oneself.

Now I will give you both some individual guidance. When your three internal entities are not unified, your heart is sad, your mind is full of ideas, and your soul is depressed. This is a poor way to live. A good healthy life comes from the union of your mind, your heart and your soul in one piece. This is like the sun and the moon and the stars in an orderly sky when everything is shining and there are no clouds or storms, no rain or snow, just a beautiful sky. People whose lives are full of rain and storms never experience the wholeness of these three as one.

The first practice is never to pull any external thing into your internal being to obstruct the wholeness of your internal energy. When the three inner beings are together, we call it concentrated or converged energy. A rigid practice would block such convergence. It must be accomplished through gentle, methodical practice.

The second is that when you discover you are thinking in your meditation, immediately unite the initial energy of the thought with the awakening energy of stopping the thought: join the head and the tail of your consciousness to become one. If you get stuck anywhere, your meditation and your peaceful mind can be destroyed or disturbed by your thoughts, and the effects of your meditation can be nullified. You must realize that thoughts are energy movement. When you discover that you are thinking, immediately combine that awakening energy with the thought energy: let the two points come together without being separate, like a snake gradually swallowing its own tail.

A thought can be a solidified energy form. When you break through its form, tremendous energy and power are released.   Such power is illustrated when an atom is split; the tightly bonded, interacting energy pattern of yin and yang is then integrated back into the oneness of the all powerful subtle origin.

The third thing is that on a moonlit night, when there are clouds, would you drive away the clouds or the moon? It is important to think of your mind as the moon. Take away your cloudy thoughts, but keep the bright and shining moon.

The fourth thing is to maintain centeredness. When emotion and insufficient knowledge are underlying your thoughts, extremes will be expressed in two ways: one is to go to the left and the other is to go to the right. You should stay centered in the mid-point, remain neutral and above the pull of either side. When a thought arises in your meditation, do not follow or join it, and do not try to counteract it with emptiness. Do not do anything. Let what is be the way it is. This will store and dam up the subtle chi. In this way you will eventually attain clarity and objectivity which will enable you to reach the deepest essence of the mind.

These principles are applicable to your general daily life as well as your spiritual cultivation. First, the union of the three: your heart and mind and soul should always be together without any separation. Second, always be alert when you fall into thought and your peaceful mind is disturbed. As soon as you wake up from the flow of thoughts, use that point of awakening to unite with the beginning point of the thoughts. When a point starts moving, it produces time and space. If it stops moving, then it does not produce experience or time in the common sense. It is not necessary to have the feeling of concrete gravity, but it is important to make the beginning of two thoughts immediately hit each other to stop further wasteful thinking. Third, is to remove the clouds without removing the bright moon. Fourth, is to cut away all extremes and remain in the center. In this way, your spiritual energy will become stronger and stronger. The purpose of stronger spiritual energy is to save you from mistakes and from causing trouble for yourself and for other people. If everyone achieved this, there would be no more wasteful trouble in the world.

Most human problems are the result of conceptual conflicts among mentally and spiritually undeveloped people. Even though they think they are very intelligent and wise and developed, they are not at all. In reality, they are just like teenagers who think they know everything. They have the ability to make trouble, but their minds and their spirits are not developed enough to not make trouble.

Q: When you talk about maintaining our center, I find that easy to do in nature, but I get thrown off very easily when I come back into the world.

Master Ni: Spiritual achievement does not mean staying in the mountains. Real spiritual achievement is assessed by how you manage your daily life in all circumstances. A person who is spiritually strong will not necessarily stay in rural places; his mind is flexible enough to adjust to any situation. If we live wastefully, even if we live in a royal palace with great wealth and power, it is not a life worth living. When people want to stay in the mountains, they think of benefiting themselves, but who is the "me" they want to benefit? The entire world is one being.

Q: *My problem is that I don't know how to handle people.*

Master Ni: You mean you are afraid of aggressive people. Let me give you some examples of power. The first type of person is strong and aggressive, taking advantage of others for his own ends, mistreating and abusing people. The second kind of person appears to be in an unglamorous position, is usually quiet, not very visible, and sometimes mistreated by others. He seems to be the low man on the totem pole, the underdog. But in the end, when the balance sheet of Heaven's computer comes out, these are the ones who, through their quietness and gentleness, reap the profits to balance what they thought they suffered.

Q: *Then how do I live a long and happy life?*

Master Ni: This is related to your previous question. There are basically two kinds of people in the world. The first kind thinks of himself: taking care of himself is his number one priority. He wants to get as much as he can, thus most of his time and effort is spent obtaining things for himself. The second kind of person thinks not only of himself, but about all people concerned in a given situation. He can be content to have less than the best if it benefits the situation as a whole. He is interested in other people's happiness also.

Which kind of person gets the greater benefit in the long run? You might think that it would be the first type, but it is not; it is the second type of person. Because they are more flexible, they are happier and Heaven will benefit them. They benefit themselves by being what they are.

Let me give you another example. There is a kind of person who is very picky in everything of life and in particular about what he eats. The food must be cooked a certain way, only certain foods can be eaten, and he won't eat something if he doesn't like it. What he likes is the emotional best, as in gourmet foods, designer clothes, or luxury cars. There is another kind of person who is glad to eat whatever is served, although whenever possible he eats food of a healthy nature. Which person benefits in the long run? The first kind of person may not really eat well enough to benefit his health. Thus, he will not enjoy a healthy life. The second kind of person usually enjoys a longer life. This illustrates the benefit of being broad-minded.

An individual can be either the slave of the material sphere and spiritual underdevelopment, or a master of spiritual freedom. The pursuit of enlightenment is what enables one to attain spiritual freedom.

To end this meeting, I offer this poem from an ancient achieved one in the great tradition of Tao, the path of wholeness and naturalness.

> **If you vacuum your mind frequently,**
> **no trouble can harm or bother you**
> **any more.**
> **There is also no more threat from death.**
> **Nothing can bind you.**
> **Before giving up the frame of life,**
> **you can still be a great person**
> **of high spiritual freedom.**

CHAPTER SIXTEEN

June 14, 1987: Malibu, California, to visitors
(Four Guidelines for Ones Aspiring to Attain Tao)

For a person who is seriously practicing spiritual self-cultivation, this guidance will help clarify how to correctly align one's mind. First of all, it is important to distinguish between true value and false value in external things which are considered artistic achievements as well as expressions of spiritual solemnity and sublimity (temples, stained glass, statues, etc). What is true spiritual value? Spiritual value is what is truly serviceable in a person's life, from the inside out. It is what assists the development of the soul and is, in fact, the developing soul itself. What is of true spiritual value in your life is what directs your life along the correct path so that your inner strength is fortified by upright behavior. Spiritual inner strength is different from the other elements such as desire, ambition, psychological imitation, competition and revenge which generally motivate people's actions. Spiritual inner strength helps you increase your spiritual health and enables you to push through obstacles. It also enables you to see the nature of all things so that you are not obstructed by any of them.

Something of true spiritual value cannot be exchanged for anything else; it is priceless and cannot be bought. As a student of Tao, the first thing to learn is how to distinguish true from false spiritual value. True spiritual value can be proven by oneself through consistently and persistently cultivating and refining the spiritual essence that is manifested in one's own being. This is far more valuable than any artistic or philosophical expression that attempts to describe or portray it.

The second thing a person of spiritual cultivation must understand is the difference between socially motivated spiritual activity and the attainment of spiritual freedom. Anyone who follows a socially motivated religion can also achieve spiritual freedom, if he knows that participating in a religious service is only a step toward further development. It is not necessary to reject collective spiritual activity, but spiritual freedom cannot be achieved through the teachings of social religion alone. Spiritual freedom is the fruit of one who has achieved himself through spiritual cultivation and discipline. To him no religion is rejected; all religions are within his paramount spiritual mellowness.

Spiritual freedom is an achieved power that enables one to enjoy oneself in whatever life situation one encounters without losing spiritual awareness and its sweetness. One can sponsor and participate in any healthy spiritual activity that supports the achievement of spiritual freedom.

The purpose of social religions is obviously socialistic, and once you join a religion you are more likely to give up your personal spiritual responsibility in exchange for a pillow to rest your head on in the dark hours.

A religion can present one side of the truth or another, but the truth itself has no particular form. Whoever wishes to formalize and organize it will only destroy its gentle subtlety. It can be seen in a circumstance where right or wrong is shown, but even right and wrong are not the truth itself; they only help you reach the truth in the moment that you distinguish between them.

To overemphasize group activity is not helpful. Human beings have social and emotional needs which are natural. These are of a different nature and value than the desire for spiritual freedom. All of the basic sources of supporting worldly life (good books, religion, sports, etc.) do not produce spiritual freedom; one must eventually dissolve all attachment to such activities.

A being who is spiritually free can express itself in any way at all without being obstructed by the form of expression it chooses. That is why it is called spiritual freedom. There is no need for such a person to start a war over this belief or that or to reject anyone or anything over a different custom or idea. Different teachings and religions are expressions of different stages in the spiritual development of mankind; they are not the final truth. It is the responsibility of each individual to attain his own spiritual growth, and it is the responsibility of one who knows this to gently guide others to the awareness of their spiritual duty to themselves. This is how people mutually help each other.

One who has attained the fruit of spiritual freedom is never unkind, but uplifts others so that they too can learn and cultivate spiritual freedom. He knows the true benefit of spiritual mellowness and freedom that enables people to move freely through the cracks of universal physical laws that otherwise bind one to the lower levels of life. He therefore promotes this attainment to all people and likes to unite with those who share this spiritual viewpoint. One thereby turns to face the undeveloped world, effecting change through gentle, sensitive activities and finding the balance point between spiritual individualism and healthy socialism. This is the standpoint of the great tradition of Tao.

The third thing a person of spiritual cultivation must understand is the difference between God, self-nature and Tao. "God" generally refers to a powerful spiritual divinity outside oneself who rules the world and can be relied upon for help. This notion is prevalent in the East as well as West and has shaped people's minds toward dependency. Theologically this is merely a shadow of the primitive stages of human life. God has simply become a psychological compensation for mental or emotional weakness. While the discovery of spiritual self-nature originally developed in the East, most people there are on the same level of ordinary worship as the majority of Westerners.

The cultivation of self-nature is the truthful way to develop one's own soul. All souls are caged by the body and bound by the undeveloped intellectual mind, and spiritual problems are thus caused by those who have not yet discovered their own spiritual self-nature.

Self-nature is another term for one's own spiritual nature which, at the deepest level, is the universal nature. When one is really achieved, one's own spiritual nature and the universal nature are one and the same.

Each culture, whether Eastern or Western, develops itself differently and affects human life according to its distinct, formal patterns. A truthful person will engage in self-cultivation to refine his self-nature and unfold the universal spiritual nature within himself. Others will join together as a group which usually observes an emotional practice of worshiping an imaginary or conceptual God.

At the deepest level, God and the individual are united. The difference between spiritual self-cultivation and ordinary worship is that one is direct and the other is indirect. Even if one follows an external path of worship, one will someday be inspired to know one's true self-nature. This is like taking a detour to your destination. Even so, the problems involved in knowing God and in discovering one's self-nature are actually the same. What is unfortunate is that external religions are often so strong and rigid that they cause people to lose sight of the true spiritual goal. The difference between the two approaches is essentially whether you look for spiritual support outside yourself or from your own development: either you worship God from the outside in or follow the path of self-cultivation that leads from the inside out. Either way, some people will succeed and some will fail. From the point of view of spiritual freedom, the external and internal approaches are two ways to reach the same destination. This has been validated by important points in Jesus' teachings and also in the example of his personal life and spiritual practice. From both ways one can learn to observe God, worship God, observe godly disciplines, and refine oneself in order to develop spiritually. All of these lead to Tao, but Tao itself is not any one of the practices. Tao is the highest spiritual reality, higher than either God or self-nature.

"God" can be defined by a shape, by a name and by certain characteristics, and the methods of self-development are many. Everything that has shape and quality falls into the after-Heaven stage of life. Tao is that which is before anything that is shaped or formed. After-Heaven is the stage of manifestation, and "God" is something that has become what it is. Tao is the totality of things and beings before becoming. It is the origin of the universe, of all things and all beings, before they become. One who loses his original freedom by becoming entrapped in a shape and form has lost Tao. One who can still maintain his original freedom without being spiritually obstructed by shape or form, can be considered one who has attained Tao.

Tao is one; its manifestations are many. God cannot be only one because once a thing or being falls into the sphere of manifestation, it can be multiplied; it is no longer the absolute one. It exists at a secondary level which is disputable and discussable and can be a source of conflict to anyone who has not moved from the external level of life to the deepest internal level, from bits and pieces to the final source. Such things and beings therefore face the difficulty of separation.

Tao is the universal spiritual essence. The proof of attaining Tao is a person who cultivates his personal spiritual awareness or who engages in observing God by linking the inner voice, internal subtle thought and the subtle reflection of the nervous system to directly engage in any moment of life as an extension of the universal spiritual nature. By this impersonal and unconscious help, one is guided to do the right thing and thus sow the seeds that will become good spiritual fruit.

The thoughts and motivations of the deep spiritual sphere are so gentle and subtle that strong impulses can easily overshadow them and blind a person to the subtle guidance from within. This inner voice or subtle thought that expresses the subtle law lives in each person's life but is blocked by spiritual undevelopment. Unless one maintains a spiritual practice, one's physical impulses are so strong that the internal subtle guidance cannot manifest in one's life. One therefore has difficulty knowing oneself and reaching the divine self-nature.

The internal path of self-cultivation and the external path of religion, if performed in a healthy way, can both bring you to a balanced condition by softening and transforming your impulses. At this stage, the subtle guidance of your spiritual energy starts to respond with natural spontaneity. By letting your chi reach a pure spiritual condition, you will reunite with the subtle law of yourself and of the universe. It will correct and protect you by its subtle vibration, by subtle thoughts, and by voluntary reflection and movement of the body. Then your being is in accord with the universal subtle law of which you are a manifestation.

Each life manifests the universal spiritual nature. Thus, once a person cultivates himself, his physical impulses will resign their tyrannical hold over his life-being and allow the subtle truth within to grow unobstructedly.

Tao is universal spiritual energy. It does not stop supporting you once you come into being. As long as you continue to soften and transform your physical impulses, Tao will continue to permeate you and support the further development of your being. As your impulses decrease and your indulgence is restrained, you allow the subtle law to unfold and guide you in your life.

Although people are born in the world with a material form, their nature is spiritual. Cultivating Tao is the way to unblock oneself and communicate with the universal spiritual energy. After attaining Tao, individual life is an extensive model demonstrating universal oneness, spiritual harmony, and united spiritual natures.

If a road is blocked, it does not go through any more; it cannot be a road any more. Tao also means the unbroken road, the unobstructable path, the gentle way. It is not a partial path in the cultural sense of religion; it is above all else.

When people come to me to learn Tao, their minds are not fresh. They come from many cultural and religious backgrounds, but once they start to learn Tao they reach a different stage and wish to go further.

Students of Tao never become hostile or prejudiced toward someone of another religion, because they recognize their own former stage of undevelopment and understand it. While it is immature to accept all religions without putting them in the right perspective, a student of Tao knows how to use good spiritual and physical practices from different traditions to help his own growth and develop his spiritual energy. A student of Tao knows that the purpose of his life is not to support one specific religion over all others, but to accomplish spiritual development through nurturing his life energy in everyday life. A student of Tao uses his life energy to live a healthy life, not to promulgate a religion. To this end, he should use any observance that can restore his original spiritual nature. A person of Tao, therefore, can be on any path and do any practice and still be a person of Tao. Many important practices were developed by people in the tradition of Tao. These practices are very effective in helping one achieve oneself, but they are not easily obtainable by the general student. Through personal growth the door to one's sincere search is opened. To the people who can reach the stage of seeing the subtle light between the lines and words, the door is not a door, but a way. The way is the door. The heart of the matter is to realize Tao in one's personal life.

An individual can be either the slave of the material sphere and spiritual underdevelopment or a master of spiritual freedom. The pursuit of enlightenment is what enables one to attain spiritual freedom.

To end this meeting, I offer this poem from an ancient achieved one in the great tradition of Tao, the path of wholeness and naturalness.

> **Whoever wishes to know spiritual truth**
> **first needs to purify the mind**
> **until it is as clear and profound**
> **as the sky.**
> **Avoid all self-disturbance.**
> **If you do not pick anything up**
> **from the deep abyss**
> **of conceptual entrapment,**
> **Then wherever you go,**
> **you are totally free**
> **of all obstacles,**
> **As one of pure spiritual nature.**

CHAPTER SEVENTEEN

Malibu, California: June 23, 1987

The four guidelines I gave at the last meeting are the conclusion of this book. This talk is given as a special service and reward to all those who follow and help me closely. First I would like to give you some further guidelines with which to assess different spiritual qualities. In this day and age, when communication is extensive, it is not hard to learn about religious and cultural practices of different times and places. It is important to be able to distinguish the spiritual qualities of such practices rather than rely upon your personal preferences to guide you. Once you are spiritually achieved, you immediately know which category something belongs to, as easily as you would distinguish people's personalities. Because such achievement takes a long time, I would like to give you some guidance in this important area of your lives.

You should know the three kinds of spiritual paths. The first is spiritual emotionalism: paths which support your emotions but not your spiritual development. This is the category in which most popular religions belong. Because people like to have an emotional outlet they know they can rely on, such religions provide easy answers which contain very little spiritual truth and which are therefore of no real spiritual benefit.

The second category is that of spiritual idealism which establishes high hopes and fanciful ideas that promise beauty, grandness, and a totally joyful, carefree life in some faraway place. This, too, is a misrepresentation of the natural spiritual reality.

The third category is spiritual pragmatism which, in a constructive sense, looks for facts and their practical application. This is the category to which the tradition of Tao belongs. From its very beginning, the path of Tao is one of natural development. Among all other paths, its distinguishing feature is that of spiritual pragmatism in everyday life. In general, it has no particular doors or gates, but such receptiveness should be applied with caution. In the East, you see, especially in China, most spiritual practices call themselves the path of the Tao. They are not the Tao that I have shown you and are not what I wish to share with my friends.

In the larger as well as the smaller scope, therefore, all practices should be objectively inspected and carefully scrutinized before being accepted. You should determine whether or not they will truly support your purpose.

Practically speaking, spiritual emotionalism and idealism are luxuries and a waste of time; they are not what we are looking for. What we need are truthful, practical, useful things that are basic to life itself.

One thing is certain: the individual soul takes form, or reincarnates, again and again. This is what we call spiritual evolution. In the process of spiritual evolution, life continually re-forms itself. In popular terms, this could be expressed as cause and effect. For example, the commonly accepted classifications of astrology (both Eastern and Western) contain twelve "houses" which are twelve areas or aspects of an individual's life: the relationship with one's parents; the relationship with one's siblings and friends; the relationship with the opposite sex (and marriage); the relationship with one's children; the relationship with social and financial life (with the possibility of achieving leadership or a high position); the area of personal health and longevity; and whether one enjoys his good life or suffers difficulties. All of these make up a person's life. No one has good things in all twelve houses or facets of his life. You might find some examples that come close to perfection, but they still go through cycles in which there are bound to be some difficulties. So you can only generalize by saying that some people do better than others. It is useful to understand that there is no one who is perfect in all areas.

The attitude of one who is spiritually pragmatic does not regard wisdom as something lofty; it must be useful. Seeing, therefore, that no one is perfect, the question becomes: how do we support and complete our good spiritual qualities? This is the recognized purpose of the spiritual self-cultivation for all individuals. The innate spiritual awareness and responsibility of human nature guides one to look for spiritual completeness, perfection, satisfaction and improvement for the purpose of realizing universal nature and fulfilling one's internal evolution to meet the pace of external evolution.

To further classify spiritual qualities, there are spiritual individualism and spiritual socialism. Spiritual socialism imposes the beliefs of one person or a group of people on others, while spiritual individualism does not care about the spiritual situation of others. Each approach has its own shortcomings. The learning of Tao is neither of these; it is based on individual development so that one can then offer oneself to the world or whoever reaches out for help. This puts the learning of Tao in a very different category. You might call it "spiritual democracy" in contrast to a spiritual dictatorship or spiritual arbitrariness.

Now let's return to the principle of cause and effect and how it applies to life in general. In spiritual socialism, things are imposed on people. There is an authority in Heaven who is spiritually above all other beings and who punishes or rewards you depending on his judgment of whether you are being good or bad. The principle of cause and effect in the teaching of spiritual socialism, therefore, depends on a third party to execute it. If you behave, you are rewarded. If you are bad, you are punished. And rewards or punishments can be postponed for a thousand years or more. This is old-- fashioned religion. It represents a stage of human development before people were intellectually achieved.

In natural spiritual reality, punishment and reward are always close at hand, and neither needs a third party to execute it. You execute both by the way you form your own thoughts, emotions and behavior. At each moment of life, a person's soul forms and reforms itself, internally and exter- nally, thereby determining the reality of one's life and the level of development one can reach. Many people don't see the internal truth but look only for external satisfaction, especial- ly in the areas of material expansion or emotional indulgence. "I need this. I want this. I like this." If they do succeed in getting what they want, they can't tell whether it will be harmful to their spiritual health or not. If it is harmful it will only reinforce the shortcoming and worsen one's spiritual condition.

In general, things evolve from the subtle to the solid level, from the inside out, from the invisible to the visible, from the intangible to the tangible. What you do every day (in thought, desire, impulse and emotion) forms you and makes you either more spiritually fit or unfit. You must therefore be spiritually responsible. There is no other choice. You must achieve yourself wisely and completely, not just partially. If you form yourself each day by thinking only of what you want and what you like, without considering the benefit of balance in all things, you will destroy the natural balance and organization of your soul by becoming extreme and partial. When you become more partial, you become more incomplete and crooked, contorting your original soul. When you enter worldly life again, you suffer and produce poison in yourself and your surroundings.

The main point in this is that all of you suffer from something; all of you have one shortcoming or another. The trouble is that you pay more attention to your suffering than to the rest of your life, thus aggravating the suffering. You don't know how to utilize what you have already achieved. If you focused instead on the satisfaction of your present achievement and continued to cultivate yourself by doing good deeds, both for yourself and for others, this would be both a personal remedy and salvation as well as a way to mend your shortcomings and suffering.

For example, if you desire money only for yourself, you might undermine your health and be cruel to the people close to you. This would only take you further from the truth of life and from normalcy and completeness. The lives of prominent people can be the subject of much useful reflection.

Spiritually speaking, the defect that a person creates by such imbalances not only affects one's present life but consequent lives as well, due to the constant needs and wants that result from spiritual imbalance. Someone who lives a good life and does good deeds is self-rewarded. Those who are greedy, covetous and jealous of others are self-punished. In both Eastern and Western religions there is a hell. In ancient times, hell was taken very seriously; it was considered endless darkness, suffering and punishment for doing and being morally bad. Factually, hell is the experienced effect of one's actions lifetime after lifetime; it is simply the truth of the individual's life. The individual is a small universe that creates energy which manifests both internally and externally so that the person himself can actually become either heaven or hell. The whole of human society is made up of individuals who are developing themselves in one direction or another. New inventions, as well as social conflict, are the result of the direction in which a society develops as a whole. You need, therefore, to watch the cause, because the cause produces the effect.

At a practical level, say someone has a forked tongue and spreads scandal about someone else in a serious manner. Traditionally, according to the stories of some conventional religions, executioners in hell would put burning charcoal on the person's tongue. Although this was the old-fashioned way of moral education, the reality is that the person will doubt-lessly punish himself with self-created problems that are not limited to the tongue.

What you suffer in your life today comes from two sources: a near cause (the result of doing things that have spiritually affected you), and a far cause (punishment from remote trouble in a past lifetime). As life continually forms itself, the spiritual effects of one's behavior will definitely emerge, either immediately of at a later time. Punishment and reward do not come from other people or from a divine authority. The unadorned reality is that they come from the way in which you have formed yourself.

People who kill other people must be killed themselves; killing invites killing. If you kill an innocent person, you will be killed for no reason. People should take responsibility for their society as well as for themselves. Today's world has reached a critical stage because of a lack of self-awareness and spiritual responsibility.

The facts gathered by spiritual pragmatism encourage people to attain spiritual self-awareness so that they can recognize the problems that they cause from day to day. As one develops oneself, the problems of the past can be dis-solved by refining oneself daily. Spiritual blessing and development are both attainable by continual spiritual discipline and cultivation. Your shortcomings and bad fortune are not reason to be discouraged. You are alive with creative energy. You can therefore reform yourself immediately through undaunted spiritual cultivation which will produce the self-awareness that can guide you toward spiritual completeness, abundance and balance.

Q: Does this mean that we should not focus on the bad things we have done in the past, but on how to improve ourselves now?

Master Ni: Each person also carries the spirits of their parents, grandparents, and great-grandparents. Someone who does bad things, therefore, punishes his descendants, not just himself. The shortcomings of a person's life are thus due also to the fact of carrying related spirits. One's entire spiritual organization is what enables one to progress or leads one to digress, brings suffering or enjoyment, makes one's life blossom or wither. These elements unfold in one's personal life, but you cannot teach your parents after they are dead. The responsibility now is yours and yours alone.

If you are going to marry, you should develop yourself spiritually so that your bad energy is not passed on to your sons and daughters. Each generation starts with you, so you have to correct yourself and your own crookedness. By your willingness to improve and actually reform yourself, you can achieve a different and better stage of life. You will also not cause your descendants to suffer needlessly from your acts of irresponsibility.

Those who choose not to marry will still carry their rewards and punishment with them when they are reborn, and the damage they have done themselves spiritually, their incompleteness, reappears in their new life all over again. Self-cultivation and spiritual development are very practical matters. The gift of the teaching of Tao is quite pragmatic.

Some of you have been married several times, each time unhappily. This could be because, although you were a spiritual person in the past, you still retained a desire for paired life. The qualities of paired life had not been nurtured.

So, when you attempted to fulfill your desire, things did not turn out well. Without the qualities of tolerance and patience that a paired person should have, nothing can happen correctly.

It is also important to realize that desire is not the proper direction of human life. Ambition is contrary to nature, and instinct is nothing more than a physical reaction. The most important thing to remember is that you have achieved the opportunity for a new life. Even though you may not have much good in the twelve areas of your life, you can still attain greater self-awareness and straighten yourself spiritually whether you live ten days, ten years, or more. Self-straightening should be your fundamental practice. Do not look for the effect or the reward; just take care of the causes and diligently sow the seeds of regaining a complete life.

I have mentioned before that each individual has three selves: spiritual, intellectual and physical. The physical self can be further divided into the instinctual self and the emotional self. Sometimes your spiritual self knows exactly what is right, but your physical self rebels against it. Spiritual self-cultivation and discipline are not a fanciful, easy matter with partial effects. They are a great enterprise for each individual's entire being. Other things are far less important, even social and material achievement.

Modern society is much more intellectually developed than ancient society, but people do not suffer less than they did in the past. In fact, they suffer more from a greater worldly crisis that is the result of people over-developing their instinctual, emotional, physical and intellectual side rather than their spiritual self. This tendency causes the majority of undeveloped situations in a person's life and pushes the real master away.

Such partial development is like someone whose body is fully grown, but whose brain is still the size of an infant's. Such a youngster can make trouble that many adults could not fix. This is the situation in the world today.

I appreciate the sweet friendship you give to me, and I think I need to reward you with the most earnest, grassroots instruction. None of us can afford to be bad, do bad or mistreat other people. Spiritual development is an individual matter of how hard you work and how wise you become. The spiritual essence that you gather is yours alone, but in matters of life we have to treat other people fairly, including our enemies. A spiritual person has no enemies. When someone does something that bothers you, it is the best of all possible mirrors to show you the shortcomings of your own spiritual condition. An enemy is therefore a blessing in disguise; it can help you cultivate yourself better and improve yourself correctly.

Spiritual emotionalism and idealism and all other unrealistic religious attitudes can be put aside, but you cannot put aside your own spiritual self-responsibility. Everyone has shortcomings of one kind or another. For example, I am sometimes not exact in my money calculations. I would not, therefore, be the world's best mathematician or financier. This is simply a shortcoming in personal capability. What we should be concerned with are moral shortcomings which are much more serious than limited capabilities. The friends around me are not necessarily those with the highest skills or capabilities, but people with whom I feel safe and happy because they have no problem morally.

Achieving Tao is not an idealistic or ideological matter. It is the way that makes you well, prosperous, happy and blessed by your own actions. Be a friend to people of moral character and support them. Then your own life will be improved and the world will also be improved. If you have felt that the world was mistreating you, that is because you are unconscious of what you have given to the world in this lifetime or past ones. The way to change the world is by mending the shortcomings of your own personality, not by attacking other people with violence. Improvement comes about through effective spiritual practice; this is how we distinguish ourselves from other spiritual paths.

We must be careful, though! It sounds as if I were preaching spiritual idealism here. There are some truly immoral people in the world. Is it your responsibility to suffer because of them? What is one to do? Please listen to what I have to say with an objective mind. These next words, given to you and to myself, could be considered a confirmed message in a world situation such as the one we live in.

Spiritual courage could be considered the same thing as moral courage when it is applied to a life circumstance. Moral courage, therefore, is spiritual courage in life. Spiritual courage can give birth to moral courage. Spiritual courage is what we were born with. Knowledge, especially intellectual knowledge, is what we have produced or learned as the result of experiencing different life circumstances. No one can expect the external circumstances of their personal life to remain the same forever. What is important is to use your original life spirit to improve life circumstances. This is why spiritual courage is more important than all kinds of knowledge. Good knowledge assists one's moral courage in life. Life will never be totally trouble free, and you will never be above making mistakes, but you must have the courage to keep going and do better.

Is this message different from Wu Wei? Wu Wei means original spiritual completeness and perfection as expressed in spiritual integralness. It also means to embrace spiritual courage. Wu Wei, in the life sphere of after-Heaven, thus means the achievement of original spiritual wholeness in an individual.

If spiritual immortality is not your goal, it might be a life of innocence as described by the Garden of Eden; if not that, then health, spiritual independence, and spiritual freedom must mean something to you.

What, then, is spiritual freedom? Is it not the fruit of your spiritual progress? I hope that you can use my work as a daily source of friendly advice for your personal achievement. The spiritual goal of individual life is to break through the limitations you have created in the after-Heaven stage of your life in time and space by developing yourself spiritually. In that way you can enjoy a life that is not limited and which can extend itself without obstruction. You will then prove to yourself that the essence of life is not limited by form, except insofar as you allow it to be. Foolish programs and rigid customs, whether your own or others', all make your life stiff and your spirit suffocated. Such chains are spiritually deforming. Do not be defeated in the game of life that courageous people play. Do not be disappointed by the trouble that people brew for the world. Do not tire of being a student and continually learning. Do not sit still and withdraw from the healthy movement of life. Do not stop being virtuously creative and celebrating the creative universal nature in your own life.

An individual can be either the slave of the material sphere and spiritual underdevelopment, or a master of spiritual freedom. The pursuit of enlightenment is what enables one to attain spiritual freedom.

To end this meeting, I offer this poem from an ancient achieved one in the great tradition of Tao, the path of wholeness and naturalness.

> The original oneness is what exists
>> throughout pre-Heaven.
> It cannot be described,
>> but it is the pure subtle law
>> and the essence of nature.
>
> If a person is entrapped
>> by his own troubles
>> in the after-Heaven stage of life,
> He will spend his lifetime
>> accomplishing the tragedy of his life.
>
> If he could only trace back
>> through all lifetimes,
> Before even the first life was formed,
> All the tragedies he has suffered
>> would disappear,
> And he could restore the pure joy
>> of his life.

CHAPTER EIGHTEEN

Malibu, June 25,1987: Meeting continued

Q: How should I nurture my energy if I want to be happily married in the future?

Master Ni: Men and women who wish to be married should nurture their own energy first. The appropriate attitude and appropriate energy will enable a marriage to happen easily; you will naturally attract someone who is serious about marriage.

A spiritual person can be single or married, although marriage does affect one's concentration and demand a great deal of compromise. If you wish to be married, you must have great respect for those who follow the path of married life. It is much harder than single life; it is not simple at all. Do not think that married people are foolish or vulgar. This is a common attitude among many spiritual people. All you can say is that the path of married life is different.

A spiritual person can be married if he or she has achieved internal unity and there are no more contradictions within one's own being. Someone who wishes to be single and spiritual, but who also desires a marriage partner will not really accept a marriage or a fixed relationship at a deep level. In the next relationship, or the next life, the person will still not be happily married unless this basic conflict has been resolved. If you wish to be married, you must form your deep inner structure accordingly and not carry on an inner battle over it.

The second thing to remember, if you wish to be paired, is to never try to force a relationship on someone else by your own will.   Neither should you interfere in other people's relationships or teach or support any doctrine that disrespects the marriage relationship, interferes with the fulfillment of obligations of either party in a marriage, and thus damages the union of a family.

In order to live a spiritual life, you must learn to see and accept people as they are without differentiating between them on the basis of sex. People are people. If you expect to enter the path of married life, you must respect both sexes and not think of your own sex as either superior or inferior. If you think of men as devils or of women as foxes that are out to steal your energy, then you cannot be happily married in this or a later life.

Q: What kind of cultivation should I do if I want to be married when I am older?

Master Ni: You are attractive, charming and young. If you want to have a beautiful marriage someday, then do not have loose relationships with different men, mating with one today and another tomorrow. If you just want to have some fun, then marriage will not happen. If it does happen, then it will be short-lived and have an unhappy ending.

Never exchange your body for a cup of wine. You need to respect the other person and yourself too. Let the man understand you, your interest, and what kind of woman you are. If he is not a suitable marriage candidate, then you should not have sex with him. Set a right price on yourself; do not place yourself for sale on the clearly understood but unlabeled sexual market. When people who have no respect for their own bodies and lives do things for the satisfaction of the moment, they destroy the hope of a good marriage.

What is important is how a woman manages her life; if temporary sexual satisfaction is readily available to a man, then who will bother to be married? If you hold steady in your good attitudes, the right person will come along. People with keen intuition will sense that you are a respectable person, if they are looking for such a person with whom to share their life.

You say that you do not want to end up an old maid, but as I see it, different flowers open in different seasons. Why must it be in the Spring? There is a saying that "haste makes waste." So what if you never get married? It is okay! Whether you are married or not, you need to have a sweet personality and character. Bees and butterflies always come to flowers that are fresh and fragrant. Even if there are no flowers in the garden of your life, there may be bamboo and pine trees to give you strength. If you do not find the right person to marry, it is better to remain single, complete and untouched than to invite unnecessary trouble.

One of the problems of today's society is the lax attitude toward sexual responsibility. This causes contagious diseases and also brews murderous criminals. Whose responsibility is it? I believe it is both men's and women's.

Q: You are saying, in essence, that unless women withhold sex, men will not behave responsibly - both emotionally and materially. what value is there in marrying a man who needs to be controlled by the threat of no sex? What joy is there in manipulating another person on the basis of their instinctual needs?

Master Ni: Thank you for asking this; it is truly a question of emotional despair which brings up many important issues. Should a person have sex before marriage? Should sexual activities only be allowed after the formal marriage ceremony? Which is right? Are both wrong or are both right? Should sex be applied as a social tool? Should it be a recreational social game? Wars have been fought over a single sexy woman. Many women have known how to utilize their bodies to gain power and make political alliances. A beautiful, intelligent woman may use her charm and looks to make good things happen or she may use her sexual attraction to invite misfortune and trouble. If you ask me what I support, first of all, I do not agree on using sex as a social tool, form of entertainment or recreation, or as marriage bait. I also do not think that sex is the foundation of a good marriage; there are many other important areas of compatibility, such as spiritual and moral values, personal interests, individual dispositions, life goals and so forth. As for sex outside marriage, it depends on how one manages the matter and whether it is accepted by the society in which one lives.

In general, sexual attraction and activity is of great importance to most people. A person can change one's whole life by doing it right. It can earn you the friendship and devotion of another person or it can become a destructive force that undermines your life. How it is used and with what results depends on the balance one has achieved between intelligence and impulse. I support anyone who can utilize this power to benefit themselves externally or internally.

The traditional teaching of Tao adopts two ways: if you are talking about the value of a family, harmonization is what is emphasized. If you wish to concentrate only on the development of the individual, you would focus on how to apply sexual energy to support your spiritual achievement.

My instruction in this area of life is that, in essence, whether one is a man or a woman does not matter; each individual should have self-respect, and not abuse or misapply himself by improper sexual behavior and habits or by an improper marriage or relationship. I recommend personal control in sexuality rather than using sex to control other people. Each of us should guide ourselves to health and increase our inner worth instead of manipulating other people. I have mentioned the word "price." By that I mean self-worth. This is very important for all people, young or old, married or single.

I remember a rural place where different communities lived around the two banks of a beautiful river. On the eastern hilly side were well-to-do farmers and shepherds. on the western side were ordinary farmers and fishermen. In one of the eastern villages there lived a rich family with ten beautiful daughters. On the west side lived a family with ten strong sons who were earnest and diligent. In those days it was the custom for a young man to bring a cow as a gift to the family of the girl he wished to marry, but the father of the ten beautiful daughters declared that each of his daughters was worth ten cows!

The ten daughters in the eastern village all possessed good qualities as young women, and it was the same with the ten sons on the other side of the river to be good young men or husbands. A strong admiration became built up between the young people of the two families. But the son's family were ordinary farmers, and it would cost them a fortune to marry the daughters of the other family, since ten cows each would mean a hundred cows. Nevertheless, a mutual admiration between the young people grew to be very strong. Finally, the father of the daughters found out about it and strongly opposed the social closeness of the young generation of the two families for fear that he would lose his daughters without gaining any cattle.   You know, parents have a different understanding of marriage than young people do. Parents usually look at the material aspect of life and are sometimes too realistic.   Young people look more for love.

After some natural disasters happened to the region, the father began to learn the quality of these young men who rebuilt their lives quickly and then gave helping hands to others who had suffered.   So he agreed to the friendship and accepted the proposal of marriage for his daughters.   Not only did he not take any cattle from the young men, but he gave them many sheep and land, as well as his daughters.

I believe that the father learned to become wise, and that the young women were also wise to appreciate good quality rather than material strength alone.   The foundation of living together, the future of a marriage does not depend on the material foundation alone, but also on the love and quality that each individual offers to the other.   If you marry the right person, your whole life is improved; if you marry the wrong one, your whole life is ruined.   Precaution is what I emphasize, not post-marriage complaints.

At the time of the story, people were naturally religious. Marriage was not just a matter of external bonds; there was a kind of spiritual understanding and devotion to each side. Marriage definitely requires the virtue of self-denial and commitment to helping the other person.   Therefore, it is important for young men and women who wish to be married to work on building good qualities and personal self-value.   A person should give himself to another only if there is great appreciation and great understanding, not just a social agreement.

Secondly, once you have worn out your energy with a very loose lifestyle, even if you can manipulate another person into needing you, you cannot manipulate their honest respect for you.   This is true even if the other person likes to be manipulated and even if you ar equal intellectually.   Only divorce or damage will happen.

I would like for all my women students to have self-worth, regardless of their age. I come from a tradition that respects women. Personally, I still highly respect anyone who values and understands the spiritual meaning of virginity and chastity.

According to the Bible, it was God who created man and woman, but we must understand that God did not build the world only for men or only for women. Nor did he build separate worlds for each sex. There is only one world in which both men and women must live together and assist each other. You can see how perfectly God planned things. If the ancestors of human beings had stayed in the Garden of Eden and obeyed God's discipline, there would have been no need for clothing, housing, agriculture or industry, and no problem with overpopulation. The only mistake God made was to give the woman a vagina and the man a penis. When they set out to look for fun, then all the trouble started.

Woman is thought to come from the rib-bone of man, but this could be interpreted as being at the side of man to assist him closely. As I see it, from the experience of being a man, I think man is also the rib-bone of woman. It is not really a question of which is superior or inferior.

In the after-Heaven stage of life, men and women are incomplete physiologically, psychologically and emotionally, but not spiritually; however, the lower foundation affects the higher building. Therefore, there can be different kinds and levels of marriage. Within a marriage, there are different practices to complete one's energy both internally and externally. A higher sexual energy exchange is performed without the usual form of making love and sometimes without any at all. This involves special instruction which I have given on other occasions and which you can find in my books.

Marriage is a good system for raising children. Once a couple decides to be married, if they would like to have children, they should have the patience to stay married long enough for the healthy psychological development of the children to be assured.

Also, marriage is an important way of settling the mind, but it could make a person too narrow, living only for their own children without considering others who are young, worthy and needy in the world. The principle of balance should always be maintained, whether one is married or single.

I hope my answer is useful to you. People's knowledge and behavior around sex and marriage do not necessarily improve as they grow older unless they set the right values for themselves and put the whole of their precious life energy into tackling the issue.

My simple instruction to all of you is to use your sexual energy constructively. If it cannot be fulfilled in a healthily paired life, or even if you are paired satisfactorily, this energy can be transformed into valuable alternatives such as artistic creativity, improving one's life in all aspects, study, service, scientific research, etc. Most significantly, you can use this energy to lengthen your life, improve your health, sharpen your confidence, and attain higher spiritual development.

If you look into the questions we all have discussed in depth, you can see the people have been programmed by a culture which lacks emotional support and thus focuses on intensified sexual energy exchange between one man and one woman. In addition to this are added the conventional spiritual beliefs and commands of religion and artificial political pressures. All of these forces require people to spend their lives learning, respecting and accepting unnatural requirements. Finally, people accept these bandits as their saviors.

The learning of Tao teaches people to re-write their programming afresh, according to the universal renewal of life and nature. To learn Tao is to know all the kinds of "software" that you can make use of on different occasions, but not be bound or managed by them. To learn Tao is to trace the inexhaustible source of life back to the Subtle Origin and thus to refresh one's life continuously. You can rewrite your own program of life, based on the life of universal immortality, not the short span of a hundred turns around the sun. Your life can be one of universal vastness rather than one which is restricted to some lines on the back of a tiny turtle, the earth. As a snake grows, it sheds its skin. The growing panther adds stripes to its hide. The spiritual growth of a human being is expressed in breaking through conceptual barriers to directly reach the truth.

Some of you may wonder about personal destiny, either in marriage or in general. Most people hope to achieve something in life, but no one can demand beautiful flowers and plentiful fruit in all twelve gardens of their natal chart. Nor can they expect their gardens to all bloom at the same time as other people's or to be in constant bloom. To describe this real-life situation, I have written the following verse for you:

> *"Each of us has been given twelve gardens.*
> *None of us works on his twelve pieces of land,*
> *Yet we expect fields of flowers in each garden*
> *all the time.*
> *Our anxiety is like a fire which bakes the land,*
> *causing it to give no flowers at all."*

Fortunately, all twelve gardens only cover the surface of life. In the great path of learning Tao, you are not asked to give up anything, but are encouraged to nurture your root. The roots of a tree are the bottom of the plant. They communicate with the earth. The root of human beings is in their head which communicates with Heaven. The spiritual practice in learning Tao is to nurture your spiritual root of life with the head and reach Heaven. Once you take good care of the root, flowers will grow and bear good fruit in the right season without your having to demand it.

I have recommended both internal and external practices in *The Heavenly Way* and *The Workbook for Spiritual Development*. At this time, I would like to offer you an essential spiritual practice that directly works on developing your spiritual self-nature evenly and abundantly.

You should sit calmly and quietly in your own room, free from any disturbance, both internal and external. The hands should be held together with the thumbprints together, thumbs pointing upwards, and the backs of the fingers of each hand meeting together from the knuckles to the fingernails. This is done in order to link the energy of both sides of the brain. Sitting thus, gently recite the Invocation for

Reaching the Divine Source of Universal Life and Blessings: **"Hsuan Tsr Yu Hsuan Chung Miao Chi Men."** Recite the words over and over again until you can feel your spiritual center awaken. You may visualize the characters or not; the visualization can intensify your spiritual strength.

By practicing this daily in your meditation and in your dreams, you can nurture and awaken your spiritual energy and become more centered. The pure, high spiritual being that you mold within yourself will be expressed through prosperity, health, longevity, peace and joy.

With sufficient practice and cultivation of your spiritual energy, you can apply your nurtured strength to a secret wish naturally when the right occasion arises, at the right time and place; things will happen as you wish. You can also store up your strength and grow "wing" energy with which to ascend to the Heaven of spiritual freedom. Then you can do and be whatever you wish. You can do and be Wu Wei, the highest being of the Being of Non-Being.

The Heaven of Wu Wei is the Heaven of Naturalness where you do not need to do anything extra or interfere in anything. You can simply be happy with whatever and wherever you are. You live with courage and joy a life which makes no demands. You can discover that everything supports your great freedom. No one and nothing can harm you. Friends and enemies alike contribute to the cruise-fare of your free roaming, as described in the first chapter of Chuang Tzu.

> *"Be the life which possesses the high freedom*
> *of birds flying in this ky*
> *and fish swimming in the deep ocean.*
> *Be the life that nature endows*
> *with great and free transformation.*
> *Be the life of nature itself;*
> *be the life behind the mechanical*
> *and physical universe.*
> *Be the life of the subtle origin*
> *before all things were born.*

Be the life of the great oneness
  when all gods and goddesses
  were still in its testicles.
Be the life of no intimidation,
  facing all social, emotional
  or material difficulties
  and the difficulties of religious
  or political darkness by going forward
  in your own spiritual development
  and sharing it with other people.
Be the life of a fixed spiritual goal
  without wandering here and there
  along the sidelines of petty paths
  or turning back.
Undauntedly correct and improve your
  spiritual stature and condition.
Be the life of knowing schemes
  and of remaining honest and simple,
  not changing to accommodate
  the dishonesty of the world,
  but going forward
  with the refreshed breath of life
  in each moment to reach the eternal light.
Be the life of self-set spiritual standards,
  firm but flexible so that you can move
  to the left or right, to the back or front,
  or any angle, without losing
  your spiritual direction
  toward naturalness and integrity.
Be the life of spiritual and moral courage
  with gentleness, tolerance and patience,
  not forcing anyone to conform to a mold
  that you have set.
Be the life that dares to differ
  from custom and convention
  that has been brewed by
  the spiritually undeveloped majority
  and its leaders.
Do nothing, however, which expresses difference
  or assists its growth.

Only apply reformation and improvement
    in your own life
    and in the life of those who share
    your awareness.
Be the life that shows light to those
    who need your help and service,
    but do not remain their teacher all the time.

Give them the chance to become better students
    of themselves.
A good teacher also needs to maintain
    his or her own flexibility to grow.
Be the life that never forgets to say
    "happy birthday" to itself each morning
    by regenerating and revitalizing
    itself and others
    and by naturally utilizing the treasures
    of the ancient achieved ones daily."

AFTERWARD

I quote the afterward in the first edition of the book which has been divided into two books under the two titles, *The Gentle Path of Spiritual Progress* as the original and as *Spiritual Messages from a Buffalo Rider, a Man of Tao*, which was the subtitle of the one volume edition.

"This announcement was made at the annual New Year Celebration on February 1, 1987, Year of the Rabbit. I would like to use it as the afterward to this book, thus "saving" two birds with one stone, using one piece of material for two purposes.

The aim of my work is to serve you in particular and directly, so here are a few words to you especially as individuals who are looking for guidance in following a life of natural truth.

First of all, I would like to point out the nature of modern, industrial development and the social standards it has created which affect the quality of life today. The direction in which people are heading, how they look and how they act, what they design and what they work for, are oriented in the present without considering the future. People see only what is good for the moment; they do not look for long-term benefits. They are excited by new beginnings, but do not look deeply into what the end will be. What they are drawn to, therefore, are things that look good on the outside, but have no internal goodness. When they are young, they look for comfort and excitement and don't care about the health or happiness of their old age. It is like caring about whether the blossoms on the branches flourish without ever considering whether the root of the entire tree is strong or not. People value the short-lived advantages of emotional highs, but not the subtler advantages that come slowly in small increments. They want an immediate remedy, not a long-term cure. They only see beautiful faces, not good-natured hearts. The evidence of this trend of modern culture is endless.

A person who follows the eternal truth will have the courage to turn away from something that looks good now, but is bad later. They would rather endure a little discomfort today and wait for something of long-term benefit. They do not look for things of outward goodness, but respect inner worth and value. Even if they come from a family that has provided them with good financial support, it is more important to them to have things that come from their own personal achievement, no matter how small. In other words, it is more important to them to be a respectful and trustworthy son or daughter than to have a powerful or famous father.

A person who follows the eternal truth knows that it is good to build themselves while they are young and enjoy themselves when they are old, thus they work at building a strong root as well as producing flourishing branches. They do not look for immediate remedies, but for long-term cures.

In today's society there are many beauty parlors and cosmetic products, but nothing that helps people beautify their minds and emotions. There is plastic surgery to make your face and body look good, but there is no market at all for beautifying your heart. The ruler that is used by a person who follows the eternal truth does not measure what can only be seen with the eye. Its only rule is the integral truth of wholeness, not the sum of its parts.

A person of eternal truth is not someone who struggles for brief victories. He is a slow turtle compared to the swift rabbit in the race of life. The attractive beauty of peach blossoms in the warm spring and that of chrysanthemums in frosty autumn, but the hardy plum undauntedly blossoms in the heart of winter, long after all the other flowers are gone. A strongly built personality is not easily crushed by difficulties and adversity.

Beloved friends, a person of natural truth must learn to maintain his nature without entering the wasteful competition of exhibiting his beauty among that of others. His undefeatable spiritual essence is symbolized by the fearless plum flower. He is the one who gives flowers to whatever work he does. Although the flowers of his life may not always be visible to many people, the true beauty of his nature is not decreased by maintaining simplicity or by living in a plain background for all beauty to be shown upon. That virtue is ignored by many, but valued by people of the universal, subtle truth.

Now, on this occasion I would like to announce a few things in connection with some newly adopted terms for this ancient tradition. All people who share the philosophical standpoint expressed in the *Tao Teh Ching* and its elucidations, such as my written work, are to be called students of Tao or students of the Integral Truth. Whoever uses this truthful spiritual understanding and practice to develop themselves and to help others in a unifying sense are following Tao and can be referred to in their entirety as the Fellowship of Integral Truth. Regional names may differ: for instance, the center in Australia is called the Fellowship of Universal Natural Spiritual Truth; the center in Miami is called the Fellowship of the Subtle Light But all express the same truth.

The abbreviation for the Fellowship of Integral Truth is "FIT," which expresses that this joint effort is directed toward total fitness in all aspects of our lives: physical fitness, mental fitness, and spiritual fitness. This is our practical goal as part of one, connected universal life.

The California organization known as the Union of Tao and Man, or the Union of the Integral Person, was the first such regional group, and it continues to help new study groups and centers develop, as other regional fellowships should also do.

Regional leaders, leaders of study groups, teachers of intellectual understanding, teachers of Tai Chi, etc., should all be called 'mentors.' In fact, all teachers, workers, ministers and the master share this title both functionally and socially.

According to the specific function of their work within the Fellowship of Integral Truth, ministers are leaders in a specific region or community. They are also teachers and workers in those regions. For the sake of spiritual distinction from the religious term minister, we define minister as a mini-ster. Mini means small, while ster, as in the word youngster, means person. Mini-ster thus means the one who undertakes the small work. As Lao Tzu said, 'The sage does not undertake the big, thus he can accomplish the bit,' and also, 'A journey of a thousand miles begins with a single step.'

Teachers who perform ceremonial activities and conduct group spiritual cultivation are 'officiants.' That means that they offer worship to the universal divine nature and by their offering they guide all participants to merge their individual divine nature with the subtle origin of the universal divine nature.

Formal authorization will be given to all mentors, ministers, teachers and officiants by the master. Personally, I welcome the good contribution of new spiritual teachers, whatever teachings and techniques they offer from other traditions. If a teacher wishes to represent the teachings and material presented in my books, then I think that personal authorization from me is appropriate so that the material will not be confused with other teachings. Whoever wishes to represent my teachings should also follow the necessary traditional discipline which I recommend.

As I see it, the master is also a minister, and his undertaking is still smaller than the general ministers, because the foundation of the Fellowship of Integral Truth is the different regional communities whose purpose is the extension of the spiritual well-being of individual persons. The fulfillment of a regional society is to promote the well being of society, expressed through assistance toward the well being of each other.

The master, in this tradition, can be considered the spiritual founder, the one who provides a healthy cultural basis from which to grow. The culture itself is the spaceship which carries people to a new range of life. All mentors, ministers and officiants are the different harmonized strengths that give a balanced, even support to the undaunted ship as it travels on its way toward the subtle light.

All those who offer their help and strength to achieve their own individual well-being as well as that of the society are true masters. Being a true master is a self-paid job, unlike paid positions in society. They are not traditionally supported by the society, but their social contribution is the natural and spontaneous response of one who engages in spiritual cultivation and achieves himself. Being aware of their spiritual responsibility, such people are willing to take on the trouble of dealing with the poisoned world while continuing to support themselves materially.

As I see it, the integral truth as presented by me will not become only a cultural appreciation, just like enjoying fine arts, but the direction which a new human society must firmly take. True masters respond to the problems of their time. False heros take advantage of troubled times. In times of darkness, true masters are treated like impostors, while the impostors are treated as masters. It is people's own darkness which is still the master.

In the future, with or without a recognized master, the leadership of mankind should rest with those individuals who live the integral truth. They are the true masters who never forsake the world. Who, then is the true master of their life? We will say the universal conscience of those achieved ones. If there is a recognized master in the world, he is the point of connection of each individual's universal conscience. He is the concourse of universal divine heart. The function of coordination among different centers and study groups in different regions and individuals in places where there is no formal center or study group, but who would like to share the joint spirit, is taken care of by the newly organized Taoist Order of Global Mission which is another name for The Order of Universal Heart.

With the above clarifications, I would like for all teachers and workers to have a better understanding of their function. Newly developed centers, fellowships and study groups can likewise have a clearer direction and firm spiritual standpoint.

All people following the integral truth are students of Tao. All workers and teachers, whatever their function, are mentors. All people in the fellowship of different regions are brothers and sisters in Tao. All of them share this kinship of integral truth.

All fellowships in each region are to conjointly realize each individual's virtuous fulfillment and well-being in order to promote the well-being of the entire society."

APPENDIX

THE INTERRELATIONSHIP OF NATURAL ENERGY:

The Creative, Destructive, and Competitive Cycles (or Phases)

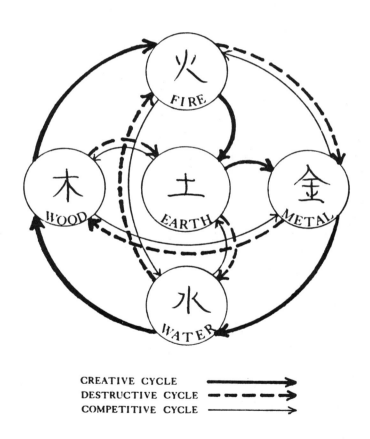

CREATIVE CYCLE	⟹
DESTRUCTIVE CYCLE	⇢
COMPETITIVE CYCLE	→

THE CORRESPONDENCE OF:

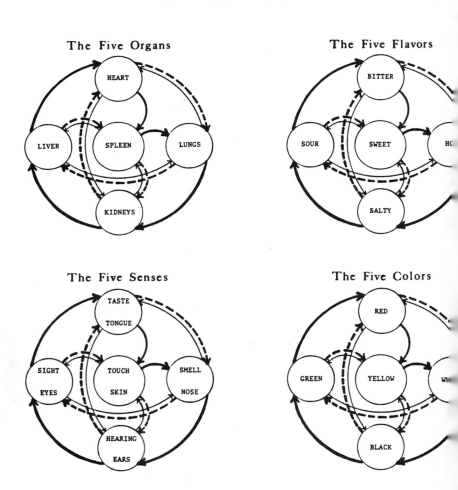

TO THE ELEMENTARY SYSTEM OF FIVE NATURAL FORCE

THE CORRESPONDENCE OF:

The Five Body Components

The Five Physical Responses

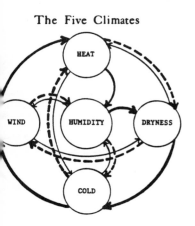

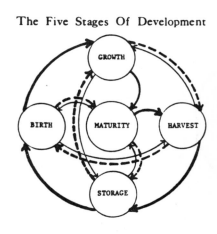

The Five Climates

The Five Stages Of Development

TO THE ELEMENTARY SYSTEM OF FIVE NATURAL FORCES

THE CORRESPONDENCE OF:

The Five Internal Energies

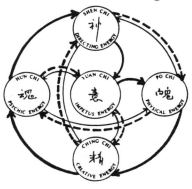

The Five Bodily Fluids

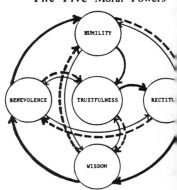

The Five Attributes Of Mind

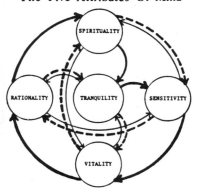

The Five Moral Powers

TO THE ELEMENTARY SYSTEM OF FIVE NATURAL FORCES

THE CORRESPONDENCE OF:

The Five Emotions

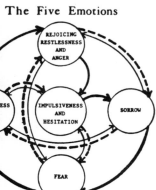

The Five Voices

he Five Negative Drives

The Five Potentially Corrupting Influences

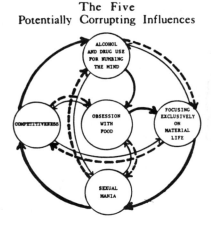

O THE ELEMENTARY SYSTEM OF FIVE NATURAL FORCES

FIVE ELEMENTS: A COMPARISON CHART

ELEMENTS	FIRE	EARTH	METAL	WATER	WOOD
ORGANS	HEART	SPLEEN	LUNGS	KIDNEYS	LIVER
PLANETS	MARS	SATURN	VENUS	MERCURY	JUPITER
FLAVORS	BITTER	SWEET	HOT	SALTY	SOUR
SENSES	TONGUE	SKIN	NOSE	EARS	EYES
COLORS	RED	YELLOW	WHITE	INDIGO (BLACK)	GREEN
BODY COMPONENTS	VESSELS	FLESH	SKIN & HAIR	BONE	MUSCLES & TENDONS
PHYSICAL RESPONSES	ITCHING	HICCUPING	COUGHING	SHIVERING	TWITCHING
CLIMATES	HEAT	HUMIDITY	DRYNESS	COLD	WIND
DEVELOP-MENT	GROWTH	MATURITY	HARVEST	STORAGE	BIRTH
ESSENTIAL ENERGIES	DIRECTING ENERGY	ENERGY OF IMPETUS	PHYSICAL ENERGY	REPRODUC-TIVE ENERGY	PSYCHIC ENERGY
BODILY FLUIDS	BLOOD	GLANDULAR FLUIDS	PERSPIRA-TION	SEXUAL HOR-MONES, BONE MARROW	DIGESTIVE
ATTRI-BUTES OF MIND	SPIRITUAL-ITY	TRANQUIL-ITY	SENSITIVITY	VITALITY	RATIONALITY
MORAL POWER	HUMILITY	TRUSTFUL-NESS	RECTITUDE	WISDOM	BENEVOLENCE
EMOTIONS	REJOICE, ANGER, & RESTLESSNESS	IMPULSIVE-NESS	FEAR & & WORRY	SORROW	SHOCK & NERVOUSNE
VOICES	LAUGHTER	SINGING	CRYING	GROANING	CALLING
NEGATIVE DRIVES	AMBITION, DESIRE	GREED	STUBBORN-NESS, DIS-HARMONI-OUSNESS	SCATTERED-NESS & COLD-NESS	JEALOUSY
CORRUPT-ING INFLU-ENCES	ALCOHOL & DRUGS TO NUMB MIND	GLUTTONY	AIMING ONLY TOWARD MATERIAL GOALS	SEXUAL MAN-IA	COMPETITIVE-NESS

CHECKLIST FOR SPIRITUAL SELF-CULTIVATION #1

Exaggerate, Lie, Cheat, Mislead

Gossip, Spread Rumors, Slander, Defame

Argue, Criticize, Insult

Depend on or Make Demands of Others

Hold a Grudge, Seek Revenge

Complain, Vent Frustration on Others

Abuse Others or Allow Them to Abuse You

Stay in a Bad Environment or Corrupt Company

Meddle in Others' Affairs

Favoritism, Judgemental

Show Off, Boast, Feel Superior

Lewd Conduct or Language

Boredom, Discontent, Negativity

Laziness, Idleness, Inertia, Stagnation

Uncleanness

Waste Time, Energy or Resources

Slipshod Work, Reckless Behavior

Overindulgence, Excessiveness, Fanaticism

Eat Bad or Unhealthy Food

Covetousness, Greed, Miserliness

Hold Narrow Viewpoints, Dualistic Thinking

Attachment to Worldly Excitement

Inconsistent Spiritual Practice

Berate Yourself for Not Keeping These Observations

Truthfulness																					
Respect																					
Harmony																					
Self-responsibility																					
Forgiveness																					
Self-Control																					
Respect																					
Purity																					
Respect																					
Impartiality																					
Plainness																					
Purity																					
Freshness																					
Vitality																					
Purity																					
Conservation																					
Conscientiousness																					
Moderation																					
Purity																					
Contentment																					
Broadmindedness																					
Contentment																					
Constancy																					
Progressiveness																					

CHECKLIST FOR SPIRITUAL SELF-CULTIVATION #2

The most effective way to begin to improve yourself spiritually is to work earnestly with the observances listed below. Study them, consider them, accept them and follow them in your life. As your thinking and your behavior improve and become more refined, the subtle response of the universal energy will change the quality and quantity of your life. This begins self-cultivation, or the practice of Tao.

How to use the checklist: make a calendar for the present month. Hang the calendar on your wall or keep it in a place where no one can see it.

Begin with today. At the end of the day, before you go to sleep at night, review the observances one by one. If during that day you have done something against the subtle law, put a black mark in the box for that day. If during the day you have done the opposite action that helps your improvement, put a red mark. This will record your spiritual development or lack of it.

At the end of a month, you can see at a glance how you are doing. Then display your record to the subtle realm with incense and flowers and request the subtle realm to witness how you have purified your negativity and misfortune.

Remember, self-cultivation is a process. Improvement comes from steady self-observation and correction. At first, your results might be disappointing to you, but if you keep working at it, you will improve yourself naturally and gradually. The strength is built by keeping this practice. If you realize how much your harm yourself by doing such things, you will naturally stop acting them out.

At the bottom of each page of observances, there are some blank spaces. You may use these spaces to write in any personal bad habits or areas which go against the subtle law that you would like to improve.

Habits that harm your spiritual well-being:

1. Seeking a connection with people just because they possess a socially important position, and making marriage ties with someone just because they are wealthy.

2. Harming, threatening or suppressing others.
3. Borrowing something or accepting things from people without returning or repaying it.
4. Expecting repayments for doing a good deed.
5. Being unreasonable in your requests of people.
6. Using vulgar or obscene language.
7. Outwardly expressing your values, virtue or wisdom.
8. Being elated when people honor you, or being depressed when you are disgraced.
9. Being critical of the affairs of others but not practicing your own cultivation.
10. Exaggerating or lying, or being deceitful or devious in your actions.
11. Revealing the shortcomings or secrets of another.
12. Disgracing the talents or virtues of another.
13. Being vain, conceited or superior to others.
14. Being overly emotional.
15. Being moody, fussy or pessimistic.
16. Always being needy and dependent.
17. Being greedy or overly desirous.
18. Being jealous of someone more successful than yourself.
19. Being angry or holding hatred towards others or yourself.
20. Being bored, discontent or incapable of enjoying things.
21. Being fearful and apprehensive.
22. Being meddlesome.
23. Disrespecting anyone, whether young or old.
24. Engaging in idle talk or gossip, or speaking without reason.
25. Arguing.
26. Complaining about your life, the weather or the food you eat.
27. Taking advantage of people's weakness.
28. Seeking revenge.
29. Being a middleman to any unethical or immoral business.
30. Cheating, misappropriating or taking bribes.
31. Blaming others for your own irresponsibility.

32. Being unreasonable or stubborn.
33. Holding prejudices.
34. Failing to forgive others for their wrongdoing.
35. Ignoring a main principle and following what is of minor purpose.
36. Doing anything that must be hidden from parents or superiors.
37. Jumping to hasty conclusion or rushing into things.
38. Being easily impressed with power.
39. Rejecting the simple and frugal way of life.
40. Being untidy, dirty or living in filth.
41. Wandering about or traveling without purpose.
42. Behaving recklessly or irresponsibly.
43. Overindulging in anything.
44. Making any disturbance when you move or stop moving.
45. Being undutiful or doing shoddy work.
46. Being lazy, slothful or inert.
47. Wasting your time or energy.
48. Eating strong meat or bad food or other improper food or drink.
49. Being irresponsible for your life.
50. Bending your virtuous principles for popular interest.
51. Being lazy in the cultivation of your spiritual essence.
52. Becoming discouraged if you fail in keeping one of these observances.
53. Add any of your own personal disciplines, such as smoking, overeating, driving too fast, etc.

If you know something about your own natal chart or learn about it with the help of a friend, it is not hard for you to know the bad influence from your birth hour. To put together those shortcomings on a checklist as part of your spiritual self-overcoming project will be part of your individual spiritual quality changing.

Also, if you hear people who live or work with you complain about the same thing several times, it must be a real personal problem of yours. You should include those things on your checklist for your own improvement.

BOOKS IN ENGLISH BY MASTER NI

Stepping Stones for Spiritual Success - New Publication - In Asia, the custom of foot binding was followed for close to a thousand years. In the West, people did not practice foot binding, but they bound their thoughts, for a much longer period, some 1,500 to 1,700 years. Their mind and thinking became unnatural. Being unnatural expresses a state of confusion where people do not know what is right. Once they become natural again, they become clear and progress is great. Master Ni invites his readers to unbind their minds; in this volume, he has taken the best of the traditional teachings and put them in to contemporary language to make them more relevant to our time, culture and lives. Stock No. BSTE. $7.95

The Complete Works of Lao Tzu
Lao Tzu's Tao Teh Ching is one of the most widely translated and cherished works of literature in the world. It presents the core of Taoist philosophy. Lao Tzu's timeless wisdom provides a bridge to the subtle spiritual truth as well as practical guidelines for harmonious and peaceful living. Master Ni has included what is believed to be the only English translation of the Hua Hu Ching, a later work of Lao Tzu which has been lost to the general public for a thousand years. 212 pages, 1986. Stock No. BCOM. Softcover, $9.50

Order The Complete Works of Lao Tzu and the companion Tao Teh Ching Cassette Tapes for only $20.00. Stock No. ABLAO.

The Book of Changes and the Unchanging Truth
The first edition of this book was widely appreciated by its readers, who drew great spiritual benefit from it. They found the principles of the I Ching to be clearly explained and useful to their lives, especially the helpful commentaries. The legendary classic I Ching is recognized as mankind's first written book of wisdom. Leaders and sages throughout history have consulted it as a trusted advisor which reveals the appropriate action to be taken in any of life's circumstances. This volume also includes over 200 pages of background material on Taoist principles of natural energy cycles, instruction and commentaries. New, revised second edition, 669 pages, 1990. Stock No. BBOO. Hardcover, $35.00

The Story of Two Kingdoms
This volume is the metaphoric tale of the conflict between the Kingdoms of Light and Darkness. Through this unique story, Master Ni transmits the esoteric teachings of Taoism which have been carefully guarded secrets for over 5,000 years. This book is for those who are serious in their search and have devoted their lives to achieving high spiritual goals. 122 pages, 1989. Stock No. BSTO. Hardcover, $14.00

The Way of Integral Life
This book can help build a bridge for those wishing to connect spiritual and intellectual development. It is most helpful for modern educated people. It includes practical and applicable suggestions for daily life, philosophical thought, esoteric insight and guidelines for those aspiring to give help and service to the world. This book helps you learn the wisdom of the ancient sages' achievement to assist the growth of your own wisdom and integrate it as your own new light and principles for balanced, reasonable living in worldly life. 320 pages, 1989. Softcover, $14.00, Stock No. BWAYS. Hardcover, $20.00, Stock No. BWAYH

Enlightenment: Mother of Spiritual Independence
The inspiring story and teachings of Master Hui Neng, the father of Zen Buddhism and Sixth Patriarch of the Buddhist tradition, highlight this volume. Hui Neng was a person of ordinary birth, intellectually unsophisticated, who achieved himself to become a spiritual leader. Master Ni includes enlivening commentaries and explanations of the principles outlined by this spiritual revolutionary. Having received the same training as all Zen Masters as one aspect of his training and achievement, Master Ni offers this teaching so that his readers may be guided in their process of spiritual development. 264 pages, 1989. Softcover, $12.50, Stock No. BENLS. Hardcover, $18.00, Stock No. BENLH

Attaining Unlimited Life
The thought-provoking teachings of Chuang Tzu are presented in this volume. He was perhaps the greatest philosopher and master of Taoism and he laid the foundation for the Taoist school of thought. Without his work, people of later generations would hardly recognize the value of Lao Tzu's teaching in practical, everyday life. He touches the organic nature of human life more deeply and directly than that of other great teachers. This volume also includes questions by students and answers by Master Ni. 467 pages, 1989. Softcover, $18.00, Stock No. BATTS; Hardcover, $25.00, Stock No. BATTH

The Gentle Path of Spiritual Progress
This book offers a glimpse into the dialogues of a Taoist master with the public. In a relaxed, open manner, Master Ni, Hua-Ching explains the fundamental practices that are the keys to experiencing enlightenment in everyday life. Many of the traditional secrets of Taoist training are revealed. People also ask a surprising range of questions, and Master Ni's answers touch on contemporary psychology, finances, sexual advice, how to use the I Ching as well as the telling of some fascinating Taoist legends. Softcover, $12.50, Stock No. BGEN

Spiritual Messages from a Buffalo Rider, A Man of Tao

This is another important collection of Master Ni's service in his worldly trip, originally published as one half of The Gentle Path. He had the opportunity to meet people and answer their questions to help them gain the spiritual awareness that we live at the command of our animal nature. Our buffalo nature rides on us, whereas an achieved person rides the buffalo. In this book, Master Ni gives much helpful knowledge to those who are interested in improving their lives and deepening their cultivation so they too can develop beyond their mundane beings. Softcover, $12.50, Stock No. BSPI

8,000 Years of Wisdom, Volume I and II

This two volume set contains a wealth of practical, down-to-earth advice given by Master Ni to his students over a five year period, 1979 to 1983. Drawing on his training in Traditional Chinese Medicine, Herbology, Acupuncture and other Taoist arts, Master Ni gives candid answers to students' questions on many topics ranging from dietary guidance to sex and pregnancy, meditation techniques and natural cures for common illnesses. Volume I includes dietary guidance; 236 pages; Stock No. BEIG1 Volume II includes sex and pregnancy guidance; 241 pages; Stock No. BEIG2. 1983, Softcover, Each Volume $12.50

The Uncharted Voyage Towards the Subtle Light

Spiritual life in the world today has become a confusing mixture of dying traditions and radical novelties. People who earnestly and sincerely seek something more than just a way to fit into the complexities of a modern structure that does not support true self-development often find themselves spiritually struggling. This book provides a profound understanding and insight into the underlying heart of all paths of spiritual growth, the subtle origin and the eternal truth of one universal life. 424 pages, 1985. Stock No. BUNC. Softcover, $14.50

The Heavenly Way

A translation of the classic Tai Shan Kan Yin Pien (Straighten Your Way) and Yin Chia Wen (The Silent Way of Blessing). The treaties in this booklet are the main guidance for a mature and healthy life. The purpose of this booklet is to promote the recognition of truth, because only truth can teach the perpetual Heavenly Way by which one reconnects oneself with the divine nature. 41 pages, 1981; Stock No. BHEA. Softcover, $2.50

Footsteps of the Mystical Child

This book poses and answers such questions as: What is a soul? What is wisdom? What is spiritual evolution? The answers to these and many other questions enable readers to open themselves to new realms of understanding and personal growth. There are also many true examples about people's internal and external struggles on the path of self-development and spiritual evolution. 166 pages, 1986; Stock No. BFOO. Softcover, $9.50

Workbook for Spiritual Development

This book offers a practical, down-to-earth, hands-on approach for those who are devoted to the path of spiritual achievement. The reader will find diagrams showing fundamental hand positions to increase and channel one's spiritual energy, postures for sitting, standing and sleeping cultivation as well as postures for many Taoist invocations. The material in this workbook is drawn from the traditional teachings of Taoism and summarizes thousands of years of little known practices for spiritual development. An entire section is devoted to ancient invocations, another on natural celibacy and another on postures. In addition, Master Ni explains the basic attitudes and understandings that are the foundation for Taoist practices. 224 pages, 1984. Stock No. BWOR. Softcover, $12.50

Poster of Master Lu

Color poster of Master Lu, Tung Ping (shown on cover of workbook), for use with the workbook or in one's shrine. 16" x 22"; Stock No. POS. $10.00

The Taoist Inner View of the Universe

This presentation of Taoist metaphysics provides guidance for one's own personal life transformation. Master Ni has given all the opportunity to know the vast achievement of the ancient unspoiled mind and its transpiercing vision. This book offers a glimpse of the inner world and immortal realm known to achieved Taoists and makes it understandable for students aspiring to a more complete life. 218 pages, 1979. Stock No. BTAOI. Softcover, $12.50

Tao, the Subtle Universal Law

Most people are unaware that their thoughts and behavior evoke responses from the invisible net of universal energy. The real meaning of Taoist self-discipline is to harmonize with universal law. To lead a good stable life is to be aware of the actual conjoining of the universal subtle law with every moment of our lives. This book presents the wisdom and practical methods that the ancient Chinese have successfully used for centuries to accomplish this. 165 pages, 1979. Stock No. TAOS. Softcover, $7.50

MATERIALS ON TAOIST HEALTH, ARTS AND SCIENCES

BOOKS

The Tao of Nutrition by Maoshing Ni, Ph.D., with Cathy McNease, B.S., M.H. - Working from ancient Chinese medical classics and contemporary research, Dr. Maoshing Ni and Cathy McNease have compiled an indispensable guide to natural healing. This exceptional book shows the reader how to take control of one's health through one's eating habits. This volume contains 3 major sections: the first section deals with theories of Chinese nutrition and philosophy; the second describes over 100 common foods in detail, listing their energetic properties, therapeutic actions and individual remedies. The third section lists nutritional remedies for many common ailments. This book presents both a healing system and a disease prevention system which is flexible in adapting to every individual's needs. 214 pages, 1987. Stock No. BTAON. Softcover, $14.50

Chinese Vegetarian Delights by Lily Chuang
An extraordinary collection of recipes based on principles of traditional Chinese nutrition. Many recipes are therapeutically prepared with herbs. Diet has long been recognized as a key factor in health and longevity. For those who require restricted diets and those who choose an optimal diet, this cookbook is a rare treasure. Meat, sugar, diary products and fried foods are excluded. Produce, grains, tofu, eggs and seaweeds are imaginatively prepared. 104 pages, 1987. Stock No. BCHIV. Softcover, $7.50

Chinese Herbology Made Easy - by Maoshing Ni, Ph.D.
This text provides an overview of Oriental medical theory, in-depth descriptions of each herb category, with over 300 black and white photographs, extensive tables of individual herbs for easy reference, and an index of pharmaceutical and Pin-Yin names. The distillation of overwhelming material into essential elements enables one to focus efficiently and develop a clear understanding of Chinese herbology. This book is especially helpful for those studying for their California Acupuncture License. 202 pages, 1986. Stock No. BCHIH. Softcover, 14.50

Crane Style Chi Gong Book - By Daoshing Ni, Ph.D.
Chi Gong is a set of meditative exercises that was developed several thousand years ago by Taoists in China. It is now practiced for healing purposes, combining breathing techniques, body movements and mental imagery to guide the smooth flow of energy throughout the body. This book gives a more detailed account and study of Chi Gong than the videotape alone. It may be used with or without the videotape. Includes complete instructions and information on using Chi Gong exercise as a medical therapy. 55 pages, 1984. Stock No. BCRA. Spiral bound $10.00

VIDEO TAPES

Crane Style Chi Gong (VHS) by Dr. Daoshing Ni, Ph.D.
Chi Gong is a set of meditative exercises developed several thousand years ago by ancient Taoists in China. It is now practiced for healing stubborn chronic diseases, strengthening the body to prevent disease and as a tool for further spiritual enlightenment. It combines breathing techniques, simple body movements, and mental imagery to guide the smooth flow of energy throughout the body. Chi gong is easy to learn for all ages. Correct and persistent practice will increase one's energy, relieve stress or tension, improve concentration and clarity, release emotional stress and restore general well-being. 2 hours Stock No. VCRA. $65.00

Eight Treasures (VHS) - By Maoshing Ni, Ph.D.
These exercises help open blocks in a person's energy flow and strengthen one's vitality. It is a complete exercise combining physical stretching and toning and energy conducting movements coordinated with breathing. The Eight Treasures are an exercise unique to the Ni family. Patterned from nature, the 32 movements of the Eight Treasures are an excellent foundation for Tai Chi Chuan or martial arts. 1 hour and 45 minutes. Stock No. VEIG. $49.00

Tai Chi Chuan - I & II (VHS) By Maoshing Ni, Ph.D.
This exercise integrates the flow of physical movement with that of integral energy in the Taoist style of "Harmony," similar to the long form of Yang-style Tai Chi Chuan. Tai Chi has been practiced for thousands of years to help both physical longevity and spiritual cultivation. 1 hour each. Each Video Tape $49.00. Order both for $90.00. Stock Nos: Part I, VTAI1; Part II, VTAI2; Set of two, VTAISET.

AUDIO CASSETTES

Invocations: Health and Longevity and Healing a Broken Heart By Maoshing Ni, Ph.D. This audio cassette guides the listener through a series of ancient invocations to channel and conduct one's own healing energy and vital force. "Thinking is louder than thunder." The mystical power by which all miracles are brought about is your sincere practice of this principle. 30 minutes. Stock No. AINV. $5.95

Chi Gong for Stress Release By Maoshing Ni, Ph.D.
This audio cassette guides you through simple, ancient breathing exercises that enable you to release day-to-day stress and tension that are such a common cause of illness today. 30 minutes. Stock No. ACHIS. $8.95

Chi Gong for Pain Management   By Maoshing Ni, Ph.D.
Using easy visualization and deep-breathing techniques that have been developed over thousands of years, this audio cassette offers methods for overcoming pain by invigorating your energy flow and unblocking obstructions that cause pain.   30 minutes.   Stock No. CHIP. $8.95

Tao Teh Ching Cassette Tapes
This classic work of Lao Tzu has been recorded in this two-cassette set that is a companion to the book translated by Master Ni.   Professionally recorded and read by Robert Rudelson.   120 minutes.   Stock No. ATAO. $12.00

Order Master Ni's book, The Complete Works of Lao Tzu, and Tao Teh Ching Cassette Tapes for only $20.00.   Stock No. ABLAO.

How To Order

Complete this form and mail it to: **Union of Tao and Man,**
117 Stonehaven Way, Los Angeles, CA 90049 (213)-472-9970

Name:

Address:

City: *State:*   *Zip:*

Phone - Daytime: *Evening:*

(We may telephone you if we have questions about your order.)

Qty.	Stock No.	Title/Description	Price Each	Total Price

Total amount for items ordered_____

Sales tax (CA residents, 6-1/2%)_____

Shipping Charge (See below)_____

Total Amount Enclosed_____

Please allow 6 - 8 weeks for delivery.
Thank you for your order.

U. S. Funds Only, Please
Please write your check or money order
to Union of Tao and Man

Shipping Charge - All Orders Sent Via U.S. Postal Service, unless specified.
Domestic Surface Mail: First item $2.00, each additional, add $.50.
Canada Surface Mail: First item $2.50, each additional, add $1.00.
Other Foreign Surface Mail: First item $3.00, each additional, add $2.00.
Foreign Air Mail: First item $18.00, each additional, add $7.00.

Spiritual Study Through the College of Tao

The College of Tao and the Union of Tao and Man were established formally in California in the 1970's. This tradition is a very old spiritual culture of mankind, holding long experience of human spiritual growth. Its central goal is to offer healthy spiritual education to all people of our society. This time tested tradition values the spiritual development of each individual self and passes down its guidance and experience.

Master Ni carries his tradition from its country of origin to the west. He chooses to avoid making the mistake of old-style religions that have rigid establishments which resulted in fossilizing the delicacy of spiritual reality. Rather, he prefers to guide the teachings of his tradition as a school of no boundary rather than a religion with rigidity. Thus, the branches or centers of his Taoist school offer different programs of similar purpose. Each center extends its independent service, but all are unified in adopting Master Ni's work as the foundation of teaching to fulfill the mission of providing spiritual education to all people.

The centers offer their classes, teaching, guidance and practices on building the groundwork for cultivating a spiritually centered and well-balanced life. As a person obtains the correct knowledge with which to properly guide himself or herself, he or she can then become more skillful in handling the experiences of daily life. The assimilation of good guidance in one's practical life brings about different stages of spiritual development.

Any interested individual is welcome to join and learn to grow for oneself. You might like to join the center near where you live, or you yourself may be interested in organizing a center or study group based on the model of existing centers. In that way, we all work together for the spiritual benefit of all people. We do not require any religious type of commitment.

The learning is life. The development is yours. The connection of study may be helpful, useful and serviceable, directly to you.

- -

Mail to: Union of Tao and Man, 117 Stonehaven Way, Los Angeles, CA 90049

_____ I wish to be put on the mailing list of the Union of Tao and Man to be notified of classes, educational activities and new publications.

Name:_____

Address:_____

City:_____State:_____Zip:_____

INDEX